"One of the finest books on the astrology of the family, *Planetary Threads* is among those rare works that change how we view astrology and its potential to heal our lives and relationships."

— GREG BOGART, author of *Planets in Therapy*

"In Part One Lynn's innovative exploration of the patterns of thinking, feeling and behaviour, which run back through generations, is enhanced by her unique adaptation of the genogram (a map utilised in family therapy) to highlighting particular planetary placements and aspects that recur in families. Her often dramatic case material, presented in fascinating detail, is rich and revealing, and we are gradually offered a profound vision of the intricately woven tapestry of the family matrix from which we spring, and the ways in which we repeat—or transform—the astrological and psychological inheritance which each of us carries.

"Part Two focuses on Siblings and Friends. The 3rd and 11th as relationship houses are often ignored or trivialised in astrological texts, but this seminar reveals the depth and importance of these two houses. An exploration of the enormous power of sibling relationships is enhanced by historical and contemporary case material as well as audience contributions, and the ancient but innovative idea of the 11th house as the *bonus daimon*, and of friends as the carriers of or catalysts for individual destiny, is presented with revealing insight.

"Together, these two seminars present a new perspective on relationships within the family and amongst friends—those "non-romantic" bonds which are so often either overlooked or overloaded with too much emphasis on pathology. This volume offers refreshing and exciting new perspectives and new practical tools for the astrological student and practitioner."

—BRIAN CLARK, author of *The Sibling Constellation*

"In the two parts of this book, Lynn Bell demonstrates how the fabric of a family is woven, in a continuum of planetary and aspect threads, to create a unique entity. In Part One, using individual horoscopes and planetary genograms, she confirms how families are inextricably linked, and how individuals live out ancestral aspects of their dynastic and interactive patterns.

"The conversations with students enhances the reality that the horoscope and its family patterns are akin to DNA. Each of us is unique, but living out—and individuating through—the embedded emotional, psychological and physical configurations of our parents and ancestors.

"In Part Two, we see how those bonds are further extended into sibling formations and the complexities of groups and friendships. How those relationships are inevitably replicated in our attractions to friends and social affinities is elegantly confirmed in the astrology."

—ERIN SULLIVAN, author of *The Astrology of Family Dynamics*

Planetary Threads

PATTERNS OF RELATING AMONG FAMILY AND FRIENDS

LYNN BELL

IBIS PRESS
Lake Worth, FL

To my sister, Jean,
in recognition of the inheritance she carried

Published in 2013 by
IBIS PRESS
an imprint of Nicolas-Hays, Inc.
P. O. Box 540206 • Lake Worth, FL 33454-0206
www.nicolashays.com
Distributed to the trade by Red Wheel/Weiser, LLC
65 Parker St., Unit 7 • Newburyport, MA 01950-4600
www.redwheelweiser.com

Charts have been calculated using Placidus Houses and True Nodes.

Library of Congress Cataloging-in-Publication data available on request.
ISBN: 978-0-89254-206-2
VG
Cover design by Henrik Drescher
Text design by Kathryn Sky-Peck

Printed in the United States of America

CONTENTS

PART ONE: PLANETARY THREADS, 25

PART TWO: SIBLINGS & FRIENDS, 169

ACKNOWLEDGMENTS

Over the years, clients, students, and friends have generously shared their stories with me, and these are an integral part of this book. Gabriel Schneider, Peggy Hancock, Lisa Davidson, and Ralph Petty all helped greatly with the evolution of this material, even though their stories are not included here. The Reseau D'Astrologie Humaniste first invited me to teach these seminars on family, and the group in Lyon was a valuable seeding ground for many ideas.

There is always a sense of excitement and discovery working for the CPA and its fine students, and this seminar would not have happened without it. Many friends have played the role of *agathos daimon* for me, in small and large ways, both ordinary and exceptional. You are too numerous to mention here—the list would be very long, but I marvel at our coming together and touching each other's lives. I'd like to particularly thank Lynn Imperatore for her willingness to participate in this material. I drank deeply of conversations with Darby Costello, who has shared her own experience of writing, among other things, with generosity and wisdom. Her husband Stephen helped me wrestle a difficult passage into shape. Everyone should be graced with friends such as these

A heartfelt thanks to the wonderful participants in the Sunday genealogy groups in Paris for their valuable contributions. I am grateful to Pam Pacelli for her helpful read-through of this material. I wish to thank Myriam and Christophe, who let me into their family in more ways than one, for their trust and generosity. Alexander shared his family story and maintained a kind, attentive presence throughout the writing of this book. Liz Greene has been an inspiration and a support on so many levels—through her work, through her faith in this material, and even her patience in constructing the genograms found in this book.

For the new, 2013 edition by Ibis Press, I want to thank Yvonne Paglia for her confidence in this book, which is in the hands of a visually gifted editor, Kathryn Sky-Peck. And I also want to acknowledge the support and enthusiasm of Caroline Myss, who has offered her home and extraordinary insight, as well as endless cups of tea, at exactly those times I most needed support. As to the cover design by my dear friend, the witty and talented Henrik Drescher, I couldn't be more delighted.

Family Inheritance

The individual and the family system,
and the matrix of invisible threads
that connect us to those who came before us

GHOSTS OF OUR ANCESTORS

Sun and Moon, Saturn and Venus are first experienced through the great ruling forces of our childhood: our parents. We interpret the world using the cues they give us, while their responses were in turn influenced by others, the extended families and ancestors whose successes and failures, quirks and talents, are found through placements in our own charts. The closer we look, the more we see mysterious repetitions of dates, parallel events, strange twists of fate that mirror stories from earlier generations, and these are often reflected in intergenerational aspect patterns. Life brings us up against the unlived energies of our ancestors; they often reappear in our own lives as powerful, sometimes compulsive, forces. The pattern of events runs under the surface of our lives, an unconscious pulse that becomes visible as events repeat. The ghosts of the ancestors are calling us, and we need to know how to answer them.

How do we identify and work with these patterns? There are rich family stories to be found within individual charts. A strong Saturn may reveal a link to another time, and to the gifts and burdens of particular individuals in a family tree. Those who have Neptune prominent may absorb the unspoken dreams of others along with their own aspirations. Each chart contains a complete picture of the world, an individual narrative reflecting a unique inner experience. This first chapter will serve as an introduction to the imprint of family in our own lives, through the individual birth chart.

At the same time, there are generational elements; outer planet patterns, repeating aspects or house positions that link us to the tribe. We will explore these in the seminar potion of the book that follows. Throughout this book we will move back and forth between the two perspectives, between the individual and the larger family system. As individuals, we are all connected to a greater pattern, each in our own way. We grow out of the family soil, out of our heredity into our unique self.

Often, we are not aware of just how much the place we have been assigned in the family affects our imprint in the world at large. It is only when we see these connections that we understand how we as individuals are embedded in a mysterious matrix. As we follow the planetary threads that link members of a tribe, we may come to a place where part of the story began. These threads can be felt as the energetic tug of affection and shared history, or as the irresistible pull of the puppet master. As we become aware of what is being worked on, we begin to glimpse the outlines of the family constellation, and we can then choose differently. The integration and recognition of the family inheritance happens in different ways at different ages, with the many threshold crossings of our lives. Just as astrology shows us our alignment with the universe as a whole, in *Planetary Threads,* we connect it to the second circle of being, the family and the ancestors.

FAMILY INHERITANCE
REFLECTED IN THE INDIVIDUAL'S CHART

The 4th house

Most work on family begins with the fourth house and extends out to the tenth, the root and crown of family life. People often come to astrology to know about the future, and just as often enough end up understanding the influence of the past in a much deeper way. Astrology reveals the deepest pattern of self, and it is the knowledge of this inner imprint and the way it unfolds that is one of the gifts of a consultation. The early years of our life and the kind of parenting we receive play a crucial role in the development of the psyche. This first emotional container can be spacious or harsh, too narrow or just good enough.

It is important to remember that the fourth house, the *Immum Coeli,* is hidden from view. It describes influences that may not be visible to the outer world, but these influences run deep within us. Some of them are hidden from our conscious memories, but remain active, flowing under the surface of our lives. They emerge into our later experiences of intimacy. The fourth house is linked both to our deepest sense of self and to our earliest experiences of home. It also contains echoes from a more distant past, traces from the lives of our parents and grandparents.

This house is a starting point for any exploration of family inheritance, and at the same time we must look to other areas of the chart to see the larger imprint. Much has been written in astrology about the Sun and the Moon and their relation to the parental *imagos*, as well as Saturn in its role of parental authority. These are the first steps in family work.

Our family story launches us on a journey to the center, and planets in this house set a tone in early childhood, as well as in later life. What makes one person take root in a very different soil, while others stay close to their place of origin, closely entwined with their clan? Some of the answers to these questions may be found in the signs and planets found here. Uranus will often push an individual to break from the tribe; while Neptune placed here can make separation from the family more difficult. Not everyone has planets in the fourth house, and in this case the house ruler will be a primary indicator for family issues.

Personal planets in the fourth are strongly colored by signs and aspects. Planets like Moon and Venus will generally create strong bonds and deep affection, a sense of shared history and interests. They support the security so fundamental to our early years, and bring the energy of the feminine into flower. With many difficult oppositions and squares to these planets, the story may be quite different; there can be a great deal of emotional unsettledness, and troubles surrounding the role of women.

Saturn in the fourth house often brings a powerful sense of responsibility towards the past. That past can be collective or personal, and while being responsible may give a sense of strength, it can also feel crushing at times. Our experience of Saturn is rarely balanced and as a result there will often be issues around the father. This may the heavy-handed patriarch, the child-swallowing Kronos of myth, or a pattern of missing fathers going back generations. An individual who is born with

Saturn here is often asked to give something to the family they did not themselves receive.

Either the Sun or Jupiter in the fourth tends to give a positive experience of family and a strong bond to the father, or another masculine figure. However Jupiter can be a more ambiguous planet than one imagines, it can call us outside our home, to a far away place or a family of adoption, especially when difficult aspects are present. Planets in the fourth are part of the story of who we will become, and no matter what we have inherited; they also give us the means to find ourselves at a deeper level. In those cases where traditionally benefic planets do not reflect childhood experiences they nonetheless provide resources for the individual later in life.

Sometimes our task is to say no; to walk away from an old way of doing things, to say no to the toxic land, to humiliation, or ill-gotten gains. Each generation does things differently; there are always changes to be made. Pluto in connection to the parental houses makes the issue of transformation more urgent. Mars here means we may fight with the family, or for them, and it can mean there is competition between the generations. Mars often indicates movement of some kind, and this can be true of Mercury as well.

For some family members the urge to individuate is primordial, and as children this can bring a disquieting sense of otherness. Uranus can heighten this sense of being an outlier, or even an alien to the family in question. Such an individual may be given the task of starting a new chapter, of beginning a new story. This Uranian ability to step beyond the boundaries of the tribe can bring healing, often in an unexpected manner. Those who separate, who take a completely different path, may also be working for the family.

Transits and progressions to the 4th house

Even those who live on their own, far from home are emotionally connected to the pull of family, often without being aware of its power. Important transits to the fourth house may bring us to a phase of deep structural change through dreams and in real life. They invite us to engage with our beginnings, to embark on the work of knowing what lies beneath us. In sessions people often bring dreams at these times or begin to ask questions they had not been especially interested in before. Stories emerge, boxes of old letters are opened, and we may touch on some of the mysteries that shape our present.

A woman who had been with the same man since her teenage years, separated after she learned he had been having an affair. At this time, the progressed Sun had just entered her 4th house. Her husband's lack of clarity, his unwillingness to be there as the father of their children became unbearable for her, and this was reflected by transits to her 7th house. She had grown up as the only child of an emotionally difficult single mother, the child of an American soldier stationed in France after WWII, so it is easy to understand how difficult such a situation could be for her. The Sun is one of the symbols for the father in astrology and often the masculine in general. Often, when a planet enters the fourth house, a new level of integration is called for.

Soon after she separated, she received information about her father after many years of fruitless searching. She learned he had returned to his native Italy, that he had a number of children there, and with joy was told that they were interested in meeting her. Although her father was no longer alive, she was welcomed by her half-sisters, and their mother, and even moved there for a time, learning the language and culture. The progressed Sun illuminated the past in the most unexpected way. It enabled her to see where she came from, who she might have been, and led her to a new foundation for her life. She found she was happier living with her children on her own. All these events brought healing to the story of her own difficult early years. It was fascinating to see a similar emphasis in her solar return with an angular Pluto on the IC, symbolizing the hidden dimensions of the past.

The past emerges into our life when we are ready to absorb what it has to offer. A man, who had inherited family letters when his mother died, put them aside for a time. When transiting Uranus entered his fourth house he took them out and found someone to help decipher the old-fashioned handwriting and indecipherable German. Though the letters were rather ordinary, the context was not. His grandparents had been writing as German Jews in the late 1930s to a son they had managed to send to safety. The letters' abrupt end brought home their later death in a concentration camp, and sent a shock wave through his sense of his own father's experience. It helped him make sense of things that had not fallen into place before.

It is fascinating to see the synchronicity between information that flows in from the outer world, and the activation of our chart by transit. One man, adopted at birth, embarked on a sea voyage in search of his birth mother, just as Jupiter transited his IC. By the time he landed in Canada, connections had been made through a program that flashed his photo for just a few minutes. He had intuitively chosen the perfect moment to embark on his quest. He found the hidden treasure that is symbolized by this house in traditional astrology, and along with it he found a whole new emotional ground. In each of these cases the activation of the fourth house allowed integration of something missing.

Outer world events that accompany transits or progressions to this house often bring underlying emotional issues to the surface. Each time this happens we are invited to digest feelings, to clarify the past, and our own emotional landscape can be redefined. A move, a flood, the departure of a family member, a wedding, or a birth, may all come at such a time. For every wall knocked down or every room repainted, there can be a subtler shift in our relationship to the past. It is not the physical events themselves that are important so much as the inner changes that accompany them. We are rather invited to go down a level, into the deeper strata of our own being. A door opens, the invitation beckons.

BEING GOOD ENOUGH:
VALUES IN FAMILY DYNAMICS

The 2nd house

It is easy to see that our family of origin influences our attitudes towards money and possession, even though children often end up with very different aesthetics and interests than their parents. Whether the tribe saves or spends, loves books, food or bank accounts, all these interests shape a child's attitudes. Inner values are often less visible, and no less essential to our sense of self. It can happen that a child's gifts are of a very different nature than those of other family members. One child may be short in a family of tall people, or bookish in a family of athletes. These differences can evoke admiration or envy, fear or disappointment. Squares to the second house from the fifth are particularly powerful in this regard.

If a son feels he doesn't measure up, he may express this later in life through an inability to deal with money. Often enough, issues around indebtedness, greed, avarice, are rooted in the psychological terrain of values. When a mother values beauty and her daughter likes to run and climb trees, a subtle sense of disapproval may waft through their relationship. This in turn affects a child's sense of worth, of being valued for herself. I have met many attractive, talented individuals who believe they are defective in some way, and somehow have difficulty dealing with the material world. Despite all evidence to the contrary, they carry an interpretation of their gifts that keeps them from being correctly re-numerated. The fifth house has to do with being seen for our gifts, for feeling loved. Difficult planets in these two houses, or aspects connecting them may tell a story of struggle around self-esteem. They ask an individual to differentiate, to have the courage to follow what they love.

Any square to a second house planet will create tension around our choices. Carl Gustav Jung had Neptune and Chiron in the second house, reflecting the religious values of his pastor father. At the same time Jung felt disconnected from the god of his father's church, and pursued a medical and scientific career. His Sun Neptune square drew him to psychoanalysis, where he flowered, until after a time his spiritual values were at odds with the 'father,' this time incarnated as Sigmund Freud. Sun square Neptune also required dissolution of self. He was plunged into a long period of near madness, of inner exploration, before emerging with his own theory of the psyche. We can consider this in part to be the fruit of a square to planets in the 2nd house. In Jung's case, Neptune is close to the 3rd house and the Sun almost in the 7th, which heightens the value of ideas as part of the conflict in relationship.

The film *Billy Elliot* showed the struggle of a young boy from a mining town to become a ballet dancer. His father was humiliated and threatened by the thought of an effeminate son. Billy had enough passion and talent, as well as support from a teacher, another authority figure, to move through the considerable opposition of both family and community. Such clashes over values do not always have fairy tale endings. At times these conflicts can undermine self-esteem, and make it impossible to move forward in life. Difficult aspects to Venus, whether they link to the second house or not, may have a similar resonance. When an individual steps outside the circle of community or class, aspects to the eleventh house may be involved.

Other people may want very different things for us than we want for ourselves. When a child loves something that is at odds with what other members of a family think is important, it can leave a lasting imprint on her sense of self worth. Later, we shall see how values are reflected as part of the larger pattern of aspects throughout the family system. In some families, the Venus thread may reveal a particular approach to values, and how each person resonates to the larger pattern. Questions around self-worth are at the core of many complex family dynamics. How liberating to recognize that those closest to us cannot see or taste or hear the world in the same way.

Money, loss, and love

Oppositions between the 2nd and the 8th house often create anxiety around the flow of money in the family. There may be enough resources to go around, but these are given only when an individual complies with certain conditions. These attitudes may reflect underlying power issues and often rebound in areas like sexuality. Giving and withholding happen on many levels of relationship, and complex emotional and psychological dynamics are common in the 8th house terrain.

Resources can be siphoned off to the desires of one individual, rather than being shared by everyone, and for a long time the cultural pattern gave strict control of finances to the head of a household. In

France, until 1965, a married woman could not have a bank account in her own name without her husband's permission, and similar constraints still exist in countries in the Middle East, and elsewhere. Until the middle of the 20th century in the UK, a working woman was obliged to resign a post once she married. While external constraints of these kinds are gone in most places, the generational imprint has continued to resonate psychologically, and may be reflected by difficult planets in the 8th house. At times we fall under the spell of a situation from the past; we may resist or cooperate, submit or transform. As a first step we need to uncover the emotional power moving through this area of the chart.

Stories around loss and gain may underlie the family's attitude towards sharing, whether emotional, financial, or sexual. The eighth house can symbolize bankruptcies, sudden loss or gain, or guilt around the source of an inheritance. Loss can be of another nature altogether, for the 8th house also contains deaths and disappearances, the unacknowledged mourning for those who have, or might have been. In this sense it is a house of ghosts, of situations that continue to claim power over us, often outside the margins of our conscious awareness. It is rich with secrets, with the hidden energies that no one speaks of, with temptation and desire.

Those with 8th house planets may be invisibly connected to family secrets, and to energies that lie beyond ordinary awareness. They can sometimes be seized by premonitions or anxieties because of the nature of their connection. It can also create a very tight defense system, a power and dominance based psyche that refuses to allow real intimacy. This house often comes with a feeling of being driven, sometimes to the point of possession. Emotions held in this part of the chart can invade the psyche, and so the family stories contained here may need to be exorcised. This can lead to a journey though the *nigredo*, an encounter with the underworld of the psyche. Such a journey can bring a profound understanding of what underlies the human condition. Once this has happened a particularly rich dimension may open, and there is a sense of flow reestablished in a person's life.

Mother and father, the family of origin

The Sun and Moon, ruling in tandem over day, then night, are the archetypal pairing of masculine and feminine. Sometimes they clearly describe the parents in an individual chart, but it is important to keep in mind that our image-making gifts are complex. I have seen charts where a tenth house Venus symbolizes a socialite mother, beautifully dressed and perfumed, while the 12th house Moon is carried by a Spanish-speaking maid. We will discuss these questions in depth throughout the seminar portion of the book.

In practice, I use the fourth house for the father and the paternal inheritance, while the tenth house more often describes the mother and the matrilineal line. That the outer world is a witness to our birth is the explanation that most appeals to me. We emerge physically, indisputably, from the mother's body. The father is the invisible parent, and until the advent of DNA testing it was impossible to know if any man were truly the father of a given child.

It is best to establish these correlations through dialogue, for it is the inner experience of a parent that concerns us. It is natural that as children, we live our aspects of our chart through the people around us. Part of the process of growing up consists of reclaiming those energies that have been projected onto mother, father, and other family member, a process that can happen, layer by layer, over many years.

There is a much larger range of possible parental significators than we might imagine, and it is particularly interesting to look at house rulerships, at the signs on the cusp of the fourth and tenth houses. When parents are older, Capricorn or Saturn becomes a likely significator. Some children are born when their parents are children themselves, or still involved in schooling; they may have Mercury as a parental significator. Mars may best describe an athletic, dynamic, father. In these situations, the more structured part of the father archetype can be carried by another family member such as a grandfather, an aunt, or an older brother. Jupiter can be a significator for a parent who is exceptional in some way, one who carries an almost mythological presence, or who is an invention of a child's wishes.

Research in Hellenistic astrology attributes the tenth house to the mother, and fourth to the father. It also gives Saturn in a night chart as significator of the father, while the Sun symbolizes father for those born during the day. This idea resonates deeply with me, and I am observing it in my work with clients.

SUCCESS, SACRIFICE AND REDEMPTION

The 10th house

The oldest child often carries the needs of the family for success. But what happens when he is a she, or has the wrong temperament to follow in the family tradition? The tenth, like the second, is part of the earthy triangle, where planets call things into form. Our ancestors pull us forward as well as back. Part of what we do is for them, something easy to see in the children of first generation immigrants, whose successes make everything their parents did worthwhile. When there are tensions between the individual's needs and the family's demands, a son or daughter may sacrifice a talent to fulfill the family's dreams, and this can impact the generations that follow. At some point the need to live one's innate abilities will come up against family responsibilities. Without the care, encouragement and sustenance of our families, we would not be where we are, and yet the individual's path is always more than this, there is a moment to break and make our own way, with or without their approval. The tenth house is both our own calling and the expectations that family have for us. These can be subtly intertwined, or more powerfully linked.

An individual with strong transpersonal outer planets in the 10th may find it difficult to be part of an ongoing tradition, to simply continue things as they have always been. They can also be breakthrough agents for families that have struggled to make things work. One woman I know, with Venus, Uranus and Pluto conjunct the MC, was born into a North African family of twelve children. She has stepped completely outside her circle of origin, and become an avantgarde artist. Without this being a conscious choice, her success has redeemed the disappointments of previous generations. Her calling is both totally personal and fed by the efforts of those who came before her. Planets here can therefore function on many levels. In her case, Uranus could be seen as instructions to break free from the traditional role of women in her family. Parental indicators are often planets closest to the Midheaven, those factors activated by secondary progression or solar arc direction early in life. Her own mother showed considerable courage, both in her desire to immigrate, and her push for her daughters to be educated.

Oppositions and squares involving the tenth house can further define the struggle an individual may have with a particular parent. Another man, with Jupiter in Pisces in the 10th house, recently wrote his family memoir. His mother was a legend in the New Orleans restaurant world, a highly regarded businesswoman. At one point, her image was splashed across billboards throughout the US, and she is still spoken of locally on a first name basis. Despite his intellectual brilliance, he felt he could never measure up to her particular standards, and he writes about the constant sense of being put down, of not being good enough. Jupiter opposes a fourth house Saturn, while Saturn in turn, squares his Sun in Gemini. In his family men were below, and women on top. Not only has this pattern wreaked havoc in relationship, it has been the spur for many years of work on himself.

He used to jokingly refer to himself as 'the prince', but his mother made sure neither he, nor his brother, would ever be king. She sold her business before her death, and never allowed the 'kingdom' to come into their hands. He received the light of her accomplishments, the reflected glory, and much of her wealth, while on an intimate level, he felt empty of maternal care, and denied recognition. While the opposition to Jupiter is part of this, and the square from Saturn to the Sun, even stronger, it is a 12th house Moon that shows this profound sense of emotional invisibility. Jupiter in the tenth also describes his pull to accomplish something exceptional. Not only does he have a PhD from a prestigious university, he is also a compassionate philanthropist, financing well-chosen causes, artistic endeavors and projects that honor his mother by bringing food education into disadvantaged neighborhoods. On a personal level the struggle with the exalted mother continues. Out in the world, they work hand in hand.

Honoring the ancestors

And so it is also possible to honor a parent without being in agreement. It is said we carry the genetic imprint back eight generations, far enough that we may no longer remember the names of our ancestors. Their strengths and accomplishments are part of our foundation, as are their trials and difficulties. Often, mysterious connections and parallels are found between their lives and ours. We may be asked to finish something they began, without even knowing anything about it. Invisible family loyalties have greater power than we imagine, influencing the choices that we make. We may need to honor our inheritance through a particular task, without abandoning our own path. Planets in the fourth and tenth houses often point the way, while oppositions between them can describe conflicts that function as obstacles in our path. Only then can we be released to live our own life.

Communication and exchange

Communication issues and the third house are treated in detail in the seminar portion of this book. Each family has its own communication style. There are tribes of talkers, and quiet clans. When they marry each other, misunderstandings may ricochet from one generation to another. Even when words seem to flow, every family has areas that are not spoken about. When there are too few words, or language is too harsh, families often drift apart. Without a flow of ideas, and the ability to be understood, a family is merely a unit of survival. Difficult planets in the third house, or those with conflicting aspects often highlight the need for communication, and can push an individual to learn skills that will help resolve the original conflict. Mapping the positions of Mercury in a family is a powerful tool for unraveling this dynamic, and understanding that no matter how close you are you aren't seeing things the same way.

Light and shadow in the family

Many families single out one individual as the odd one, the black sheep or the problem child. Difficult fifth house planets, stressful aspects to the Sun, or luminaries in the 12th and 8th houses often constellate the shadow. A child born with these house placements is intuitively connected to those things the family has chosen to deny. Difficult aspects to Sun or Moon may also mean that a given child mirrors a parent's least liked traits. When a son or daughter rejects or denies these aspects of self, they can feel unloved in some way. One woman grew up with an abusive brother and as her first son grew, she saw her brother's character traits in him. In such cases it is helpful to consider the synastry between the two charts. This son had the Moon at almost the same degree in Virgo as his mother. He reflected her unresolved emotions back to her. The rest of their charts were indeed quite different. A child who is noticeably different from a parent can be perceived as a threat to the family's narrative, and made to carry the collective shadow. Children are ruled by the fifth house in astrology, and planets here may describe the energies we ask our children to carry for us, good or bad, light or shadow.

At the same time 12th and 8th house planets denote susceptibility to the negative projections of others. In this case, the son had an 8th house Moon, and the mother had many 12th house planets. Her parents had ignored her own needs and anxieties, and she felt, orphaned, invisible. For a time she had been addicted to heroin. As an adult she moved to the other side of the world to find her own purpose in life. As her children move into adulthood they have all chosen to live in different countries, continuing this pattern

At times however it is a child with a very strong personality, the gifted athlete, the star of the school play, the beauty or spelling champion that the others cannot compete with. A child with a special gift may have many first or tenth house planets, a shining fifth house, and take up more room than other family members. They don't mean to, but their presence demands the energy of parents, and their talents delight, but also consume a family's resources. Sometimes parents will attempt to balance things by each giving their particular light to a different child. The one the father loves may be cold-shouldered by the mother, and the mother's darling dismissed by his father. These painful patterns rebound on self-esteem and can take hold over several generations. For the successful child they may invoke guilt, and create mysterious shadow rivalries in their professional or personal lives.

Envy and rivalry

Light and shadow come strongly into play in sibling relationships where rivalry and envy are often revealed in their clearest form. They can strengthen families or leave them divided. When these issues have been unresolved in the past, they can resonate between a parent and child in unconscious ways, and affect both trust and confidence. Sibling conflicts may also have their origins in tensions between the parents, and hold up a mirror to them, especially, but not exclusively in brother sister relationships. These are discussed in great detail, along with the third house in the second part of Planetary Threads: Siblings and Friends.

Servants, orphans and invalids

When the 6th and 12th houses are strong, an individual can become the family servant or the scapegoat, the one who carries the many burdens of the tribe, the one who does the healing or the suffering for others. This is another aspect of shadow, one that has seeped into the biology of an individual. Our bodies come from the genes of our forebears, and their health or brokenness can often express family issues that have not been able to find resolution. Liz Greene speaks of this in her fine book, *The Astrology of Fate*. While the birth of a handicapped child or one carrying a defective gene, is a tragedy for the people involved, it also calls up immense reserves of courage and forbearance. The willingness to do what needs to be done is part of the tribe's healing.

One woman suffered from severe migraines as early as preschool age. As the middle child of five, and a 12th house sun, she probably didn't have much room for herself. The migraines meant she needed to stay home from school with the curtains drawn. This solitude and quiet is fundamental to a 12th house sun. This is not to imply there was no physical cause for her migraines, for both her mother and grandmother suffered from these debilitating headaches. Her strict, unaffectionate upbringing, the pressure not to say or do anything that might be out of bounds, no doubt also rebounded physically. Slowly she is finding the triggers for the pain, and beginning to look at the highly critical environment she grew up in. Often it is the most sensitive child that develops a physical or psychological symptom. Like a canary in a coal mine, their difficulty alerts others to an untenable environment. Symptoms in a family can sometimes find their origin in unresolved family dilemmas, in a family system that is too tight. While it would be naive to interpret every illness in this way, giving meaning to these kinds of difficulties can often be quite liberating.

Symptoms that involve mental illness often carry a different kind of stigma than the merely physical. These distorted mental patterns also layer themselves throughout the emotional atmosphere of a family. A young man born with many 6th house planets became the caretaker for his mother, who suffered from mental illness. At 11, he would listen to her, calm her fears, cheer her up. As a result he became the "good" child. Of course being the good one comes with a cost, the cost of putting other's needs before one's own. His Uranian brother was "bad," he broke all the rules and ended up in trouble with the law, struggling with a drug problem. Both boys reacted to the difficult family situation in very different ways, and the 'bad' son needed the strong presence of his father into his late 20's. This presence helped him find inner guidelines, until he moved into a mature relationship. The good child did everything right until he got to college. Without everyone telling him how good he was, he stopped feeling much of anything. He needed to fall apart, to screw things up, to fail, and he managed to do this as a university student. In doing so he was able to see that the role of the good son might cost him everything. This difficult period obliged him to think about his own needs and he was able to move into responsible work. Although he still feels pulled by his mother's difficulties, he was able to say no to her request that he take care of her full time when his father died.

In some cultures the youngest daughter was singled out to be the caretaker of her parents in old age, but often enough we choose these roles ourselves. The sixth house can mean a son is valued only for the help he gives in relations to others, for the work he contributes to the family. Parents can unconsciously undermine a daughter's beauty or talents to keep her tied to them, dependent in some way, so that she will remain close when they are old. When the twelfth house is strong the sense of exile, of being in the wrong place, even being orphaned, can be very powerful.

These houses, the 6th and 12th, are mysterious. They do not function according to ideas we may have about conventional justice or fairness. They contain notions of karma and spiritual reparation that are beyond the bounds of the purely psychological. They often come with powerful family themes, issues that require healing, and they can gift an individual with the skills to help others. Many doctors and therapists have emerged from family environments of this kind. The 12th is also a place of family ghosts, of half-lived lives, and forgotten stories. It often resonates keenly to ancestral work.

Houses above the horizon

Houses above the horizon are in the visible part of the chart and they are generally more engaged with the larger world. We have already seen how the eighth tenth and twelfth houses are a key part of the ancestral paradigm, and even more, how the tenth house of accomplishment reflects the family's push for success. Even houses that we see as outside the personal can contain family themes.

Relationship models

The very first template for partnership comes from the parental relationship, and this is often described by planets in the seventh house. This is not to say that we will necessarily follow the parental model, only that it needs to be acknowledged and transformed for an individual to form a successful relationship in the future. There can be an overlay in the pattern, a warp or a twist, that draws situations unconsciously. This brief description of the way family affects relationship, can only serve as a cursory introduction to the very rich and complex issues found in the seventh house.

We fully receive another in this house, so planets here can be perceived as belonging to another person. They can be projected, or even seen as something outside the self, as "not me." With Jupiter the other can be seen as extraordinary, exceptional in some way, and this may reflect an idealization in the parental marriage. Neptune can speak to a pattern of rescue, redemption, disappoint, or loss. Uranus can indicate an unusual pairing, or a break in the pattern. It is not uncommon in the charts of those who come from families with multiple marriages. Each of us will resonate to a particular aspect of the parents' marriage, described by the sign and planets in this house.

Planets here may also describe other significant early influences in an individual's life. With difficult planets here we can feel pushed back, even rejected by someone. It can be a sibling, or even a parent for the seventh house is the place where we came face to face with another person. The seventh is also the house of open enemies, and sometimes the birth of a child can encounter immediate resistance. Oddly enough a father may feel displaced by his children, for he is no longer the center of attention for his partner. A very young child can then be innocently involved in a triangle with his parents' relationship. Later, with planets like Mars or Saturn, the rivalry may be experienced as rejection or hostility and erupt into conflict. Or these conflicts may be seen as part of the parent's relationship.

The Moon in the 7th can signify a particularly close relationship to the mother. This can be even more powerful if the father is rarely home, or indifferent to his partner's needs. It may mean the mother has a stronger emotional connection with her child than with her partner. In later life such an experience may then lead to a tendency to mother, or be mothered. This may need to be worked through before a more equitable adult relationship is possible. The Sun in the 7th sometimes creates a similar bond to the father, and this can be true of other planets as well. One unmarried woman with Saturn and Jupiter together in this house, stayed close to her successful boss as his personal assistant. Her other primary relationship to a man was with her gay best friend. The early relationship with her father taught her to be a companion for the men in her life, and her admiration came with a certain distance.

Squares to 7th house planets can describe tensions between the family of origin and an individual's choice of partner. Such a choice would reflect a pressing need for individuation, which could come through the kind of man or woman one chooses to marry, and the way they connect to the tribe or clan of origin. The family inheritance may contain a narrative of this kind.

The family Weltanshauung

Families often come from a particular culture; they share certain beliefs about the world. When an individual family member interprets the world differently, turns liberal in a clan of conservatives, or steps out of a shared religious vision, family identity can be threatened. Questions of religion, belief, philosophy and ethics belong to the 9th house, Strong planets here, may describe an environment where moral authority cannot be questioned. This has always been considered a fortunate house; there may be a wise grandmother or grandfather, a history of deep reflection or brilliance in the family. A young woman with Jupiter in the 9th has been strongly influenced by her aunt, a well known author and teacher. This has helped with the anger she feels towards her parents. Mars in her seventh house describes a long battle of attrition in their marriage, unable to reconcile different desires and values. Her 9th house offers a welcome respite from these family tensions,

Stresses to planets here, particularly oppositions, can give rise to profound disagreements that may call family unity into question. It can be hard to know what to believe, or to trust one's own judgment. A member of the tribe who follows a different path through education or travel may sometimes need to leave the family behind for a time. This can be particularly intense for those who grow up in a family with strong traditional beliefs, and yet feel a need to call the tenets of religion into question. They can be treated as crazy or wrong for thinking about the world differently, and even be ejected from the family for a time. A Jewish son who marries a Catholic, the prayerful child of scientists who reject any belief in God, or an individual who grows up in a cult may all need to seek the freedom to view the world in their own way. These differences may be encoded by parents from different cultures, religions or temperaments, or when children surpass their parents through education. A 9th house individual may be called to interpret the world in a new way. Their task can be to bring in a larger vision, to inspire, to connect the tribe to wisdom and respect for knowledge.

The social interface: the 11th house

Families, like countries, each see the world in their own way. Some are survivalist, protecting themselves from perceived threats in the outer world; no stranger ever crosses their threshold. Others welcome outsiders and are active members of their community. Questions of status and integration, of social class, of one's place in the world at large, are often seen in the 11th house. Growing up in a housing project where drugs are rife may undermine a loving family with solid values. The son or daughter of an aristocrat, while benefiting from privilege, may also find it difficult to let go of social convention. The groups we belong to, the schools we go to, in most cases mirror the world of our parents. A family that shuns people of color, or avoids poor neighborhoods, offers a limited vision of the world. Oppositions or squares to planets in this house can activate tensions between a family's value and the larger community.

This is also a house of individuation, of breaking through to a wider circle of connection. The possibility of friendship, of non-blood ties, is one of the antidotes for a difficult family situation, and the choices we make create an opening in our lives. This subject is treated in detail in the second part of the seminar portion of this book.

FROM THE INDIVIDUAL TO THE FAMILY SYSTEM

Our own story begins before we were born, just as the DNA in our cells links us back over many generations. When we lay the astrological map of our world next to that of people close to us, we may see many connections, and not always the ones we imagine will be there. Sometimes charts may not match closely at all. Siblings can have radically different visions of family, even with shared memories and experiences. These elements of connection and difference are revealed as we place the charts side by side.

First, we can look at the individual synastry, the way two charts work together. We can elaborate differences between family members through chart aspects and placements, and see through to the dynamics of a particular relation. The comparison of any two charts reveals tensions, harmonies, and contrasts. When we add the larger context of the family narrative, it can help us understand that a conflict between a father and son may be more than it seems. It may have its origin in an earlier father and son relationship, and the power of such emotional history continues to run through present time. These patterns seem to replicate themselves, until they are made conscious, or until some kind of reparation is possible. This book invites you look at both the individual and the family system, to understand the invisible threads that connect you to those who come before you. You are part of something larger, much larger than you imagine.

PART ONE

Planetary Threads

*This seminar was given on 27 June 1998 at
Regents College, London, as part of the
Summer Term of the seminar programme of the
Centre for Psychological Astrology.*

THE NEVER-ENDING STORY

Working with astrology and family patterns gets overwhelming quickly—there are so many charts, so much data to absorb, that we can easily become lost in the complexity. One of the things that I want to do today is give a fairly simple technique for pulling information out of a group of charts. I've been doing this work for about ten or twelve years, starting from looking at parental images, which all of you have worked on in other seminars at the CPA. I enjoy pulling family stories out of individual horoscopes, and prefer to begin in this way, to tap into the extraordinary richness contained in each one. Each chart gives a complete picture of the world. You don't actually need groups of charts to get an image of the family, but any one chart gives only a partial point of view—a brother or a sister may see things quite differently. When we put these individual pictures side by side, they take on an entirely different quality.

So, take a deep breath, gather up the charts of family members, and open your mind. When we plunge into our own charts and those of other people, it can feel as though our experiences are so entangled we'll never be able to get clear of them. Connections leap out, and we begin to follow a trail that soon gets smeared and confused, not only by too much information, but also by our own images and impressions of those close to us. We need something that helps us stand back. Without perspective, it can feel very lonely within the boundaries of our own chart; tracing the threads of connection with other family members can help us step out of a sense of individual limitation. We begin to see ourselves within a wider context, and to understand how others are placed in the family constellation. This opening of our vision can be a powerful tool for change. I'm sure that all of you have noticed connections between your own chart and that of other family members. Sooner or later, we all get curious. Does anyone here have Moon conjunct Saturn? Yes? And have you looked to see whether your own mother has a Saturn-Moon aspect of some kind?

AUDIENCE: I have looked at my mother's chart, but I can never remember it! But my daughter has a Moon-Saturn trine. I suppose that's a kind of heredity.

LYNN: Students often say this about family charts, and sometimes even their own! There seems to be an issue of timing, of being ready to see whether a parent's chart fits your image of them. Often students wait many years before they look at their mother or father's charts for the first time, perhaps not daring to discover unwanted resemblances. We spend a great deal of time talking about the parental images in our own charts, but when we really start to look at their charts, our attention can flag mysteriously. Sometimes we walk away perplexed by aspects that clash with our idea of the person—or we may even be confused by the lack of it between the image of the mother or father in one chart and a totally different signature in another. It can all be quite disconcerting. Others eagerly draw up the charts of brothers and sisters, parents and grandparents, building up monumental amounts of information. Then, having gleaned a few insights, they sigh and put the charts away It can be even more stressful for a mother to look at the Moon or the MC in her own child's chart. What kind of maternal image does that child carry with her? It can all be very hot to handle. Today I'd like to open it up a bit, to place it in a larger context.

Imagine a woman with the Moon conjunct Saturn in her birth chart. This means that she carries an image of Moon-Saturn inside her. She will lave a heightened response to anything in her environment that corresponds to this image or picture of the Moon: a hardworking, responsible, perhaps frustrating or rejecting mother. Moon-Saturn will interpret the world in a particular way, often with a feeling of lack and constraint. Now, it is quite possible for someone to be born with this kind of aspect into a family where everyone else has the Moon in aspect to Uranus, a placement which demands a great deal of freedom and autonomy. Since Moon-Saturn needs structure to feel safe, the frustration could come from something "missing" in the family context. This woman's picture of the mother may not fit her mother's chart at all. I think we have all seen examples like this and puzzled over them. This Moon-Saturn would be very different from one where the mother, grandmother, and great-grandmother all have Moon-Saturn aspects, describing a Saturnian tradition passed on from one generation to the next with a weight of duty, responsibility and sorrow. Some factors in the birth chart may be specific to one member of a family, and others represent shared ways of seeing and being in the world.

The notion of family

Let's look at the notion of family. All of us come into this life through the body of our mother and the genetic and biological substance of both our parents. We are all born into a family, connected to other people, whether we like them or not! In the old myths, the soul is said to choose the family that will best suit its purposes. Whether we believe this literally or not, there are mysterious events that seem to repeat from one generation to the next, families where the men die young, where one child leaves and never comes back, where spouses go mad or develop incurable illnesses. How is it that our own life experiences often echo those of preceding generations?

Part of what we find in a chart belongs uniquely to that person, another part is generational; all those with Saturn-Neptune conjunctions and all those with Uranus-Pluto conjunctions are carrying something similar. But there are pieces of the chart—sign repetitions, aspects, house emphases—that link us quite closely to other members of our family, as if we are all working on the same puzzle, and each family member has a different piece of it. The chart connections between family members give clues to what may be tying us together, where we are carrying a particular pattern, a talent or conflict that belongs not only to us but to our kin. When the puzzle goes unsolved, the missing piece gets passed down. There are issues that reach beyond the scope of one individual or one lifetime. In many ways, looking at the family brings out the storyteller in us. We have to listen for the archetypal patterns that run down through the generations, using the planets and signs to help trace meaning and influence. There is a technique called narrative therapy, that helps a patient give meaning to suffering and difficulty by acknowledging both painful events and hard-won accomplishments as part of the story, as necessary encounters, twists and turns on the path. Each member of our family has their own story to tell, and together we are part of a saga, continuing what was begun long before our birth.

I found myself powerfully moved the other day, reading *Under A Wing: A Memoir*, written by the youngest of the five Lindbergh children, Reeve.[1] The tragic kidnapping and murder of Charles Lindbergh Jr. was one of the major media events of the 1930's. Anne and Charles Lindbergh were a charmed, famous couple, writer and legendary pilot, and the loss of their child was a public event. Afterwards they fled America for safety and privacy, raising the children that followed in England, out of the public eye, away from the cameras and the journalists. Reeve writes that she was aware of the facts surrounding her brother's death early on, but that she only really understood what had happened when her own son died of a childhood illness at eighteen months, the same age as the brother she had never known. She remembers calling her mother in the middle of the night, and her mother saying, "Whatever you do, don't let anyone take him away." Together they sat with the dead child, keeping watch through the night. It was only then that Reeve fully realized her mother had never seen her son again, never been able to fully mourn his loss. It's a shock to hear a story of this kind. How can we make sense of it?

Reeve makes it clear that the loss of her son was also an opportunity for healing in the family. No one would wish to lose a child, and yet in this family, the shock of the lost child was so strong that it was relived in the following generation as a fated event. This kind of coincidence often occurs when a child reaches the anniversary age of the original trauma, as if there is a resonant memory of an event so powerful that it is lodged in the family unconscious and reactivated like the concentric circles that spread from a stone thrown into the sea. It happens with a

---

1   Reeve Lindbergh, *Under A Wing: A Memoir,* Simon and Schuster, NY, 1998.

far greater frequency than one would imagine. Family therapists speak of the anniversary syndrome.

AUDIENCE: Is this astrological or something else?

LYNN: A great deal of work on family patterns—what is known in France as *la psychogénéalogie*—has been done elaborating these stories and repetitions within a psychological context. Family histories and stories can be meaningfully, richly described without astrology. The psychologists who work in this field are at a loss to explain the mechanism of repetition through the generations. They take note of them but skirt the notion of fate. In fact, the goal of the work is to understand what is moving through a family's history in order to unbind a possible "fated" event, through understanding and reparation of another kind. What interests me is how the astrological model presents this information, and the clues it offers for unraveling extremely complex situations. How many of you know Erin's book?[2] In *Dynasty*, Erin Sullivan has written an excellent overview of the systemic approach, linking the work that has been done in family therapy with astrology, and this is a book to read if you're at all interested in this subject. As far as the Lindberghs are concerned, Reeve has Mercury, Sun, Neptune, Jupiter, and Chiron conjunct—many of the same planets we find together in her mother's very remarkable chart.

The Lindberghs had five children, but it is Reeve, a novelist like her mother, who shared her mother's terrible loss when her own son died. Both women have powerfully Neptunian signatures, and the infinite, larger-than-life experiences of overwhelming loss and boundless compassion are at the heart of Neptune's realm. Tenderness and psychic fluidity between mother and daughter are typical of Neptune, as is the ability to stay open, to stretch boundaries beyond personal suffering to reach an understanding of the heart. Neptune often evokes a sacrifice of some kind, of personal identity or emotional happiness. The sacrifice can be unconscious or a redemptive act, a decision to take on the suffer-

---

2   Erin Sullivan, *Dynasty: The Astrology and Psychology of Family Dynamics*, Arkana, London, 1996.

ing of others, reaching its *summum* in the Christian paradigm. Besides the Neptunian signature, it is not surprising to find powerful nodal connections between mother and daughter. These are often present when there are strong fated experiences.

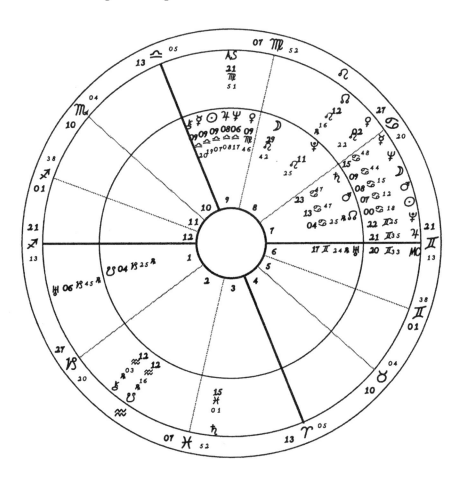

Inner chart: Anne Morrow Lindbergh, 22 June 1906, 11 15 am EST, Englewood, New Jersey, USA. Placidus cusps, true Node.
Outer chart: Reeve, 2 October 1945, no birth time.
Placements calculated for noon EST.

Here is a passage from Anne Morrow Lindbergh's *Gift From The Sea:*

We walk up the beach under the stars. And when we are tired of walking, we lie flat on the sand under a bowl of stars. We feel stretched, expanded to take in their compass. They pour into us until we are filled with stars, up to the brim;

This is what one thirsts for, I realize, after the smallness of the day, of work, of details, of intimacy—even of communication, one thirsts for the magnitude and universality of a night full of stars, pouring onto one like a fresh tide.

And then at last, from the immensity of interstellar space, we swing down to a particular beach, We walk back to the lights of the cottage glowing from the dark mist of trees. Small, safe, warm and welcoming, we recognize our pinpoint human match-light against the mammoth chaos of the dark. Back again to our good child's sleep.[3]

This passage bridges the intimate and the sublime, beautifully reflecting the Virgo Ascendant and the powerful Cancer stellium, and their link, via Neptune, to vast and mysterious reaches of the night, full of numinous receptivity to a larger world. In much the same way we will try to discern the celestial patterning running through our lives, through the stories of individuals and families.

Before we go on, I want to say a few words about today's chart. Friday night, at about the moment of the exact Saturn-Neptune square, I broke out in hives. This is not something I'm prone to doing, but a tiny crop circle appeared on my hand. I have no idea what it means, though the mysterious shape—the invisible becoming visible—seemed a jokey reference to Saturn-Neptune. The Saturn-Neptune square has to do with the dreams that are carried within, and how these bump up against external experience during this time. They can be abandoned or brought into form. Either way, a vision gets some reality testing. The square brings

---

3   Anne Morrow Lindbergh, *Gift From the Sea,* Vintage Books, NY, 1991.

up issues around inner solidity, tests the strength of these deeply held dreams, and challenges us to act on them. On a collective and personal level, fantasy and reality may collide, and certain ideals turn out to be less than we would hope. Since we are so close in time to the exact aspect, it informs and colors our understanding. When Neptune meets Saturn, our vision changes, and we can use this for working on the family With the Moon in fire, at 28° Leo, and Venus moving into opposition with Mars, the passionate side of things will come to the fore.

The water houses, which contain what is hidden beneath appearances, are emphasized by the Moon in the 12th and Jupiter in the 8th.

I always feel a kind of awe when a child is born with many immediate links to other family members: Moon/Asc, Sun/Moon, Asc/Sun. These are not the kinds of connections revealed by statistical analysis, but they are immediately visible to the astrologer's eye. As we start to look at the charts of a group, other patterns begin to emerge. Today we will concentrate on a few of these, to see how they weave in and out of a family's story. I will try not to overwhelm you with detail, but to follow these patterns like colored threads in a tapestry, coming in on one side of the family or another, creating different motifs and pictures, and then perhaps fading away, only to be picked up later in a different context. Some members of the family seem to carry the main design, while others are working on counterpoint, filling in another part of the story. These patterns are one of the great mysteries of astrology, revealing an underlying architecture of connection with no clear mechanism to explain how they get there.

I also want to say that some families have much closer links than others. One Uranus-Moon friend finds very little to connect his chart with those of his parents, and he feels very "other". The siblings see each other infrequently and have quite different interests and values. It may be that his connection to family is extremely specific, and that his real nature was not nourished in the original environment. He had a complete change of identity in his late forties. He left his job, his wife, his neighborhood, and completely re-invented his approach to life. Not everyone has the same degree of connection to his or her tribe.

Family myths

All of you are used to thinking of the power of myth in our lives, from Oedipus to archetypal connections. Powerful stories run through families as well, sweeping us along in events which often have their roots in decisions made long before we are born. In the seminar on siblings we spoke of Helen and Clytaemnestra, the sisters who marry into the house of Atreus, a family where children kill their parents or are killed by them, over many generations. These killings may be accidental, unconscious, or, in the case of Iphigineia, a sacrifice to the gods so that the ships can sail to the Trojan war. But they began with Tantalus, who cut up his son Pelops and served him in a stew to the gods. Although Pelops is miraculously brought back to life by Zeus, with only an ivory shoulder to show his lack of wholeness, he breaks an oath, and his offspring are cursed by the one he betrays. Rather than trusting to the speed of his chariot alone, a gift from the gods, he bribes and betrays a man, using treachery to win his bride's hand.

It is as if Pelops, favored by the gods, had an opportunity to emerge from his father's horrifying act relatively unscathed, but instead, reactivated a destructive force, which then became locked into the fate of several generations by the charioteer's curse. The series finally ends when Orestes kills his mother to avenge the murder of his father, and though he is hounded by the Erinyes for matricide, Apollo finally purifies his crime and ends the cycle. In the original crime, Tantalus betrayed his friendship with Zeus, while Orestes, who resolves the family curse, had a steadfast and legendary friendship with Pylades, and this points to a key element in the resolution of family issues—the need to bring in outside elements and resources to break the hold of a repeating pattern. The tragic repetitions in this family are held in place by betrayal, pride, and misjudgment. The horrible series of deaths and losses comes not from the gods, but from a mortal's curse. Although Tantalus's crime is unpardonable, his descendants were only caught up in it when they showed the same seeds of hubris as their infamous ancestor.

This story, while thankfully more extreme than most of our own experiences, shows how we can be caught up in a family myth, mysteriously bound by another's past action. And at the same time it may offer us a way to avoid awakening a tragic inheritance. It is the repetition of betrayal, the breaking of trust, which sets the curse in motion. The possibility for resolution was wasted—nothing doomed Pelops and his descendants until he broke faith. And even when Orestes is caught up in the implacable logic of revenge and retribution, he acts out of a perception of justice and inspires loyalty in those closest to him, renewing, perhaps, that original friendship between the gods and men, broken by Tantalus.

An undigested event in a family, like Pelops' shoulder, has a lasting impact on the family psyche. Heaviness, depression, strange symptoms without any obvious cause, can be particularly strong in the lives of those with strong water houses and powerful outer planet placements, because of their permeability to the family unconscious. These individuals sense the presence of the family ghosts, and in extreme cases can feel haunted by the past and pulled out of present time. A family myth has an invisible dynamic structure that pulls individuals into its narrative. One woman left home in Germany to be an au pair in London and then came to Paris. She fell in love with a Frenchman, and still lives in France twenty years later. But it was only after many years that she discovered a family secret. Her mother was an illegitimate child whose background had been shrouded in mystery After careful questioning, this woman learned that her grandfather had been Alsatian (Alsace was under French rule at the time) and had run off to join the French Foreign Legion when the grandmother got pregnant. Long before she knew this, she brought a Frenchman back into the family, weaving a lost thread back into the pattern.

A strong 8th house, with the Sun conjunct Pluto, probably shows her sensitivity to this theme of the unknown grandfather. Every family carries several different motifs of this kind, and the unwanted child has particular power in this one, along with the lost father, as we shall see later. These themes are part of a family's work, and they tend to come back with slight changes and varying degrees of difficulty until someone finds a creative solution, or steps out of the pattern altogether. We can follow this astrologically by tracing, say, a Mars-Pluto aspect over several generations until it fades out in the chart of the new generation. Something has been resolved, a new story has risen up and taken its place.

THE FAMILY OF PLANETS

The Moon

Some of you may have heard of Virginia Satir, a highly regarded family therapist. She asked the question, "What is a family for?" I've found her answers to this question provide a useful structure for exploring family patterns. For Satir, the primary business of a family is to raise individuals, much as a farmer raises carrots or apples. In astrology, the growth of the individual centers around the solar principle, and the ability to express the essential self, comes form a powerful connection to the Sun. However families are also a small group banded together for safety and protection, concerned with economic survival. What kind of planetary energy would that be?

AUDIENCE: Saturn and the Moon.

LYNN: Yes. If any of you grew up in a very poor family, you will know first hand the primacy of these issues. Security, both emotional and mate-rial, has to do with the Moon. Keeping warm enough, having enough to eat, can push other concerns way into the background. Assuming these issues are taken care of, the Moon then hopefully provides the soil of emotional needs, a place to thrive, bounded (Saturn) by the care and attention of the family circle. When the emotional and psychological environment is relatively healthy, individual essence can emerge. Just as in nature, perfect conditions are rare. External events play a part, along with a long history of lack or abundance experienced over generations. Like a lack of nutrients in the soil, missing bits from the family will affect development in a quite fundamental way. Most of you know this all too well, because work on ourselves in therapy often has to do with filling in what was missing in the very beginning.

One of the things I'd like to do is to run briefly through the planets in terms of the family, and see what specific issues come up around each one. Much of this simply carries on from their basic meanings, with an emphasis on how the family contributes to our experience of ourselves. It is after all, our very first environment for good or bad, our first mirror. Later, as we look at planetary genograms, this will give us clues to making sense of them.

Mars

Human beings are resilient, and even with a minimum of security begin to develop independence and initiative. Mars represents this need to move away from safe parental boundaries, to explore and test limits. Many astrologers have pointed out the correlation between the first Mars return and the "terrible twos". If the Saturn-Moon function is shaky, Mars can even be pushed into overdrive, compensating for a lack of security in the very beginning. Sometimes, when the early environment is extremely harsh, an infant may withdraw from the world. Remember those stories about babies left in Romanian orphanages, who were never held or comforted and became severely retarded. In cases like these, the inability to develop Mars comes from a void in the beginning. The infant simply goes away, never even reaching the stage of self affirmation.

Mars can also remain underdeveloped in an overly structured environment, although it won't have the same "feel" as one weakened by despair. A tight Saturnian family, with strict discipline and too many rules, can inhibit this next stage of development. A toddler needs to feel safe enough to say, "No!"—to challenge earlier limits; when this desire is squashed, an individual may have trouble finding courage later in life. Some writers compare the rages of the two-year-old with the crises of adolescence, where the same urge for independence erupts with a wash of hormones and a greater need for individuation. We get a replay of Mars, with some Uranus thrown in for good measure.

Venus

Each member of a family seeks to feel loved and valued, without necessarily living up to parental expectation. And here, in astrological terms, we enter the territory of Venus. A family will transmit certain values, and these turn around issues as diverse as money, beauty, learning, loyalty, religion, strength—the list is clearly limitless, and we might imagine this to be fairly straightforward in families. But Virginia Satir earmarked this as one of the main areas of conflict. Even when parents agree between them, each child loves the universe in its own way. It can be very painful when parents and children disagree about the fundamental importance of things—the artistic child in a "macho" family, or the hard-working father faced with a son who refuses to take over the family business.

Difficult aspects to Venus can indicate tension around values, or a feeling of not being loved enough, or not in the right way These issues of value and self-esteem are fundamental in early childhood, and also during adolescence, when it becomes practically *de rigeur* for a young person to invest in music, clothing and ideas that run counter to parent's values. While most of us have integrated the idea that a child may have tastes and interests different to our own, this passage often stretches parents as much as it does teens. In many systems of planetary ages, Venus is said to rule a seven- (or eight-) year period, beginning at fourteen or fifteen, the time when choices are made about who and what we love. If a parent or grandparent experienced great difficulty with any of these issues, they are likely to be reflected in our own charts. But when we share the same aspect or family of aspects, then we enter a territory fraught with generational significance, a zone of possible talent or repeated struggle.

The Sun

Venus is not the only factor connected to self-worth. We must also look to the Sun and its aspects, and this holds true in questions of self-esteem as well. Parents who have felt unacknowledged by their own families may not be able to "see" a child, and this can create problems with self-image. It is Aphrodite who holds the mirror in classical iconography, and we need to see ourselves reflected with love in the eyes of our mother or father. Through this reflection, we discover our identity. Without the other, we may remain fascinated by our own image, unable to differentiate between self and other, a danger reflected in the story of Narcissus, who confuses himself with his own image, falls in love, and drowns.

Mercury

Virginia Satir stated that problems in families always came back to three issues: values, communication, and rules. When I first read this, my astrological ears pricked up immediately I'm sure you can hear what I did: Venus, values; Mercury, communication; and Saturn, rules. Mercury is the go-between, the planet that moves from inside to outside, from the ordinary world to the underworld. When our Mercury doesn't match that of other family members, we perceive the world quite differently from those closest to us, and can feel disconnected and misunderstood. We may doubt our own perceptions and intelligence, and the natural curiosity of Mercury can turn inward into a kind of constant self-doubt.

Jupiter

Jupiter describes our faith and confidence in a benevolent universe, our belief systems, and our willingness to discover new horizons. Jupiter and Saturn together describe the interface with society, how we relate to the opportunities and constraints presented by the world at large, and the acquisition of moral and ethical values. Dissonant aspects between Jupiter and the Sun, for example may speak of the father's tensions around social status, recognition, and integration into the community

Saturn

Saturn is a key planet in family maps. It best describes the father archetype, the lawgiver and the patriarch, and often carries information about family history. The Saturn cycle defines key moments in each individual's ability to separate from the family, and to construct a solid sense of identity The ability to stand alone, to hold a firm position, to define the limits of the individual, all come from a healthy integration of the Saturn principle. But Saturn can also represent fear of authority and rules, guilt, inhibition, and control. We will be looking at this in detail later.

We could say that families are made up of individuals; mothers and fathers bring their own histories, more or less resolved, into the creation of a new family. Carl Whitaker, a well known family therapist, says that a marriage is really a blending of two foreign cultures, and not always an easy one. A mother burdened by past issues can have difficulty responding freely to a newborn; a fatherless father may feel at a loss when his son turns to him. Not all abused children become abusers or rapists in turn, though some do. Some families create healthier environments than others. They still encounter difficulties, but somehow find ways to resolve them. These solutions, these successful strategies, then become part of the family inheritance. Ideally, a family creates a place where growth is possible for each family member, and the chart patterns will describe the coloring of a particular family, giving us clues to what they did well and what may have been missing. From these descriptions, does anyone recognize a charged area in their own family? Hmm. You don't seem ready to talk about this yet; let's give it more time.

The outer planets

Carl Whitaker even questions the idea of the individual:

> After forty years in this crazy business, I've finally come to realize that I don't believe in people. There's really no such thing as an individual. We're all just fragments of families floating around, trying to live life. All of life and all of pathology is interpersonal. Focusing on intrapsychic processes within a particular person is merely a way of simplifying life beyond reality. Given this perspective, I naturally choose to work with families. That's where the real power and energy of life are found.[4]

Although we may not be ready to go as far as Whitaker in his deconstructing of the individual, the outer planets, Uranus, Neptune, and Pluto, stretch us out beyond individual boundaries and often describe how powerful undercurrents and events shape our lives. As you all know, the outer planets bring disruption to Saturn's careful structure. They create cracks in the edifice, unexpected openings in our experience and consciousness. However, the flavor and range of each transpersonal

---

4 Carl A. Whitaker, *Dancing With the Family*, Brunner/Mazel, NY, 1988, p. 36.

planet is quite unique. With Pluto present in the 4th house of today's chart, that seems like a good place to begin. Does anyone have an idea what kind of issues may be strong when a Plutonian current runs through a family?

AUDIENCE: Family secrets, power issues, and extreme emotions.

LYNN: It sounds as though you might be speaking from personal experience! And yes, Pluto connects strongly with all those issues, as well as indicating a need to respond to powerful events. Sometimes these are collective experiences that lie beyond individual control. I remember well the chart of a young woman, in primal therapy at the time, who had Pluto, Uranus, and Mars conjunct in the 4th house, and both her parents had strong Plutos. Her father, who was fifty when she was born, had fled the Nazis in Germany as a young man—his whole family had been wiped out in the camps. She comes from a broken root, born long after devastating events, and her parents needed to find a response to these events, to either die or be reborn. She felt pushed internally to exorcise emotions of rage and helplessness, to go as deeply as possible into her feelings, and this flowed into her creative talents as a singer and actress. We will be looking in greater depth at this placement later on.

A strong Uranus often breaks patterns, standing out from what comes before. Uranus looks to shake free from past conditioning, to develop something unique, and this holds true for strongly Aquarian people as well. Sometimes an individual with a strong Uranus arrives saying, "Wait, there's been a mistake! They delivered me to the wrong address! How did I end up here?" The Uranian fantasy goes like this: "These aren't my parents, and I'm not meant to live here in this house."

AUDIENCE: That's fascinating! I have Sun conjunct Uranus on the MC, and I thought that I was in the wrong family. My mother actually said that she would never have chosen me if she'd been given a say.

LYNN: Maybe you were in the wrong family. Do you look like them?

AUDIENCE: All my life I've wondered about this. I do seem to have strong connections to my father's chart. My mother had Moon-Venus in Gemini, and her way of expressing closeness was totally different to mine. Now that I'm older, I'm pretty sure I'm connected to them biologically, but it's a strange feeling.

LYNN: Do you know, it does really happen sometimes that people get switched at birth, or there can be family secrets that only come out when some of the protagonists have died. I've met people with these fantasies who learn when they are forty-five that their father wasn't really their father, or it turns out they were adopted, or their older sister was their mother, or the hospital made a mistake. Not that I want to encourage any Uranians in their wilder imaginings! Real cases of mistaken identity or parental confusion usually correspond more to Neptune. What we are touching on here is the transpersonal impulse to feel our roots in something beyond our biological parents—in the divine.

It could be that some individuals need a misfit environment in order to become themselves completely. Matching furniture and matching psyches aren't suited to everyone. It can be quite painful when your own parents are unable to "see" you, incapable of mirroring what you feel inside. After spending time trying to figure out their connections with other family members, Uranians often simply throw up their hands and get on with their lives, usually taking a path which is quite different from the rest of the tribe. Occasionally Uranus in the 4th will describe a family where everyone is odd and eccentric, or brilliant and disturbing for society at large. Do you know Mary Shelley's chart? She had Sun-Uranus-Mercury in the 4th house, and her father and mother were both brilliant social thinkers and innovators. She had a Uranian root. She came from a tribe of feminists and radical thinkers, a family capable of growing very strong personalities—independent-minded individuals who break the social pattern. But when only one person in the family has Uranus in the 4th, or Uranus on another angle, you can be pretty sure they are always going to feel out of step with their family.

I would guess that everyone in this room probably has a sense of being entangled in family patterns, to some degree. Murray Bowen, another well known family therapist, used to puzzle over the power of the family to pull him back into behaviors that he was perfectly conscious of but wanted to leave behind. He described going home for Thanksgiving as an adult with his own children. No matter how well he had prepared beforehand, or how different he was elsewhere, "something would come over him," and he'd find himself acting in the old ways, behaviors otherwise outgrown for years. We do the same, reacting to an older brother, getting peevish with Dad, overly complicit with a younger sister. How does that happen? I don't think he answered that question, except to postulate a kind of psychological force field that maintained individuals in expected roles and behaviors. I suspect most of you can relate to this.

AUDIENCE: It sounds as though you may be talking about some mysterious Neptunian force!

LYNN: Yes, Neptune is a good fit for this unconscious field. When Neptune is strong in a family pattern, it often creates confusion about who's who. This blurring of identity can mean that children never leave home, creating what family therapists call the "enmeshed" family Neptune always pushes us to move beyond the strictly personal, to leave the small self behind for a connection with the Source. Of course, the danger is that you may never learn to exist separately from the whole, or confuse Mother or Father with the divine. One way I've seen Neptune work out in the 4th house is in a family where the father is ill. The daughter, who became a nurse, still lives at home with her young son. She feels it would be a betrayal to abandon her parents, and sacrificed her own relationship to care for them. These are very common Neptunian themes, and we will see more of them as we go along.

THE GENOGRAM

I'd like to look at an example now. Some of you may be familiar with the genogram, a tool which has been widely developed in family therapy and which allows us to immediately see who is who and what place they hold in a family The diagram is fairly straightforward.

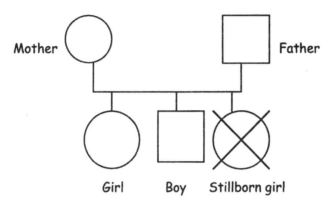

Squares represent men, circles are for women. A line is drawn between the symbols for the mother and father, and the children are represented coming off that, by small vertical lines with symbols attached according to gender, and following birth order. Miscarriages, abortions, and stillborns are all included—an "x" through the circle or square indicates the person is deceased, and the date of birth and death is usually noted next to it. Divorce would be indicated by a line that cuts vertically through the horizontal line between mother and father, and the date would be noted. Other important family events can also be added.

Here is a simple genogram (on page 46). I don't have the charts for the whole family, but the genogram places the one I do have in a revealing context. This family had three children. The first was a girl born in 1917, followed by a son born in 1920. This "x" I've put through the square for the son tells us he died, and here is the date, 1923. The third child, a girl, was born in December 1923, and we will be looking at her chart. What would you expect to find in the chart of a child born soon after the death of a sibling? What kind of planetary pattern?

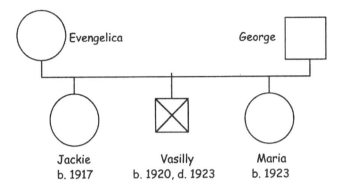

AUDIENCE: Chiron in the 5th?

LYNN: I would expect that kind of Chiron placement to correspond more to the parent's chart. I have often found a strong Pluto or powerful Mars in the chart of a child who comes after a death. Does that surprise you?

AUDIENCE: Pluto would make sense. It describes a shadow of some kind hanging over the person. But Mars?

LYNN: Mars gives us courage to move outside the family circle, and confidence in our ability to survive. The loss of a child may cause parents to overinvest in one who follows, unconsciously binding a son or daughter, who will then need a stronger dose of Mars to break away.

Let's look at this woman's chart. The data isn't absolutely clean; different birth times have been proposed, both cited by Lois Rodden.[5] The one I've chosen puts the Sun in the 12th house rather than the 1st. In any case, she is a double Sagittarius with Jupiter-Sun conjunct the Ascendant and Jupiter strong in its own sign. That powerful solar energy jumps out of the chart, and while Pluto quincunx the Sun from the 8th house gives a mournful base note, this seems to be outweighed by the vital and optimistic Sagittarian signature.

---

5   Lois Rodden, *Profiles of Women*, AFA, 1979. Very "dirty" data; several different dates and times are given. However, for the purposes of this study, which is primarily about the effect of immigration and the lost child, a speculative chart has been deemed appropriate.

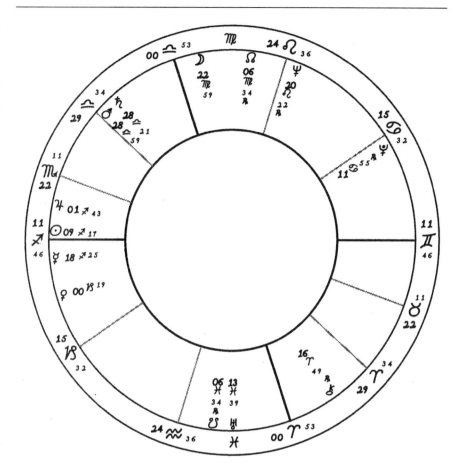

Maria, b. 2 December 1923, 7:18 EST, New York. Placidus cusps; true Node

One way of thinking about a death in the family is that the child who follows must live for two, and sometimes gets twice as much vitality and life force. But this probably occurs less frequently than the kind of Pluto signature which accompanies unresolved grieving and anxiety.

An important piece of information about this family may help to explain things. Their son died during an epidemic of typhoid fever, and almost immediately afterward the parents decided to leave their native Greece for the United States. They arrived in August 1923, when the mother was five months pregnant. A major event in the family's history also needs to be added to the genogram. This daughter, Maria, came with the energy of a new beginning, as well as the shock of a child's death.

Notice the 9th house Moon and Sun conjunct Jupiter in Sagittarius. Both describe the move from one culture to another, and the 12th house often indicates some kind of exile. Neither parent spoke English, and although her father was a pharmacist and eventually made a success of things, the family went through a period of difficult adaptation. A child born at such a moment carries the hopes of her family for a new life, reinforced by the symbolism of 0° Aries on the 4th house cusp. Mars exactly conjunct Saturn in the 10th gives tremendous determination and ambition. Do you see anything else here which reflects the family story so far?

AUDIENCE: Uranus opposes the Moon and squares the Sun. That looks to me like change, even instability. I suppose the 9th and 3rd house emphasis describes the move. Would Chiron in the 4th indicate something unresolved from the past?

LYNN: Yes, unresolved or unhealed. There is difficulty integrating the past, and on top of it, all that Sagittarian energy pushes towards the future. The 12th house often speaks of family ghosts, but also opens up to collective feelings and influences. It is said that she became a "special" child for her mother, who invested tremendous love and passionate feeling into this daughter, perhaps needing to compensate for the loss of her home and her son. This domineering mother infused her daughter with her will and hopes, and Maria became one of the great sopranos of the century: Maria Callas.

Maria Callas reached beyond ordinary limits. She had that larger-than-life quality so fundamental to the operatic mode, tapping into the transcendent quality of the 12th house. In Greek families the birth of a son is usually of prime importance. Her birth after her brother's death meant that her mother poured tremendous energy and attention into this new child, which might not have been the case otherwise. These kinds of events in a family's history become the nutrients for our own development. Often a child born at the moment of major changes, especially a decision for positive change, has access to great creative force, perhaps because the parents are full of the sense of new possibilities. The quincunx between Sun and Pluto creates a constant pressure to go further, to surpass what has already been achieved.

Callas was famous for explosions of temper. She was the archetypal diva, and the diva touches the divine. Sun-Jupiter creates a sense of limitlessness, of being close to the gods, and perhaps her parents saw her as a precious gift, following so closely the loss of their son. In other families the lost child might have cast a long shadow, but here it seems to have added to a sense of mission, giving an urgency and emotional force to her fiery temperament. As a young woman she was awkward, plump, and ungainly. Her much older husband transformed her into a glamorous star, again a reflection of that 7th house Pluto. Callas remained susceptible to powerful personalities all her life. She left her ambitious mother to marry her manager, walking out on him ten years later to pursue a love affair with Aristotle Onassis.

AUDIENCE: Would that be part of the Pluto-Sun quincunx, which gives difficulty integrating the planets involved?

LYNN: Yes, she may feel her power comes only when she is bound to another's passion and influence. It's worth looking more closely at the Saturn-Mars conjunction in Libra in this respect. It goes in the same direction, acting as a spur to accomplishment. I always find it fascinating to see some people with this aspect who can't seem to get out of bed, and others who steamroller their way towards a goal, refusing to be held back. Some years ago, in The Astrological Association Journal, I read an article about fishermen going down with their ship off the coast of Iceland in freezing temperatures. One survived, walking 30 kilometres to the nearest town, and he had a Mars-Saturn conjunction! With the conjunction in Libra, Maria Callas found other people to goad her on. Perhaps Saturn's exaltation helped keep her on track.

AUDIENCE: My daughter had a twin who died at birth, and I always wondered how that might affect her. In her case Mars is angular. She has a very strong 4th house.

LYNN: Twins are usually born quite close together, so the chances are that both would have had an angular Mars, but only one survived. As we have said, survival is a Mars issue, and some of the research suggests that twins fight for dominance, even in the womb. Is she very vital, very alive? Yes? As Rudhyar often pointed out, we cannot change events, only our response to them, and sometimes the weight of the past holds someone back for a long time. The loss of a child is a painful event for a family, and could be symbolized in many ways. A strong 4th house may give the ability to heal the circle through the activation of whatever planet is placed there. Neptune here would call up a great sensitivity to the emotional environment of the family and a need to develop compassion. In your daughter's case the angular Mars suggests that the survival needs of the family gave rise to a strong, dynamic response. A successful adaptation, a strong Mars activated early on, gives a person tremendous vitality, and this vitality may have provided an antidote for the parents grief. Perhaps this was her piece of the puzzle. When one family member moves in a healing direction, things can shift for everyone concerned. Difficult family events don't necessarily haunt us throughout our lives.

AUDIENCE: I have the Sun in the 12th house, and was conceived after my mother had miscarried.

LYNN: That's an interesting take on the 12th house, because it often has to do with something waiting to come to term, needing more time before it can emerge. How far from the Ascendant is your Sun? 10°? The closer to the Ascendant, the faster a planet will progress into the 1st house. I wonder if you sometimes feel you need more time, or that things take longer for you? A miscarriage has to do with unfulfilled potential, and its impact on a family is slightly different than that of a child brought to term. Much will depend on the mother—how she responds to it and what it costs her physically. A stillborn leaves a different imprint in a family from an infant that survives just a few days, or a child who lives for two or three years. The 12th house Sun can symbolize something left over, bumping around in the family unconscious.

AUDIENCE: I also was born after my mother had had a miscarriage, but I've never really made the connection between that and her possessiveness until now. I have Pluto conjunct the Moon, and I often felt eaten alive by her and dragged down by depression, as if I wasn't allowed to be separate. So I suppose that when she looked at me she must have felt all this anxiety, wondering if I might die. We have very strong Mars contacts, and the relationship has had a lot of conflict.

LYNN: Remember we've spoken about Mars several times already in terms of survival energy. It represents the ability to stand up for oneself, to keep others from stepping on one's toes. As I said earlier, the life force needs to be strengthened in some way after a death or a miscarriage, and Mars can do this.

AUDIENCE: My oldest child was born after a miscarriage, but I don't see any of this in her chart. She's very Uranian.

LYNN: I'm sure there must be other ways of looking at this in a family, and I wonder how we might understand that? Perhaps the miscarriage occurred early in the pregnancy, and didn't leave an indelible psychic imprint. I would imagine this has something to do with your response to the event. We human beings are infinitely creative in the way we respond to events. Perhaps you gave her more distance, as a way of protecting your own emotions.

Repeating family patterns: the Fondas

However, family patterns, even difficult ones, can also be used to great advantage—they often become part of the solution. I've brought Jane Fonda's example. She and her brother Peter both followed in their actor father's footsteps, as did her niece Bridget. Jane Fonda was married to Ted Turner for ten years, and they share something significant in common. Any ideas as to what that might be?

AUDIENCE: Money and multiple marriages.

LYNN: True enough. But besides money, on an emotional and psycho- logical level they shared family tragedies. Both have a parent who

51

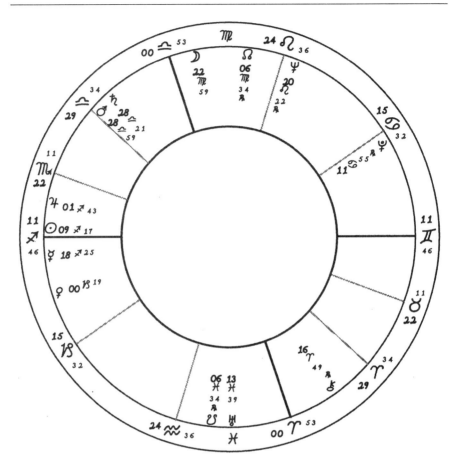

Ted Turner, 19 November 1938, 8:50 am EST, Cincinnati, Ohio.
Placidus cusps; true Node

committed suicide. Ted Turner's father shot himself in the head after accomplishing the goals he'd set for himself; at fifty-three he owned a yacht, had his own business, and had made a million dollars. There was nowhere else to go, no longer any point in continuing.

Let's look at some of the elements of Ted Turner's chart, particularly the image of the father. The Sun conjuncts Venus in Scorpio at 26/27° in the 12th house, and squares Jupiter in the 3rd. We can see tension and contradiction between a somewhat impenetrable masculine image and an outgoing social personality. But it is Mars, the IC ruler, opposition Saturn in Aries in the 4th house, that best describes

Turner's relationship with his father. Turner senior was violent and driven. He would devise punishments for Ted if he had done something wrong, beating him with a wire coat hanger, or laying down and asking Ted to beat him. He left Turner in boarding school at age six, gave him a military education, and never let him feel comfortable or at ease.

Ted Turner became driven and compulsive, pushed by the need to win and dominate, explosive and unpredictable. He was obsessed by death, and pursued sailing in ever more dangerous situations, winning a race in which fifteen people were killed in a storm. As with his father, sexual conquest and success went hand in hand. He constantly put himself in danger, and spoke frequently of suicide, convinced that he would be dead by the time he was fifty. Turner was twenty when his elder sister died of lupus, and grew up haunted and pursued by death, desperately needing to exorcise these 12th house ghosts.

Turner's role in global communication is aptly described by that Sagittarian Mercury conjunct the Ascendant, and Jupiter square Sun conjunct the cusp of the 3rd house, as well as Pluto in the 8th, trine Sun and square moon. Turner was widely ridiculed when he launched CNN, seen by most experts as a wild pipe dream, but the size of his ambitions can be understood as a way to avoid reaching the pointlessness that had overtaken his father. He only began to enjoy life when he went into therapy and began taking lithium, given an ultimatum by a woman he loved. Those who knew him well described his pre-therapy self as "scary," "explosive," and "monomaniacal, interested only in winning." This transformation had already taken place by the time he met Jane Fonda, whose own mother committed suicide when she was twelve. Now, when two people who share a similar pattern meet, a great deal depends on how much of the underlying issues have become conscious. On a very deep level, the psychological fit can bring healing, and Turner married Fonda just before he turned fifty-three, the age his father had reached when he committed suicide.

These anniversary dates are powerful turning points, often unconsciously reactivating traumatic events, but also offering a possibility for a new future free of past conditioning. However, a few years later, during the Pluto-Sun transits, Turner was diagnosed with skin cancer, a manifestation of the destructive power of the sun. He again confronted the issue of his mortality, speaking out on the need for protection. Turner has redirected his self-destructive impulses into campaigns for the preservation of the environment, global peace, zero population growth, and other lofty schemes.

Suicide leaves a lasting imprint on a family, not only because of its violence and despair, but because it creates a void when faced with the future. Hillman said that every suicide is a transformation unable to happen, an inability to give birth to a new life. A suicide in the family sends a message: "I do not know how to go forward in my life. I can't continue, I don't know how to change, or to find a way through this." This absence of a model for moving through pressure and difficulty, as well as an immense residue of guilt, can feed into a repeating pattern of suicide in a family. Hemingway's father committed suicide, and his grandfather attempted it; his granddaughter recently continued the tradition. The men in the Hemingway tradition defined themselves through machismo and courage, and refused to accept the ravages of age. Ernest Hemingway was physically broken by severe accidents and ill health before he turned the gun on himself. From one generation to the next, families tend to fall back on the same "solutions."

Jane Fonda,[6] with a fiery 5th house Sun exactly trine her Leo Moon and ruler of the Leo Ascendant, easily followed her father's path to an acting career. At first glance this seems a very positive masculine image, with a wide conjunction to Venus and sextile Mars. But on closer examination we see the Sun forms a T-square to an 8th house Saturn in Pisces and Neptune in Virgo. This suggests a shining and brilliant father—the star who regularly disappears, the squares undermining any sense of solidity or certainty. The Sun is also quincunx Pluto, and Pluto rules her Scorpio 4th house, suggesting something hidden or brooding in the father's energy. The 4th house ruler in the 12 almost always indicates uneasy issues in a family.

---

6   Data from Lois Rodden, *Profiles of Women, ibid.* The data was given by Fonda herself. Ted Turner's chart is from Michel and Francoise Gauquelin, *The Gauquelin Book of American Charts,* ASC, 1982.

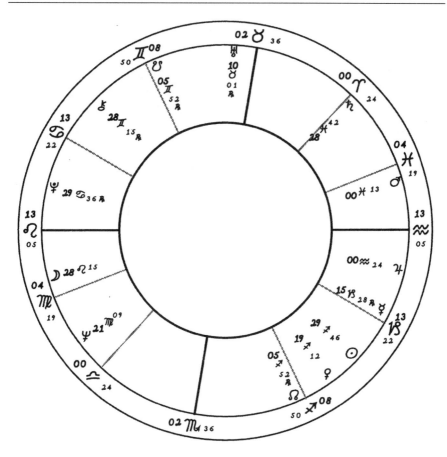

Jane Fonda, 21 December 1937, 7:57 pm EST, New York Placidus cusps; true Node

Jane's mother Frances, Henry's second wife (he married five times), was also an actress, but suffered from depression and committed suicide in a psychiatric hospital. The Moon opposes Mars and also forms the apex of a yod with Saturn and Jupiter. It's interesting to note that Ted Turner also has a yod in his chart, with Uranus as the apex to Mercury and Mars, the yod often being an aspect of sudden and radical change. When Jane's mother cut her throat, a particularly brutal form of suicide, a terse Henry told the children their mother had died of a heart attack, and never spoke of her again. Jane, whose 10th house Uranus describes an unstable, unpredictable mother, discovered the truth several years later while reading a movie magazine.

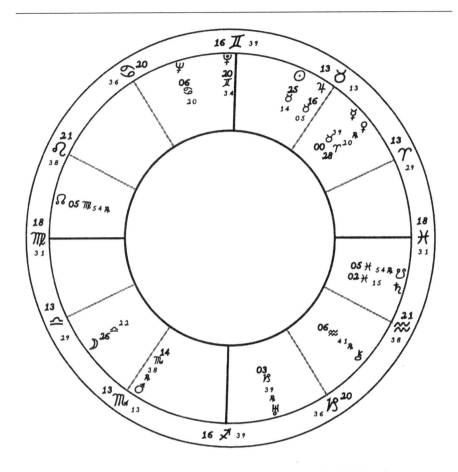

Henry Fonda, 16 May 1905, 2:00 PM CST, Grand Island, Nebraska
Placidus cusps; true Node

Both children describe Henry[7] as cold and distant, a man who found it "almost impossible to show emotion to those closest to him." His Ascendant ruler Mercury is in the 8th house, and Pluto conjuncts the MC, while Saturn in Pisces makes an out-of-sign square to his Taurus Sun. All these, together with Mars in Scorpio, correspond to the description of an introverted and foreboding father, despite a Jupiter-Sun conjunction. Peter described their home life as "dark, silent, and booby-trapped."

---

7   Data from Lois Rodden, *AstroData II*, AFA, 1988; "dirty" data.

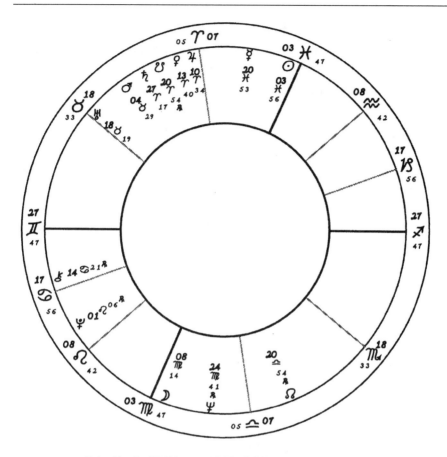

Peter Fonda, 23 February 1940, 12:09 pm EST, New York, NY
Placidus cusps; true Node

In Peter's chart,[8] Sun on the MC in Pisces again suggests a highly visible father with a Neptunian overlay, but he has Mars conjunct Saturn
square Pluto, and responded with explosive violence and wildness as a
child. When his father remarried, just six months after their mother's
death, and left on his honeymoon, Peter took a gun and shot himself in
the stomach; he was ten years old. Other suicide attempts and a history
of drug abuse followed, but after years of therapy and a stable marriage,
Peter now says his father was "a painfully shy man," and that as children they misread this as anger. Jane has parlayed that Mars opposition

8 Data from Lois Rodden, *AstroData II, ibid.* This data is from a birth certificate
and is therefore reliable.

57

Moon into great determination, and her battles have been fought in true Uranian style with public opinion during the Vietnam War, and against ageing as the high priestess of aerobics back in the 1980's. Clearly she identified with her father from the very beginning, while her brother Peter carried more of the emotional shock—he has both Moon and Neptune in the 4th house. This fits the classic birth order pattern, where the eldest child tends to be high-performing, and the second child is more closely linked to the emotional issues in a family. If you have a parent who has not survived, you must choose which side you are on, and Mars is very much a planet of survival. Jane tapped into the emotional power of the aspect, and used it to propel her forward, but her chart is also very different from her brother's. In Ted Turner she found another fighter, one who had pulled back from the edge. Both of them come from very privileged and yet destructive backgrounds, and the choice between constructive and creative use of force or destruction is central to both their lives.

AUDIENCE: Mars in the 7th opposition the Moon in Jane's chart would indicate a lot of anger in the marriage. But wouldn't Uranus in the 10th describe a more independent mother? Do you know anything about their relationship?

LYNN: I would imagine it couldn't be easy being an actress married to someone like Henry Fonda, who was running around having affairs and was not a great communicator. A lot of rage could build up. There may be an issue of feeling left in the shadow by a famous husband, but we probably need more information. Uranus can also indicate highly unstable conditions. Along with Moon opposition Mars, it could describe someone whose energy swings back and forth or, alternatively, has great courage and daring.

AUDIENCE: Could Peter Fonda be carrying his mother's chart?

LYNN: His own chart certainly reflects the impact of his mother, with a very powerful full Moon conjunct the IC, and Neptune, the MC ruler, in the 4th as well. In a way, the mother lies at the root of the chart, and that strong 4th house underlines the importance of the family story and gives an allegiance to the past—so emotionally powerful! The Saturn-Mars square Pluto speaks of tremendous tension and anger, often bursting out in self-destruction. Although he has worked as an actor for years, much of his career has been in obscure "B" movies, hardly on the scale of either his father or his sister's success, and perhaps some of this is self-sabotage. He could be reliving his mother's experience of being overshadowed professionally.

Things get more complicated. Henry Fonda remained close to his first wife, and her children by a later marriage were friends of the Fondas. Peter eventually fell in love with her daughter Bridget. When Bridget's mother killed herself, Peter was close to her, consoling her through the loss, but nine months later Bridget also committed suicide. Peter later named his daughter in memory of her. Both he and his father were initially drawn to women who at some point couldn't go on with their lives. For Peter Fonda we could see this as a way of reliving the loss of his mother, having to choose again between life and death. He has five planets in the 11th house, including Jupiter and Saturn, two different ways of imagining the future. A history of suicide in a family demands our attention, pushing those that follow to find out what makes life worth living. In the Fonda family there is either death or success, stardom or self-destruction, and we need to pay particular attention to the Sun, Mars, and Pluto. To understand these patterns in a really satisfying way, we would need the mother's chart.

PLANETARY GENOGRAMS

How can we work with this kind of information? I often draw up a sketchy genogram while I'm speaking to a client, if it seems appropriate. In Paris I set up a genealogy group. We met one Sunday a month, using the month in between to study a series of family charts and the family map, which would have been prepared ahead of time. I tried to get people to focus on a particular issue, and we'd look at the distribution of planets in houses and signs, and then set up what I call the planetary genograms.

A Mercury story

Here's an example. Early on, when I was doing this work, I asked a group whether anyone there had a family where communication was problematic. A woman raised her hand. As it turned out, her seventeen-year-old son, David, had stopped speaking to everyone else. This was a family with two sons, aged seventeen and fifteen. Their mother was in the astrology group. I said, "Where's your son's Mercury?" She said, "Oh, my son has Mercury in Taurus conjunct Saturn." I said, "Oh, that's interesting. Where's your husband's Mercury?" She replied, "He has Mercury conjunct Mars in Aries, and Saturn in Gemini. I have Saturn in Gemini too."

As she spoke, I drew up a planetary genogram, extracting Mercury from all four charts. This is what it looked like. As you can see, she has Mercury square Mars, and the second son has Mercury conjunct the Moon. Now, even without elaborating the meaning of each of these aspects or seeing the rest of the chart, I quickly got an idea of which questions to ask.

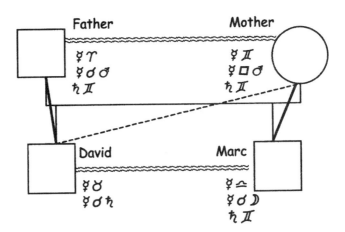

Key:
——— = close
≋≋≋ = conflict
------- = distant

How to construct a planetary genogram

1. Gather a family's charts. You may wish to begin first with only parents and children, to keep the amount of information manageable.

2. Set up a regular genogram, showing who was born when, and in what order. This will become the "template" for all the planetary genograms. Remember, men are represented by squares, and women by circles. Children are drawn in from left to right according to birth order, along with symbols for any abortions or miscarriages.

3. Think of an area in the family that seems to be problematic. If it's communication, select Mercury; if it has to do with rules and authority, you might want to look at Saturn. Choose which planet you wish to map first.

4. List the position of the planet by sign, house, and degree for each member of the family. Make sure to note the aspects this planet makes with the rest of the chart.

5. Note the planet's position for each member of the family in the family genogram (see step 2).

6. Repeat for other planets that seem interesting, or until you find a significant pattern. In theory, you could do one genogram for each planet, but you will quickly be able to "eye" the charts and judge which are significant.

7. Expand a genogram by adding grandparents, children, great grandchildren and in-laws. Plan carefully, or you may need a bigger piece of paper!

8. A Mercury genogram can be refined by adding any factor involved in communication—3rd house, planets in Gemini, and so on. Be careful not to add too much, though, since the point of the technique is to organize the data into an easily recognizable thread of meaning.

It was pure luck that this turned out to be such a striking example. A pattern doesn't always appear where you expect it to. First of all, three of four family members have Saturn in Gemini, and the other has Saturn conjunct Mercury, which immediately conjures up a family where words have great weight, or require a lot of work from everyone concerned. My first question to her was, "Whom did your son talk to before he stopped speaking to everyone else?" As it turned out, he had been quite close to his father; though he could hardly have been considered chatty, they shared a great deal. The mother had always felt slightly shut out, and had formed a close dialogue with her other son, Marc, who is generally more lively and extraverted. In this family the son with Mercury-Moon literally spoke his mother's language, and the son with Mercury-Saturn spoke his father's language. Of course, the next question to ask concerned the parents. What was communication like between them?

AUDIENCE: Did they fight? They both have aspects between Mercury and Mars.

LYNN: Yes, exactly. The parents sniped at each other constantly, and the brothers argued and fought. The family split into two modalities: being at war, with the sons mirroring their parents' relationship, or being in closed pairs of father/son and mother/son. Communication had been an issue all along, but the system functioned, more or less— everyone had someone to talk to.

I will draw in a jagged line between the symbols for the mother and father to indicate conflict, and will do the same between Marc and David. A dark line indicates a strong connection, like this one between Marc and his mother, and a dotted line represents distance or lack of connection.

Oddly enough, the Mercury-Mars aspects shared by the parents indicate a basic similarity—but they had unfortunately fallen into the impatient and wounding side of the aspect. Words tended to become weapons, and the father, who travelled a great deal for his work, had become increasingly withdrawn. He fought less with his wife, but this wasn't necessarily an improvement. The mother talked more and more with her youngest son, who was becoming a replacement spouse. Things had polarized in the family. Suddenly David stopped talking to everyone, except for a few grunts and "Pass the salt." Teenagers are diabolically clever at coming up with a behavior pattern that can send every other family member into a reactive state. After a few months like this, the mother was going mad. She and her husband *had* to talk about it. Was he depressed, angry, unhappy? What on earth could they do about him, and should they be worried?

Do you see what has happened here? At seventeen and a half, David had plans to go away to university the following year. When he left, who would his father have to talk to? When he went mute, the other people in the family were forced to talk to each other. It created some movement in the family system—the very beginning of a change. David's silence was, in fact, a shout—a cry for exchange between his mother and father, and probably much more effective than talking about his discomfort, even if he had been able to do so.

Don't immediately expect to find a communication map of this kind in your own family's charts. It may be another planet, like Venus, that holds the key to the family puzzle. But for the moment let's look at another kind of Mercury pattern, one that is revealed by sign placement.

What if everyone in a family has a well-aspected Mercury in air, but one child doesn't fit, only one, who is born with Mercury in Scorpio or Cancer or Pisces? What's going to happen? What kind of dynamic are you looking at, putting aside everything else in the family for the moment?

AUDIENCE: Mercury in water is a lot less verbal than Mercury in air signs. I would think someone with this could feel quite out of place.

LYNN: Yes, Water does not need words the way air does. Mercury in water very often absorbs and intuits, and may feel connected without talking. They could be okay in this environment up to a point, unless they begin to feel incompetent or undervalued. The family member who is different from the others may gain tremendous strength from this, by developing a special relationship to words. They could carry a quiet weight, bring attention to feeling, speak of what is easy for the others to forget. Otherness doesn't necessarily create pathology, but it can go in that direction when it is misunderstood. The opposite situation, an air Mercury alone in a watery family, could be even harder. Mercury in Gemini feels absolutely shattered by too much silence, by unopened mail and unreturned phone calls: "Please talk to me, please!"

AUDIENCE: Could the watery Mercury be an artistic temperament in a family full of more abstract thinkers?

LYNN: Yes, that's a good way to think about it. The one watery person may need to dive even more deeply to find a language for inner experience, and this can have a powerful effect on other family members. Of course there is always much more going on in terms of aspects and house placements. The signs are only one way of seeing how people interact. Elemental emphasis in families is quite common—it makes it easy to see who fits into the main pattern and who doesn't. This commonality may come through, say, Sun in fire, or similar Mars energy. Each planetary thread will reveal different kinds of connections, and each family has its own kind of patterns. This is the kind of dynamic we'll be looking at today.

A CASE HISTORY

The thread of suicide

Now we are going to turn to our first family. This will mean bringing in quite a few charts, so I'll try to build slowly. As I mentioned earlier, it's often helpful to have a question or a guiding concern to give focus.

These charts were brought to me by Christian, and his concern turns around a pattern of suicide in the family. Both his grandfathers killed themselves, as well as a great-grandfather. He feels uneasy about this and wonders whether astrology will give some clarification about what things to watch out for. Although he has never felt suicidal himself, he worries about his brother, who holds everything inside, and his

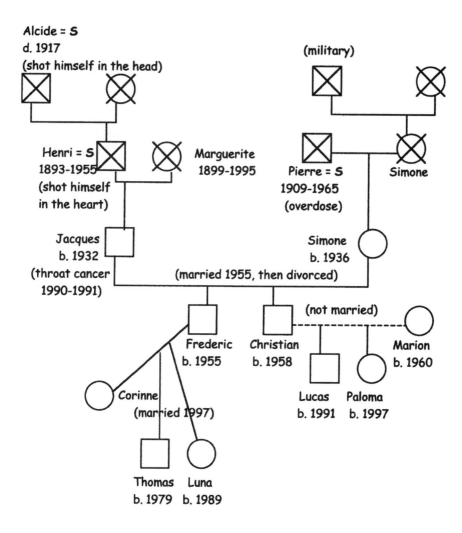

Alcide = **S**
d. 1917
(shot himself in the head)

(military)

Henri = **S**
1893-1955
(shot himself
in the heart)

Marguerite
1899-1995

Pierre = **S**
1909-1965
(overdose)

Simone

Jacques
b. 1932
(throat cancer
1990-1991)

Simone
b. 1936

(married 1955, then divorced)

Frederic
b. 1955

Christian
b. 1958

(not married)

Marion
b. 1960

Corinne
(married 1997)

Lucas
b. 1991

Paloma
b. 1997

Thomas
b. 1979

Luna
b. 1989

[Editor's note: some details have been left out of this genogram for the sake of clarity. Worth noting is that Christian's mother Simone (b. 1936) had a younger sister (b. 1939) whose child developed throat cancer, like Simone's husband Jacques. Jacques remarried after his divorce from Simone, and a daughter, Marie, was born in 1980, nine months after the birth of Frederic's first child.]

mother, who often talks about finding her father's body and makes dark hints about her own end. Although he never mentions it explicitly, the question of fate hangs over the family and the future: Could it happen again? During the time we looked at the family charts, Pluto was transiting his Sagittarian Sun.

My first question is whether the two grandfathers have anything in common, so we need to find out more about the specific circumstances of their deaths. But first I'm going to present the genogram of Christian's family. I know this looks complicated at first, so let's go over it together. As you can see, Christian is the youngest of two brothers. Remember, the squares represent male family members, and circles female. Let's concentrate on the father's side of the family to begin with. Christian's father, Jacques, is the youngest of two children. He has an older sister. Jacques' father Henri committed suicide when Jacques was twenty-three, two months after the birth of Jacques' first son, Frederic—Henri shot himself in the heart. His own father, Alcide, had committed suicide when Henri was twenty-three or twenty-four by shooting himself in the head. I've put a small "s" next to their symbols on the genogram.

Frederic's son was born when he was twenty-four, the age when both his father and grandfather lost their own fathers. And look what happens: Jacques must have immediately made his new wife pregnant, because nine months later, at age forty-eight, he became a father again. This time we have birth rather than death in the family tree. But when Christian's wife became pregnant twelve years later, Jacques was diagnosed with throat cancer. He spoke of his fear of dying and his belief that when one V. arrives, another disappears. Clearly Jacques had not yet got over the shock of his father's death, associated in his mind with the birth of a child. Henri, a negative and pessimistic man, shot himself in the heart rather than the head. Does this suggest he was wounded in love? Is there a generalized anxiety about fatherhood in this family, perhaps an unresolved paternity further back in the family tree? Or is his suicide due to an accumulation of difficulties in his past, compounded by failing health?

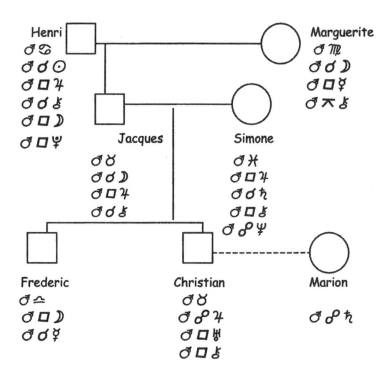

Let's look at it astrologically. What kind of signature would you expect to find?

AUDIENCE: Pluto has got to be strong in the situation you describe.

AUDIENCE: What about Mars or Uranus? There's an explosive kind of violence in a shooting death. That seems more than just Plutonian to me.

LYNN: Those are just the directions I would tend to look in. Let's go through the charts and put up the planetary genogram for Mars to start with. I don't have the birth data for the great-grandfather, Alcide, and I have no birth time for Henri, the grandfather, so I've put up a sunrise chart. In any case, most of the aspects remain within orb during the day.

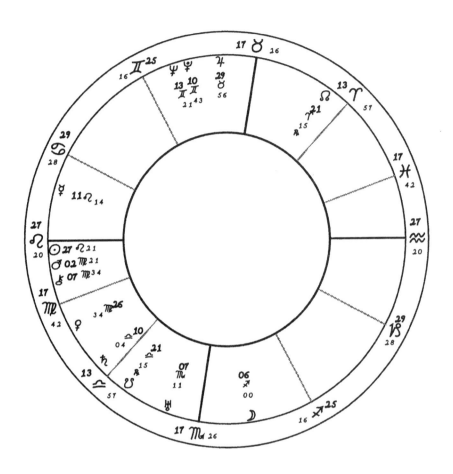

Henri, 20 August 1893, sunrise, Paris

We can find significant planetary patterns even without a birth time. The Sun is in late Leo, conjunct Mars at 2° Virgo, both square Jupiter at 29° Taurus that's definite. The Moon moves from 6° Sagittarius at sunrise to 15° at midnight. It is either square Mars or opposition Pluto and Neptune, perhaps both. A Leo Sun, and he shot himself in the heart! He married on 11 December 1924, and killed himself "around 12 December 1955"—very close to or on his wedding anniversary.

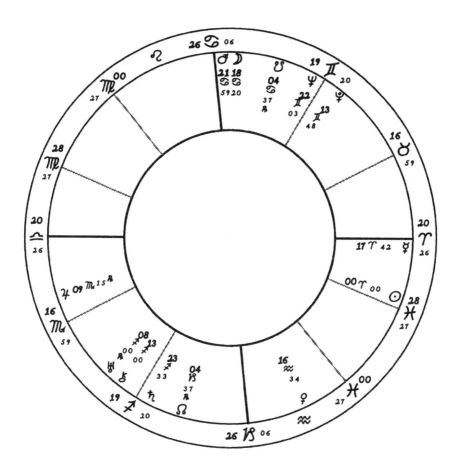

Marguerite, 20 March 1899, "evening" (here calculated for 8:00 pm LMT), Paris

The grandmother, Marguerite, Henri's wife, had Moon conjunct Mars in Cancer, square Mercury in Aries. She also had the Sun at the first degree of Aries. This means we're looking at a couple with Mars conjunct the luminaries, and we can expect issues around dominance—a strongly competitive pattern. Mars-Sun for the husband, Mars-Moon for the wife.

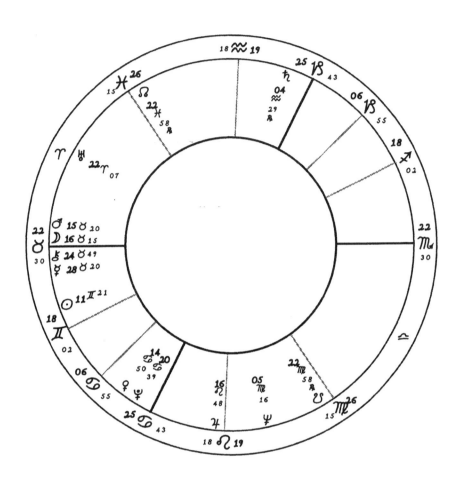

Jacques, 2 June 1932, 4:00 am GMD, Paris

Jacques, the father, has Moon conjunct Mars in Taurus in the 12th, square Jupiter in Leo in the 4th an interesting structure to find in the chart of someone who had throat cancer given that Taurus rules the throat in medical astrology.

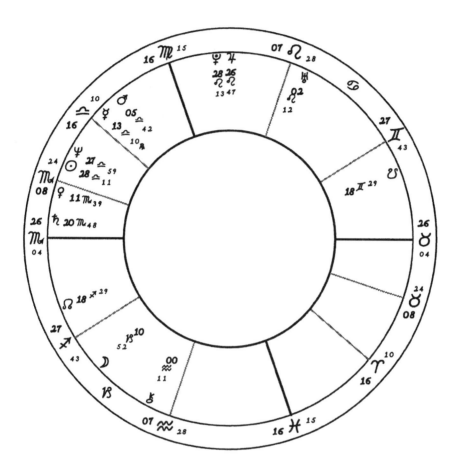

Frederic, 22 October 1955, 10:00 am, Paris

Frederic, Christian's elder brother, was born a few months before his grandfather's suicide. He has the Moon in Capricorn, square Mars in Libra. Mars and Mercury are linked through conjunction. Note that this pattern is similar to his grandmother's.

71

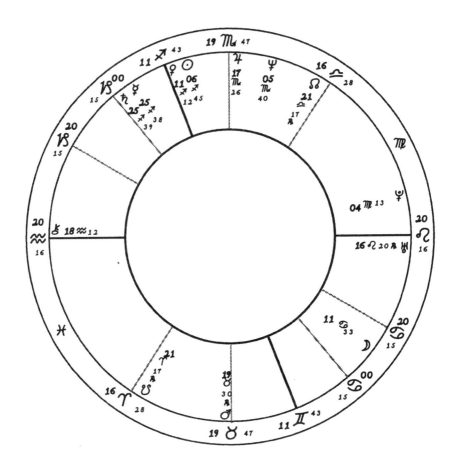

Christian, 29 November 1958, 1:00 pm CET, Paris

Christian has Jupiter in Scorpio opposition a Taurus Mars, picking up his father's and grandfather's pattern, but there is no aspect to the Moon. He is the only one in the family on the father's side without an aspect between Moon and Mars, and Moon is in Cancer trine Jupiter. Christian also has Uranus in Leo square Mars, making up a powerfully energetic grand cross with Chiron in Aquarius.

The Mars-Jupiter thread

It certainly looks as though something has been inherited. We consistently find either Mars-Moon or Mars-Jupiter. Later we'll look at Christian's children's charts to see whether they fit into the pattern, but I think this is probably enough information to take in for the moment. We have found a planetary thread, and now we need to interpret it! One of the interesting ways to think about any planetary combination is to look at what happens when the two principles interact. Are they friendly or unfriendly? What is the dialogue between the planets? Any ideas about Jupiter in aspect to Mars?

AUDIENCE: It will exaggerate Mars' violence.

LYNN: Does anybody have Jupiter Mars? Yes? Do you find that you have extreme outbursts of anger? Yes? When Mars energy comes up, it can be very strong, and it needs somewhere to go. How do you live with that on a day-to day basis? When you think of your chart, do you see Jupiter-Mars as one of the things that you really like about yourself?

AUDIENCE: I would be boring without it!

LYNN: "I would be boring without it." That's a very interesting comment. What do Jupiter-Mars people like? They like things to be happening—they like action, movement, energy. Whenever Jupiter is strong, it brings more aliveness to whatever it touches. Of course, Jupiter can get phony and inflated when it's disconnected to the center. It's still trying to make things bigger. Remember Maria Callas, with Jupiter conjunct the Sun. She was bigger than life in many ways. Mars doesn't usually resist the Jupiterian call, because both planets tend toward extraversion; instead, it can have a strong tendency to go into overdrive.

AUDIENCE: Does Jupiter-Mars need to escape?

LYNN: I would say it certainly needs to roam. This aspect demands movement of some kind. That movement can be in physical space, even becoming nomadic. There is something about the sphere and scope of action being large and spacious. Overdoing clearly triumphs over underdoing. The guys who get sand kicked in their face on the beach are unlikely to have Mars square Jupiter. Rather than hesitate, these people will often rush into things, needing to prove over and over again their fearlessness and inexhaustibility. This aspect has a strong physical and sexual component. Neither planet turns energy inward, and without other factors to balance things out, like a strong Saturn or lunar focus, escapism through a kind of hyperactivity is certainly possible. These people are more likely to get themselves in trouble by taking on too much; they probably don't hesitate enough.

AUDIENCE: I don't hesitate. He who hesitates is lost.

AUDIENCE: I have Jupiter in Pisces opposition Mars. I don't always know where I'm going, so sometimes I sit and dream about it. That's the Pisces side. But I'd rather go. I'm happier when I do.

AUDIENCE: My boyfriend has this aspect, and sometimes he exhausts me. He never seems to want to stop.

LYNN: My favorite examples of Jupiter opposition Mars are Errol Flynn, Laurence Olivier, and John Wayne. They are all Geminis with Jupiter opposition Mars—dashing, daring, and courageous. Errol Flynn had Mars in Pisces. He insisted on doing all his own stunts, even very dangerous ones. He also had problems with his limits—the quintessential Hollywood party animal, he drank too much, and got into legal trouble for seducing very young girls. John Wayne and Laurence Olivier were born within a few days of each other, and both have Mars exalted in Capricorn opposite an exalted Jupiter in Cancer. Mars is conjunct Uranus and Jupiter conjuncts Neptune, so this is admittedly more than an ordinary opposition. They incarnate forcefulness and a willingness to take risks. John Wayne eventually became the ultimate male tough guy -a macho icon to be admired or mocked. The French love to imitate him because he barely moves his lips when he speaks, something linguistically impossible in their own language: the triumph of control over morality. I always picture these three men with swords in their hands, jubilant in combat.

Jupiter square or opposition Mars demands a stretch. We find the opposition in Gandhi's chart, and the square in Larry Flynt's. Neither ever shrank from a fight. Both had major legal battles, largely brought on by their own actions, and both won against great odds. To my mind, Jupiter-Mars becomes destructive when it is held in and contained within too tight a structure. Is that clear? For all you Jupiter-Mars people, what happens when you are in a frustrating situation with limited possibilities? You're making some very bestial noises in response to that question!

It is unbearable for Jupiter-Mars to feel squashed or stuck in a very tiny space. Gandhi could bear prison because he saw it as part of the battle, and beyond that felt connected to a spiritual purpose. But generally, if a Jupiter-Mars person is told that they have no choice, or that action is pointless, it feels like death. There always have to be options and choices. In and of itself, this is normally a healthy, life-affirming aspect, if slightly over the top for the people who live with them. You need something else for it to become destructive. It is, of course, an aspect of overreaching, and often these individuals bring about their own fall by going too far.

AUDIENCE: I was just thinking that both Gandhi and Larry Flynt were shot. Do you think that has something to do with Mars-Jupiter?

LYNN: That's a fascinating idea! I hadn't thought of that at all. Jupiter in a hard aspect to Mars may not know when to stop; it may carry a battle to a breaking point, provoking an extreme aggressive response. Still, with assassination I'd expect Pluto to be involved as well. I know that's the case for Gandhi.

The Moon-Mars thread

Let's turn our attention to the Moon-Mars aspects in this family pattern. Keep in mind that, so far, we are only looking at the father's side of the family What can you say about Moon conjunct or square Mars?

AUDIENCE: Volatile emotions.

AUDIENCE: Warrior personality.

AUDIENCE: Strong, sudden instinctive responses.

AUDIENCE: Moon-Mars makes me think of cutting. Could it mean someone who gets cut off from their own feelings?

LYNN: Now, that's an interesting question. Does anybody here have Moon-Mars? Do any of you feel you cut yourselves off from it? No? My experience doesn't go in that direction. You're more likely to find emotional cut-off with hard aspects between Pluto and the Moon.

AUDIENCE: For me, it's clearly other people who get cut!

LYNN: Moon-Mars may indeed be about cutting, but one of the things you need to remember about Mars is that it puts energy outwards. The nature of Mars is to thrust forward. It is an extrovert, ex-centric planet, moving away from the center. Mars puts up a great defense, and also goes out there and gets things. The Moon, on the other hand, moves inward, and in this sense they are opposites.

AUDIENCE: The combination could make someone protective of their possessions.

LYNN: Yes, the Moon is basically a caretaking or protective energy, but it makes things safe without weapons. Mars also defends and protects, but in a different way. Moon-Mars is more like the policeman or security guard, armed to the teeth and ready to fight for you, and we may as well throw in that highly trained, slightly menacing German Shepherd for good measure.

AUDIENCE: My experience of people with Moon-Mars is that they often act as if they're under attack. You have to be careful around them, they have such strong reactions.

LYNN: This is a very, very strong aspect of reaction. One of the things the Moon and Mars have in common is motion and emotion. The Moon is the fastest-moving planet, and Mars is about movement—things go in, then go back out very quickly.

AUDIENCE: They don't always seem to notice other people's feelings.

LYNN: Their own feelings are so vivid and overwhelming that there may not be much room to take other people into account. They often respond without thinking. Both Mars and the Moon are planets of the instinctive life; they have to do with a very physical, gut-level response to things. It's almost as if their skin were more sensitive than other people's. Emotions and action well up in the same time continuum, way before they have thought things through intellectually. If you get a cramp while swimming and start to go under, a Moon-Mars person comes in handy. They will dive in to save you before they have time to think about it. This is the classical tigress mother who will save her cubs from any danger, and it really does function on that level. What one of you just said "They don't seem to be aware of other people's feelings!"—can be because they have a war going on inside, or, at the very least, a struggle to contain the emotional wildness. I once saw a friend, who has the opposition, open an envelope containing a bill for a rather large sum of money. He put his fist through the wall in anger. It wasn't as if the bill came as a total surprise—he'd been expecting it, but the shock of reading it was too strong to contain physically, and he actually hurt himself.

AUDIENCE: Could we say that Moon-Mars has trouble containing emotions?

LYNN: You could say that. Of course, this might not be true if Saturn were involved, or there were other factors to hold the energy back. A person with Moon-Mars needs to move their feelings out, to express something inside and give it back. Whether, in doing so, other people get knocked around a bit, probably depends on the signs involved, but mostly on how conscious someone is. That raw emotional power probably rumbles close to the surface even after years of therapy. That doesn't mean that feelings are always raw, but they remain strong and subject to outbursts. Much will depend on how safe the Moon feels. An insecure Moon-Mars, at its worst, turns to blame and revenge fantasies. "He did this to me, I'll get him!"

Someone with this aspect may have experienced anger from another family member, often a woman, since the Moon symbolizes the mother and other female caretakers. I worked with a woman who had Moon and Mars conjunct in Scorpio. She remembers her mother beating her head against the tiled walls of the bathroom until she started bleeding. As a mother herself, she sometimes feels "possessed" by a rising tide of anger, shouting words she "doesn't mean," words her mother screamed at her: "I wish you were never born!" It is very hard for her to stop herself, once she begins. Lillian Hellman, who had this aspect, describes an argument with her father in her autobiography:

> I sat down again, knowing for the first time the rampage that could be caused in me by anger. The room began to have other forms, the people were no longer men and women, my head was not my own. I told myself my head had gone somewhere and I have little memory of anything after...[9]

In cultures like Britain, where raging and screaming are frowned upon, the Moon-Mars person must find another outlet or somatize headaches, ulcers, tummy upsets, and depression can all be symptoms of imploded emotions. Ringo Starr has a Moon-Mars-Pluto conjunction in Leo, and happily pounded it out on the drums. As Frank Clifford has written, Mars is important for making an impact in performance charts. And yet, shortly after his divorce, at age thirty-nine, Ringo had emergency intestinal surgery, and his house in Los Angeles burnt to the ground a few years after. Even the drums didn't get it all out. I have also seen this aspect in the charts of those who have great courage, like a woman born with birth defects who, sustained by her mother's will,

---

9   Lillian Hellman, *An Unfinished Woman: A Memoir*, Little, Brown, 1969.

underwent over thirty operations before she was twenty and overcame the doctor's prediction of life in a wheelchair.

Moon-Mars can mean a mother who will go to battle for you, and, more often than not, describes women with a certain amount of forcefulness. The strong drive of the aspect can be spent in conflict or directed toward a goal. As a family pattern this may describe strong determined women, women behind the wheel. The women may run things or be the drivers, in the sense of motivating other people in the family. Or they may go to war. For your sake, you hope the war finds an external adversary and is not directed towards you or against themselves.

Warrior and nurturer come together with this aspect, in the charts of both men and women. This makes the Sun-Mars grandfather (probably both are square the Moon) and the Moon-Mars grandmother in Christian's family a particularly interesting couple, even without knowing the house placements. Normally you would think that the Sun in Leo conjunct Mars would be stronger than Moon-Mars in Cancer, but they are probably better thought of as complementary. In the re-discovered classical astrology, Mars rules the watery triplicity at night, giving it power in a water sign, and this makes sense when we think of the less conscious moments of emotional life. What kind of mother would Marguerite be?

AUDIENCE: I would imagine an argumentative, directive mother who orders people around, but allows little discussion. Moon-Mars is square Mercury in Aries. She demands that you agree with her. Other people would have to go along with what she wants, or she could make things very unpleasant emotionally.

LYNN: That's very perceptive. Moon in Cancer wants emotional closeness, but with Mars conjunct, it often drives people away. "You will respond to me emotionally the way I want you to." Christian described her as a tight-fisted, rule-bound, unpleasant old lady, whom he hated going to visit. His parents forced his hand, and the visits were full of rules: "Don't touch that. Don't do that. You have to do it this way." At the end she would open her pocketbook and pull out a crumpled note, which he always felt was meager payment for an unpleasant duty. He detested her racist talk, full of insults to *"negres et arabes,"* and her small-minded, narrow view of life.

AUDIENCE: Would Mars conjunct Moon be an aspect of racism?

LYNN: It could just as easily be the opposite. It all depends on what you choose to protect, because this aspect is as willing to fight for something as it is to fight against. Cancer describes the circle of home, family, country, that we are willing to protect and claim as our own. In the natural zodiac it is quincunx both Sagittarius and Aquarius, signs that have to do with outsiders. On an archetypal level, tension builds up between "us" and "them," tribe and non-tribe. An unhappy Moon-Mars will be angry at someone or something, and is probably not a lot of fun to hang out with, looking for a target to spill out its animosity. This can be a very difficult aspect if it isn't channeled. Moon-Mars can also be tightly contained and goal-oriented, with a profile of high achievement, drive, and determination. But watch out when it's unsatisfied.

AUDIENCE: I get the feeling of someone who nags and wounds with words.

LYNN: Yes, because Mercury is involved here. It could easily turn words into weapons. Moon-Mars in a family pattern may simply describe anger, a good guess here because the husband has Moon square Mars as well. This corresponds pretty well to the description of the grandson—a woman who won't leave you alone. She also ran the cash register in the family business, a busy restaurant.

AUDIENCE: Is that why he talks about her relationship to money?

LYNN: Yes, that's right. Later she ran a shop that sold leather goods, and would dole out small amounts of money to the grandchildren on some condition or other. When Christian was nine or ten, he remembers refusing her point blank: "I don't want your money, don't bother." If you look at his chart you'll see he also has Moon in Cancer, so it's fascinating to reflect on his highly charged response to her. Sagittarians are repulsed by tightwads, and attracted by generosity. But in rejecting his father's family he was also choosing his mother, who despised her inlaws. I don't think you'll find that surprising, given the exact conjunction of his Venus with the MC. His mother was indeed a beautiful, exciting woman, the opposite of the father's side of the family. For Christian, the paternal side of the family has a kind of tightness, an overly wound up, rigid, ungenerous feeling. For eight generations they've been Parisians, petit bourgeois shopkeepers committed to self-interest. Except for one cousin, he doesn't actually like any of them, and wouldn't voluntarily choose to spend time with them. That's pretty extreme, isn't it?

Henri's suicide shook the family. He had always tended to look on the dark side of things, and his health had deteriorated, but the suicide was unexpected. Henri's mother died of tuberculosis when he was twelve, and he and his brother were sent away to boarding school, deeply unhappy. Between his mother's death, the war, and his father's bankruptcy and suicide, he began life under terribly difficult conditions. The Moon is opposition Pluto and Neptune. Perhaps as a reaction to their mutual loss, Henri and his brother became very close—they even married sisters. His brother's painful death of cancer in 1949 had reinforced the depressive side of his personality. His son Jacques, in reaction to this dour father, became relentlessly upbeat and superficial, and never speaks of anything "difficult," which for Christian goes a long way to explain his father's throat cancer.

AUDIENCE: Didn't you say earlier that the grandfather couldn't bring himself to tell his sons about the bankruptcy?

LYNN: That's a very good point. Something was too difficult to say — with fatal consequences. Remember the story: Shortly after Christian's wife became pregnant with their first child, his father was diagnosed with throat cancer. He had a business and home in North Africa, and came to Paris for treatment. He actually moved in with them for four or five months. The shadow of death came up, but Jacques didn't die.

He was cured by the chemotherapy. The repetition of the pattern tells us something, though, because recurring events in a family usually point to an unresolved issue knocking at the door.

Jacques' Moon-Mars conjunction is in the 12th house, a house where there are often residual phantoms. At UAC I went to Darby Costello's lecture on the water houses, and she talked about the family ghosts, people and issues that you are not aware of as belonging to the 12th. I think that is a good way to talk about it. Is this ghost an angry woman, or one who has been sacrificed in some way? I even wondered if there might not have been a shotgun wedding. In fact, Jacques was Simone's math tutor, and pregnancy forced a marriage that neither really wanted. Simone was only nineteen when her first son was born. When her sons grew up, they both lived with women for many years, and even had children without marrying, which makes sense, given the parent's story. I would wonder, with all this, if the grandfather weren't also made to do something he didn't want to do?

AUDIENCE: The male image in this family seems problematic somehow.

LYNN: Doesn't it seem clear that the women are combative and the men under pressure? Mars in a family pattern can indicate striving for achievement, but it also builds a strife-filled environment. These contacts increase the possibility of conflict. Does anybody have a family that tends to go to war? Do you have a strong Mars in your family pattern?

AUDIENCE: My mother has Moon-Mars conjunct Neptune, conjunct my Pluto in the 5th house. We are always feuding.

LYNN: The Moon often holds what happened in the past, and Mars here can constantly reactivate memories and emotions. People resuscitate old battles, or never stop fighting them, like those Japanese soldiers on a remote island who only surrendered years after the war had ended. Haven't you observed a tendency for strong Cancer or lunar energy to call up past emotions into the present? "That day I came home from the hospital and you went out for a drink..." It's rerunning the family story.

AUDIENCE: Rerunning the past.

LYNN: And rekindling past battles is very common with Moon-Mars. With Moon-Mars very strong in the family, the chances are someone is carrying a lot of anger, or, at the very least, a sense of urgency We don't know whether someone is angry at their mother because she was violent, or whether a mother fought to get her way, or whether emergencies rose up in the person's early life.

AUDIENCE: If families have difficult events like suicide, does that push people to act in such a way that they confront the issue again ? Do they feel it hanging over them like some sword of Damocles?

LYNN: That's a very interesting question—particularly for Christian, who feels happy and satisfied with his life just now. The second child he'd wanted was born not long ago, and he's on track professionally. Yet he's uneasy about this family history and feels the need to understand it. He was seven when his maternal grandfather Pierre was found dead at home, old enough to remember the shock. His mother talks about finding her father hanging from a light fixture, but that's imaginative overstatement, because it turns out he took an overdose.

Christian has a mordant sense of humor, and jokes about the situation a lot, and yet the worry rides him like an afterthought. The men on the father's side of the family tend to bitterness and held-in anger, a climate which chafes at someone with Jupiter-Mars, but Christian also has a tight Mercury-Saturn conjunction, unaspected in the 10th house. Remember his frustration at the lack of communication in the family, and how he sees his father's throat cancer. It's probably no accident that he chose a woman who needs to bring the past to light and put words to feelings. The feelings in the family churned around with no place to go, largely unspoken, slowly building into compressed violence.

Christian throws himself into action in order to release some of that, but despite a provocative and biting wit, has had to work to talk about what's important. While we were working on these charts, Christian was in the middle of a Pluto transit to the Sun. Notice the Sun at 6° Sagittarius squares Pluto in the birth chart, symbolizing the tension between the life force and the destructive, transformative energy of Pluto. Often Pluto-Sun aspects demand that someone undergo a symbolic death and rebirth. Here the square reminds us of the linkage between death and birth in the family history. This kind of aspect gives either great anxiety about change or pushes someone to midwife change in himself and others.

AUDIENCE: I just remembered that my mother has Moon-Mars conjunct the MC, and her mother's chart has a similar pattern. She was a great fighter. She was brought up by her grandmother.

LYNN: Perhaps your mother was out there earning money, confronting a difficult world and coming home with all the tension and irritability.

AUDIENCE: I have a similar feeling. What happens is that I can hold the pressure in at work, but then I need to be able to let it go somewhere or I feel really terrible. I have a quincunx between the two.

LYNN: The quincunx is often linked to a certain amount of frustration, since energy tends to back up and build tension, at least for a while. An opposition releases energy much more easily, for good or bad. Planets in quincunx bind each other in self-defeating patterns until a creative solution is found. But oppositions lived unconsciously can describe constant conflict, shouting and screaming, and may resolve very little.

The Neptunian thread

Jacques has Moon-Mars conjunct, but in the 12th house, and he tended to be passive. He also has Sun square Neptune. However, he chose a woman who hated his mother and went to war with his family, living out Moon-Mars for him. His son Frederic has Sun conjunct Neptune as well, and Moon in Capricorn square Mars-Mercury, a very similar structure to Jacques'—both have air Suns and earth Moons, with similar aspects. How would the Neptunian element tend to work out?

AUDIENCE: An absent father.

AUDIENCE: A struggle to find your identity.

LYNN: Sun-Neptune gives great sensitivity, and sometimes indicates loss or sadness, a longing for another world. When the everyday environment doesn't provide uplift, Sun-Neptune can tune out and become disconnected to others, even those who are closest. It can describe a father who has checked out emotionally. His attention may be elsewhere, whether he is sitting in the same room or literally absent. He may "go away" to keep from feeling too much. In Frederic's case it may express his father's sense of helplessness, even a tendency to resignation. Often, Neptunians give up rather than fight, and let themselves drift into unconsciousness, away from pain. Perhaps we could see Frederic's Sun-Neptune as a connection to his father's sadness or helplessness around the suicide, something Jacques may be carrying from his own father.

AUDIENCE: Sun-Neptune has a tendency to avoid conflict, rather than fight. It makes the men look weaker than the women here.

LYNN: Imagine a dialogue in this kind of family "Honey, you didn't take the garbage out!" says Moon-Mars. "Mmm, what did you say, dear?" says Sun-Neptune. Neptunians wrap themselves in a little fog and the words go right by, only half-heard. We could imagine this to be Jacques' strategy in his family. This would allow him to stay emotionally on the surface in an environment that must have been full of conflict. With Mercury rising, he's quite talkative, but he can't hear what's said and can't say what he's feeling. Real communication never gets through; it's too dangerous. Frederic has a similar tendency—the same pattern is there.

Working on the family tree creates waves in the family. Christian had to call various family members to get birth data, and people would then want to know what the astrologer found out. Last fall, after he collected this information, he and his brother spoke about the suicides for the first time. They had *never* talked about them before. Simply asking these questions opens up channels of communication. The process creates a flow of energy in the family, and sets small changes in motion, which is one of the reasons this work is so exciting. Of course it's important to ask the right questions.

The other side of the family

I think it's time to explore Simone's side of the family. Christian's mother is a very striking, charismatic woman from a family of beautiful women. Both her mother and younger sister were great beauties,

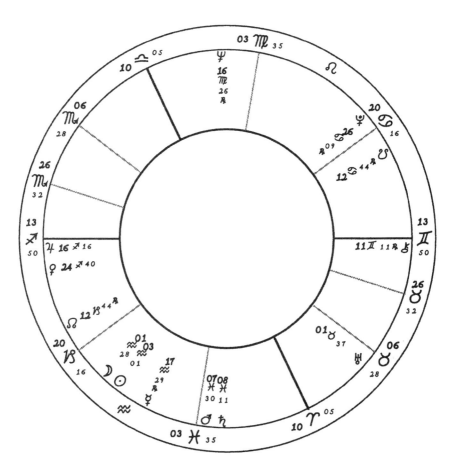

Simone, 24 January 1936, 4:30 am CET, Angers, France

but Simone had genuine Aquarian flair and irrepressible spirit as well. It's easy to see from Christian's chart, with a 5th house Cancer Moon trine Jupiter and Venus-Sun on the MC, that he adored and admired her. She made life exciting and creative. Notice how her Sagittarian Ascendant and Venus conjunct Jupiter in the 1st house, as well as Sun and Moon in Aquarius, connect strongly to Christian's own chart. He is a Sagittarius with Aquarius rising. Does anything else jump out at you here?

AUDIENCE: We've been talking about Mars. She has Mars conjunct Saturn, which gives a completely different feeling from Mars-Jupiter or Mars-Moon. I would expect some kind of tension or frustration, a tendency to control or be controlled.

LYNN: Exactly. That Saturn brings in an element we haven't seen in the family until now. Of course the conjunction is in Pisces, and Mars makes a wide square to Jupiter and opposes Neptune, which suggests both an aspiration towards something unlimited and a lock or a limit to her desire. The Mars pattern doesn't hold true in the same way for Simone's mother and sister, so I would look to other planetary pictures in her family. However, when we look at her father's birth date, the connections are astonishing. Simone married a man "just like dear old Dad." Her father, like her husband, had Moon conjunct Mars in Taurus! His Moon is also conjunct Saturn and Mars opposes Jupiter, so his chart dovetails perfectly with her husband's family pattern. I don't think this is entirely unusual, but since her father committed suicide, the similarity carries more discomfort than it would otherwise.

The Mars-Chiron thread

There is a Mars-Chiron thread, though, which some of you may have ideas about. Simone, her mother, her father, and Christian all have the square; her sister has a conjunction.

AUDIENCE: There's a side of Chiron connected to war. He invented that poison, after all, and it's his own cleverness that makes the wound incurable.

LYNN: You're saying there's a self-wounding with Mars-Chiron? That their creativity can turn back against the self? What an interesting idea to explore in this family!

AUDIENCE: Melanie talks about wounded self-assertion with this aspect, and how it tends to activate anger in others.

LYNN: That means the Mars-Chiron person could unintentionally set off Mars-Moon, and then feel wounded by them. Let's talk about some of the creative issues in this family. Christian works in film as a first assistant, one of the most highly regarded in the business, but he would prefer to be directing. He's so good at what he does that people want him to continue at it, and this represents an immense frustration, especially since he's turning forty. Pluto transiting the Sun often pushes someone to connect with a deeper strata of power in their own nature. Since suicide in a family corresponds to a lack of faith in the possibility of transformation, the stakes can be very high. Christian may need extra resources in order to pass over the threshold, and although he's put a number of changes into place, the desired breakthrough hasn't yet happened. He has great determination, which alternates with doubt, and he wonders whether the change will ever come. You can see how all this would be exacerbated by the Pluto-Sun transit.

The Sun-Pluto thread

AUDIENCE: My father had Sun-Pluto. He transformed his life when he immigrated from the south to the north of Italy. He was very strong, very proud. The northern Italians look down on Sicilians, so it's almost like being in a racist society. But there's a kind of tension in him as well.

LYNN: Yes, Pluto is rarely relaxed and easygoing! Hard Pluto aspects to the Sun contribute to a build-up of pressure and resistance as change approaches. It begins to feel like life or death—letting go of control and accepting a new life, or holding to a dwindling source of power. Simone, Christian's mother, has Sun conjunct Moon in Aquarius and opposition Pluto, and at one point she walked out of her marriage into a new life. Christian was fifteen. His father completely lost it emotionally, got a gun, and wanted to shoot Simone, her younger lover, and himself. It was the one time his Moon-Mars emerged full-blown out of the 12th house.

Interestingly enough, Christian's wife also has Sun square Pluto, and when they met, Christian had been living with someone else for several years. He went through a very painful upheaval in choosing Marion. His wife writes, reflects deeply, brings words into consciousness, and has been in analysis. She says it's no accident he chose someone who would be able to put things into words. Both their children have Moon square Pluto, perhaps reflecting this quality in their mother—the planetary thread shifts and continues.

AUDIENCE: I'm born within a few days of this man, and I have a wide Sun square Pluto. We moved around a lot in my childhood, and change seems easy to me. I don't think twice about pulling up roots, but that's only one level of change. I can relate to this desire for something that doesn't happen—I often have that feeling of being blocked in some way. Can you say more about this?

LYNN: Pluto demands something very deep. Often it takes time, long stretches of time to prepare. I suspect your sense of changing easily has more to do with Mars square Uranus, and your Sagittarian energy. I have brought another set of family charts where Pluto shows up in the pattern, but the issues are very different—no suicides. Rest assured that the rest of the day will be very different.

AUDIENCE: I am enjoying this. It's like being a detective.

LYNN: Yes, we're following clues, and Pluto tells us to start digging, to look at power issues, or an energy that's been held back. Sometimes the desire for power is a defense—a way not to take risks—and when that is the case, an individual is asked to step back and let go. Pluto often demands recognition of a higher power: the need to bend to that, to give up whom you have been, what you have known, and to step into something else. The ability to go deeply into the Pluto process gives an unshakable strength at the core. A Plutonian who hasn't done this feels constrained and even Saturnian. How many of you with Pluto aspects have felt something like this? Yes? There are quite a few of you hiding out there! And with Pluto-Sun, have you or your father had an issue like that?

AUDIENCE: Mine died when I was six.

LYNN: So your own life path and identity were immediately shaped by death and your response to it. You may have emotionally followed your father down to the underworld, locking away part of your aliveness. Or perhaps you strengthened your vitality and determination, and hardened your will to survive. Either way, the father carries mystery and anxiety, and at some point you will need to go down there and bring the father back up into your life.

AUDIENCE: I have a trine to Pluto from the Sun in the 9th, and my father came from a poor Italian family in Sicily. He became a doctor and went north. I am repeating that pattern, going north to London. My sister also has Sun conjunct Pluto and went to the north. My brother has no aspect between them, and he stayed put.

LYNN: Trines may indicate strengths that are clearly shared within the family pattern. From your description, it sounds as though the Pluto trine Sun helps affirm your sense of self, even in a hostile environment. This strength comes from your father's successful transformation. He had the power to go out and change his life, to break the pattern of poverty, and this is one of Pluto's gifts. The trine aspect gives a friendly relationship to Pluto; it tells a story with a happy ending. Sicily and the north of Italy are dramatically different, and with

Sun trine Pluto your father gave birth to another identity You have done the same. When the Sun aspects any of the transpersonal planets, this notion of re-shaping oneself becomes strong. Very precise orbs and dissonant aspects underline the importance of the process. Each planet goes about things in a slightly different fashion. Uranians reinvent themselves through opposition and reversal, while Neptunians lose themselves and stumble onto their identity almost by accident. It doesn't look as if they want to change intentionally, but they probably do. Since Christian's mother has Sun opposition Pluto, and he has a square—both difficult aspects—we could assume that resistance to transformation is greater. Sometimes that means when change does come, it takes a more disruptive form. What about that grand cross with Mars? He has Mars at 19° Taurus, opposition Jupiter at 17° Scorpio, square Uranus in Leo and Chiron in Aquarius. Could we see this as a potentially violent structure?

AUDIENCE: No.

LYNN: A very quick response from the man born a few days later!

AUDIENCE: Mars in Taurus is too slow for violence.

LYNN: I'm not sure you can generalize about Mars in Taurus like that, especially when it's square Uranus. Working in the cinema can be very demanding, and a first assistant has to pull all kinds of things together very quickly. I don't see him as slow at all, either physically or mentally, but then, Uranus is angular. Mars in Taurus expresses itself elsewhere as a kind of steadiness, and reliability in his emotional life.

AUDIENCE: That grand cross is like an elastic band.

LYNN: Yes, it's able to stretch and hold. This chart is great for organization, for taking in the maximum amount of information and acting quickly on it. Of course your metaphor would imply a danger in stretching too far. A first assistant is in charge of making everything happen, ironing out all the details and smoothing things for the director. It requires both a superb organizational sense and an ability to respond quickly and effectively. He has Saturn-Mercury conjunct in the 10th house. That's the organizational part. The Mars aspects give rapidity. With these aspects, he's travelled all over the world for his work.

The other person in the family with a Pluto-Sun aspect is Simone. Since she has a close Sun-Moon conjunction, Pluto also opposes the Moon, and both luminaries are square Uranus. How would you see this kind of combination?

AUDIENCE: It feels very explosive, and somehow contained at the same time.

AUDIENCE: Doesn't she have a Saturn-Mars conjunction, too? There could be a sense of other people controlling her life, a feeling of great pressure. It would eventually erupt or lead to difficulty, even depression.

LYNN: That's quite accurate. Simone got pregnant at eighteen, but she had a strong personality from the beginning, and chafed at the conventional aspects of her husband's family. Look at the difference astrologically. Simone has Sun-Moon conjunct in early Aquarius, opposition Pluto, square Uranus. Jacques has Sun square Neptune, with Moon conjunct Mars, and he marries a Moon-Pluto opposition. Who is the stronger personality in this couple? It is not hard to guess. No one ever feels indifferent towards Simone. Christian says she was a fantastic mother—fun, inventive, endlessly entertaining—and her husband was very much in love with her. She began to work in fashion, and had an uncanny flair for finding new talent. She discovered and promoted several designers who are now quite famous. But about fifteen years ago her eccentricities veered over the line into wild, irrational behavior. The official diagnosis is manic depression, or bipolar disorder. She now lives a marginal life in the Camargue, a region in the south of France with a strong gypsy population, and is convinced she's part gypsy.

AUDIENCE: Why does she think she is a gypsy?

LYNN: For one thing, she has jet-black hair and an olive complexion, with strong Mediterranean features. And there is a mystery about her maternal grandmother, who disappeared from her children's lives when they were small and was never spoken of again. The grandfather was Alsatian, blonde, blue-eyed, stiff and military. The children were raised by nuns in strict Catholicism. Christian, who takes after his mother, wonders if this great-grandmother might have been Jewish. In any case, she passed on the dark coloring in the family. That 8th house Pluto opposition to the luminaries in Simone's chart points to a family secret.

The power of the unknown

When you draw up a family tree and there's a question mark of some kind, it carries energy. The unknown has great unconscious power. What you don't know also propels you forward. We spoke earlier about how those with transpersonal planets in aspect to the Sun transform their identity. Simone is reinventing herself and her past. You see this sometimes in adopted children—they frequently have unknowns in their family tree, and this can give a rich, raw soil to the psyche, with the possibility of creating anew. It can also be experienced as emptiness, a deep vortex that pulls an individual away from the present. Adopted children may focus on the hopes and dreams of their adopted parents, or the abandonment and sadness of their birth parents. Usually, both forces interact in their psyches. A fundamental aspect of this family work turns around the ability to see how even a difficult event or circumstance can also become a gift, a source of strength. Often patterns are repeated; choices that your forebears made are somehow replayed in your own life, and the solutions they found become part of your talents.

In my own family, both my grandfathers were immigrants who left their native land for new opportunities. But on the other side, my mother's family never seemed to go anywhere. My mother has always lived within a radius of about five miles and still has no passport, while I followed my grandfathers back across the Atlantic. When I first came to Paris, I lived in a garret with the toilet out in the hallway, recreating some mythically uncomfortable "Parisian experience." It had lots of charm and very little heat. I had essentially chosen to live in voluntary poverty. It was only after I left that place that I made the connection to my father, who had grown up in the back woods of Michigan with no indoor plumbing and very little money. Living this for a few years was a way to understand where I'd come from, but I didn't know that at the time.

AUDIENCE: Is a part of it unconscious?

LYNN: Yes, absolutely. Perhaps even 95 or 99 percent of it is unconscious. The repetition provides a means for something to come out in the open. I only realized afterwards how necessary it was for me to tap into what it was like to be poor. It helped put something into place. I would recommend it to those who have a parent with Saturn in the 2nd house! Early on, with Taurus on the 12th house cusp, my tendency was to deny money's importance a completely polarized response to my parents' depression-scarred childhoods. Both my mother and father have Moon-Saturn hard aspects in their charts, and their fears about money pushed me into a rather extreme opposition. I could only see it once I'd gone through the experience, and chosen to live differently.

AUDIENCE: I am translating what you are saying into my own experience. I now live in a poor part of Clapham in the South of London, and perhaps that's a way to balance the rich and the poor, the north and south of Italy in my own background. Living there has made me acutely aware of what it's like to be stigmatized for being racially, ethnically different. I never understood that it might be connected to where I came from.

LYNN: Perhaps others of you can think of events in your own lives that turned out to have some kind of connection with your family history, even if you never would have made the connection at the time. We often are, on a certain level, repeating things. When you repeat something that has already happened in a family, the repetition is a way of reliving it and maybe doing it differently—maybe healing it, moving through it, saying, "Now I can get on with this piece. I understand its importance or its real place." Your past informs you. Imagine family as the soil you grow with, richer in certain nutrients, depleted in others. For good or bad, it leaves its mark on you..

Simone's mother was also called Simone. She was a great beauty, very refined and well educated, and she had Sun-Venus in Virgo widely square Pluto. Pluto may also square the Moon. Her mother disappeared from her life when she was quite young, and her husband Pierre committed suicide when she was fifty-four. Pluto's tendency to bring very profound change seems to have erupted in her life from outside, in a rather brutal fashion.

I know this is a lot of information. Are you with me? Yes?

This man Pierre, Christian's grandfather on his mother's side, was a successful entrepreneur, wealthy, magnanimous, and something of a womanizer. He lived well and enjoyed life, but lost his money during the Algerian war. He gave loans of grain to the French government on trust, and was never repaid. Bankruptcy followed, and a few years of humiliating jobs. He even worked as a car salesman, where he could barely eke out a living. He had lost everything, and went from a big luxurious house with servants to a small apartment, barely making ends meet. Finally he decided he'd be more helpful to his wife dead than alive, and he took out a life insurance policy Jacques and Simone found him in their home, dead from an overdose. Simone adored her father. You can imagine the devastation she must have felt, and the impact of a suicide is even greater for the person who finds the body. Jacques, too, had to relive the shock of his own father's death just ten years before.

AUDIENCE: The parallels between the grandparents are incredible—two suicides, two bankruptcies. Was it the grandfather or the great-grandfather who went bankrupt on the other side of the family?

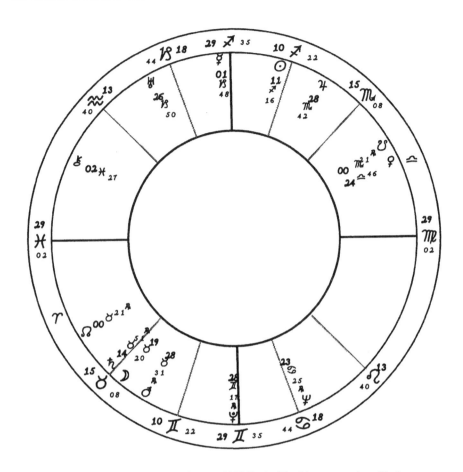

Pierre, 4 December 1911, 1:00 pm GMT, Paris. Placidus cusps; true Node

LYNN: That was Alcide, the great-grandfather. But you're absolutely right the similarities are striking. I don't think we can consider this to be entirely coincidental. In *The Astrology of Fate*,[10] Liz talks about this in terms of the family complex, acting through individuals who find exactly the right partner to keep the issues of the complex alive. Both Henri and Simone's mother lost their mothers as children.

10 Liz Greene, *The Astrology of Fate*, HarperCollins, London, 1985.

AUDIENCE: Would the Sun-Pluto inheritance indicate anxiety about change, about losing everything?

LYNN: We know that Pluto asks us to strip down to essentials at some point in our life, to accept a change of identity. This stripping down isn't necessarily financial. I would say that Sun-Pluto tests an individual's ability to maintain some sense of self in the face of enormous change, and tests the strength of one's commitment to life. Pierre felt betrayed, cast down, and kicked on the garbage heap. He couldn't find a way to pull himself back up. This is admittedly more difficult at sixty-one than it might be at thirty or forty Let's have a look at his birth chart. He was born on 4 December 1911 in Paris.

Again, I'm working without a birth time, but the main planetary patterns will hold throughout the day I've calculated the chart for 1.00 pm, which gives a strong 2nd/8th house emphasis, and coincidentally puts Pluto on an angle. But there is no Sun-Pluto aspect here. We find Mars exactly opposition Jupiter, the aspect we spoke of at length earlier in the day, a classical aspect of overreaching. And the Moon is between Saturn and Mars, so once again we find the explosive energy of a Moon-Mars conjunction. Pluto opposes Mercury, which would give a very sharp and penetrating flair for business, but can also take an individual's thinking down into some rather dark places. Pierre's suicide coincided with transiting Pluto square the Sun, although Uranus was making an even tighter square at the moment of death. Henri, the other grandfather, killed himself with transiting Pluto conjunct the Sun and square transiting Saturn. Both men were undergoing periods of extreme pressure and difficulty. But they didn't have Pluto-Sun aspects in their charts.

Those who do have Pluto in hard aspect to the Sun have to deal with this inheritance of loss and destruction. Simone's re-invention of herself as a gypsy can be seen, in part, as a desire to move away from her painful "roots." But Simone's "eccentricity" goes further than that. In the early 1980's she began to act increasingly bizarre, ending up in prison in Morocco for threatening a policeman. A period in psychiatric care followed, with a diagnosis of manic depression, and a series of relationships with younger, homeless men, often culminating in conflict or financial disaster. Simone has gone from a successful and widely admired innovator to the precarious status of the slightly mad, living with numerous dogs and cats, stoking vendettas against her daughters-in-law. Although everyone jokes and tells hilarious stories about Simone's misadventures, Christian's anxiety runs to both his mother's madness and his grandfathers suicide.

AUDIENCE: When did Simone begin to fall apart psychologically? Does she get suicidal?

LYNN: Christian thinks it began in around 1983 or 1984, but I don't have the exact details. In 1984, Pluto went into Scorpio and squared Simone's Sun and Moon, activating the natal T-square. When she gets depressed, she talks about suicide: "One day you will find me like my father." But she tends to veer towards the exalted side of things, the mania. Christian was seven at the time of his grandfather's death, and must have had Saturn square Saturn by transit.

AUDIENCE: Was Simone having her Saturn return?

LYNN: Her father, Pierre, died in 1965, and she was born in 1936. That makes her twenty-nine, so she must have been very close to the Saturn return.

AUDIENCE: I'm picking up a pattern here around success and loss. It sounds as if success in this family eventually turns into the opposite.

LYNN: That is perhaps the most important issue for Christian at this point in time. If he does manage to break through professionally, will he hold on to success, or will it all fall apart on him? His brother was a war correspondent, and still works as a well-respected journalist, and yet neither has quite broken through to the top of their respective professions, perhaps held back by the anxiety of going too far. Their father Jacques was at one time the director of a business, but lost his job for padding the expense account. He's had a number of professions, but his changes were gentler. The Pluto-Sun aspect tests one's commitment to life, and the strength of the creative core. If something were to happen, would Christian find the energy to begin all over again? An unsuccessfully navigated Sun-Pluto does not begin again.

AUDIENCE: Pluto is square the Sun in my natal chart, and I lost some property that I'd bought. I wasn't able to pay the mortgage, and even though I sold it, I ended up with a net loss. This sent me into a period of depression.

LYNN: Was that, for you, something really fundamental in your life?

AUDIENCE: It was very, very difficult, and at the same time forced me to start looking at things, to go into therapy. I have become a completely different person because of it, much more conscious. My family says I'm a lot easier to be around. I used to be unreflectively driven and ambitious, and I see everything quite differently now.

LYNN: How long ago was that?

AUDIENCE: Eight or nine years ago.

LYNN: Pluto doesn't have to take such a dramatic form, but Sun-Pluto can get locked into a compulsive behavior pattern. An individual may then become overly identified with some kind of external power. It can look like success from the outside, but they may have stopped evolving on some core level. If this is the case, Plutonian energy can eventually become toxic, subtly poisoning the psyche and affecting the life of everyone around you.

Pluto and psychotherapy

AUDIENCE: Do Pluto aspects demand some kind of psychotherapy?

LYNN: Psychotherapy creates a more conscious relationship with Pluto, but it doesn't guarantee an absence of upheaval. A willingness to question, to dig deeply into the unconscious, can slowly work through the armored zones of the psyche. Christian initially studied to be an archaeologist, another kind of digging, and we can easily identify the Plutonian impulse in such a choice of profession. He said his interest was never in field work, but in the theoretical part of it, understanding how things had come about. At the same time, his chart demands action and risk-taking. Since his Pluto-Sun square comes down through the maternal line, he probably needs to pay close attention to the problem of limits. This side of the family in particular tends to overdo things, to go too far. The other side doesn't go far enough, and his inheritance places him squarely in the middle. Sun-Pluto asks him to burn through to his own source. The information from the genealogical pattern can be very specific when you start to pull it out of the charts.

AUDIENCE: Is it possible to move through it more quickly if you've done work on yourself?

LYNN: If the therapy has built a relation to the core self, it will sustain the person even through a long period of difficulty. Terrible things sometimes happen to people. They live through wars, get seriously ill, have an accident, lose their home or a loved one. Who can say how much time it should take to get over such an event? There can be a stage when you are just full of rage at the injustice, and you don't want to go back out there you refuse to co-operate with life. When you are unable to move beyond that reaction, the energy can slowly become destructive. Pluto tests our belief in a new life, our willingness to give it another go, no matter how painful our losses have been.

AUDIENCE: Can the process be quite long?

LYNN: I think it can take a long time. A very difficult event is never resolved by easy fixes. All of us have encountered some kind of setback, and we cannot judge an event's significance from the outside. When a love relationship ends, how long does it take your heart to heal? That answer will be different for each person in the room, depending on how strong your feelings have been and, even more, how you are structured. For some, it will be only a matter of weeks, and for others, a wounded heart can take years to heal. I know a woman whose house burnt down. She has Moon opposition Pluto in the birth chart. She was in a state of total shock, but in some ways it also freed her. It helped her see whom she could count on, and she also made a decision to change countries and begin things anew much more easily. Looking back on that event, twenty years later, she says it gave her tremendous strength. A setback also changes something inside us. We can identify with it, and feel diminished by difficulty, or respond in such a way that we discover something unsuspected in our own inner nature.

Emotional planets respond differently from Mercury or Mars. It can take part of a Saturn cycle to digest something—some people take seven years to get over a divorce. I have a client with a Sun-Saturn square who left her husband and did not go near a man for fourteen years. She vowed never to have another relationship again, and became dried up and harsh—something she didn't realize until she fell in love again, and came back to life. Some people never get over a hurt; the wounding has been too deep for them to recover their courage. I think you have to respect the time that people take, and help them recognize what they're going through. Isn't that one of the things you do with transits and progressions? Moments of real integration are often shown by aspects made in progressions, or the movement of the progressed lunar cycle.

Imagine you have a Moon-Mars aspect about to be activated by a significant transit or progression. A conflict may erupt in your life which will bring an opportunity to move the energy out of the old pattern. At first you may experience the conflict as a failure: "Why does this always happen to me? Why am I so stuck?" Every repetition brings another chance to understand our own role in what is happening, though too many may defeat our sense of hope and limit our resilience.

It can be helpful to realize that some of your reactions are products of past conditioning arising, not only in individual experience—say, in this case, a scary, angry mother—but in events that happened before you were born, such as a family pushed to survive under extremely difficult conditions. Our histories play within us. We feel an imperceptible tug on invisible strings, but the moment we discover the connections running back into the family past, we realize that the solution may also need to happen on another level.

AUDIENCE: What about the Nodes?

LYNN: The Nodes can be more or less significant in family maps, like any other factor. You might want to draw them up as a planetary genogram, just as we have done with Mars, paying particular attention to the signs involved. They are connected to zones of comfort, stagnation and evolution, and may show that family members are evolving along quite different lines. But very tight connections between planets and Nodes in synastry often show strong synchronicity in the lives of particular family members.

The Venus-Jupiter thread

On the maternal side of Christian's family, there's a particularly strong planetary thread which involves Venus. Let's have a look at that now Let's go back to Simone's chart (see page 86). Notice that she has Jupiter conjunct Venus in Sagittarius in the 1st house. We've already spoken of her creative flair, sense of fun, and inimitable style. Not long ago she turned up dressed in flea market finds—boots, a long skirt, a beaded scarf, and wearing a holster with a toy gun, when she spontaneously went to pick her grandson up after school. They wouldn't give him to her! She's not exactly the traditional grandmother. How would you interpret a Venus-Jupiter conjunction?

AUDIENCE: Highly extravagant.

AUDIENCE: Pleasure-loving, in every sense of the word.

LYNN: Remember Christian's description of his mother: she was a lot of fun to be around. He and his brother had wondered for a long time what she was doing with their father. She pulled him out of his family's narrowness; she brought joy. They applauded her decision to leave. And yet the father's energy must have acted in part as a *garde-fou*. I'm thinking of the Mars-Saturn conjunction: she let his character provide the limits. Once she left that structure, there was nothing to hold her back, and although initially she flew high, she eventually went too far.

AUDIENCE: Is it the Venus-Jupiter that led her to go too far? Or the fact that it's square Neptune? Come to think of it, Saturn in Pisces probably doesn't help much either.

LYNN: As we know, there are usually many factors in a birth chart that feed into the same direction. I doubt that Venus-Jupiter alone would lead to this kind of overstepping, though I know many people with the hard aspects who find themselves in financial difficulty. Does anyone here have a Venus-Jupiter pattern in their family, or know people with the aspect?

AUDIENCE: This pattern is in my family, and there's an over-idealization of peace. We are always supposed to get along. Everyone's busy being nice, smoothing things over.

LYNN: I'd wonder about Mars in that case. Is there a fear of conflict in the family history? Every aspect, every planetary thread occurs in a larger context. Imagine a family with many Saturn-Venus aspects and Mars strong, and then one individual appears with Venus conjunct Jupiter. That will make quite a splash! Let's look at the Venus map on Christian's maternal side (shown on page 104).

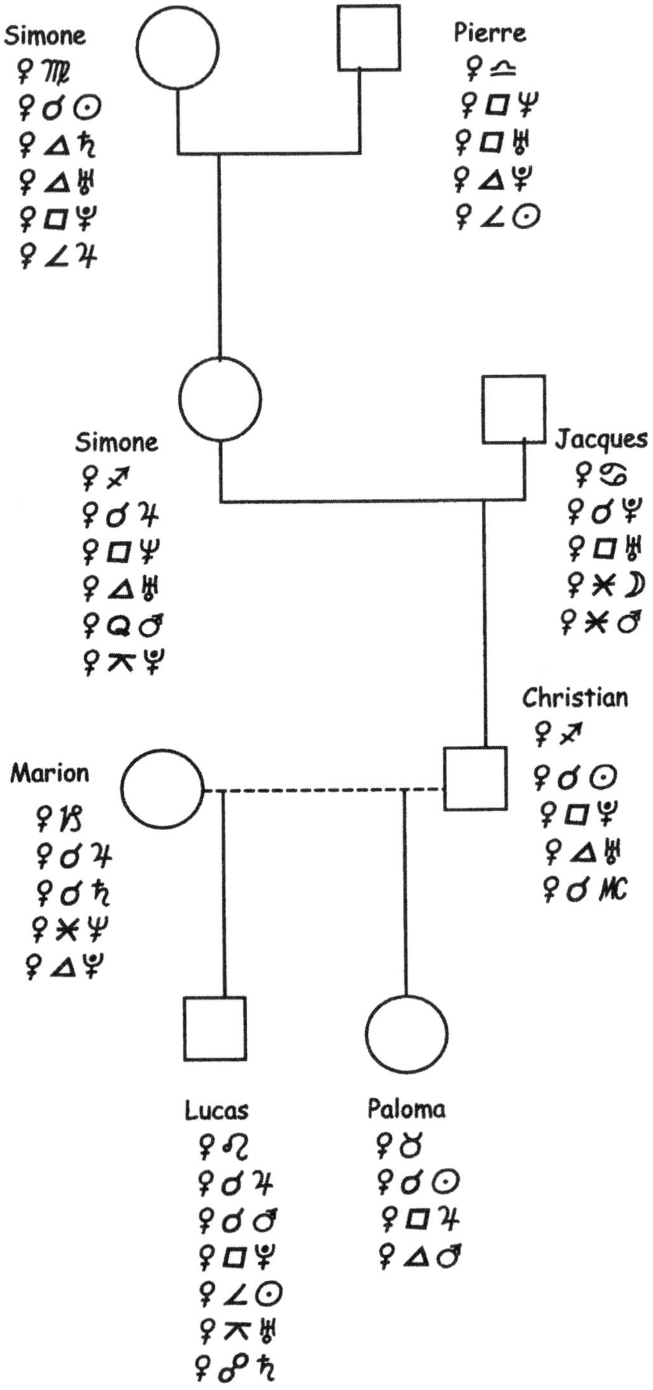
Simone
♀♍
♀☌☉
♀△♄
♀△♅
♀□♇
♀∠♃
Pierre
♀♎
♀□♆
♀□♅
♀△♇
♀∠☉
Simone
♀♐
♀☌♃
♀□♆
♀△♅
♀Q♂
♀⚻♇
Jacques
♀♋
♀☌♇
♀□♅
♀✶☽
♀✶♂
Christian
♀♐
♀☌☉
♀□♇
♀△♅
♀☌MC
Marion
♀♑
♀☌♃
♀☌♄
♀✶♆
♀△♇
Lucas
♀♌
♀☌♃
♀☌♂
♀□♇
♀∠☉
♀⚻♅
♀☍♄
Paloma
♀♉
♀☌☉
♀□♃
♀△♂

I'll make a list of the aspects:

Simone's father, Pierre, has Venus in Libra, square Neptune, square Uranus, semi-square Sun, and trine Pluto.

Simone's Mother, Simone, has Venus in Virgo conjunct Sun, in a grand trine to Saturn and Uranus, square Pluto, and semi-square Jupiter.

Simone has Venus-Jupiter conjunct in Sagittarius, square Neptune, trine Uranus, quintile Mars, and quincunx Pluto.

Jacques has Venus in Cancer, conjunct Pluto and square Uranus.

Christian has Venus conjunct Sun in Sagittarius, conjunct MC, square Pluto and trine Uranus.

Marion, his "wife," has Venus in Capricorn conjunct Jupiter and Saturn, exactly sextile Neptune, and trine Pluto. Her mother has Jupiter square Venus.

Lucas, their son, has Venus-Jupiter-Mars conjunct in Leo, semi-square Sun, square Pluto, opposition Saturn, and quincunx Uranus.

Paloma, their daughter, has Venus in Taurus conjunct Sun, square Jupiter and trine Mars.

AUDIENCE: Venus-Jupiter seems to be getting stronger in the family. It's interesting that Christian chose a woman with Venus-Jupiter like his mother. Like blonde hair or blue eyes, it's more likely to be passed down through the family.

LYNN: I wonder if it really does work this way? I'm not yet ready to claim this patterning is equivalent to some kind of genetic inheritance -but it's a fascinating avenue to explore. We could say that this family is growing Jupiter-Venus energy. I don't think any of us would object to that. Ebertin, in *The Combination of Stellar Influences*,[11] describes this combination as "the joy of love, happiness in love." Christian and Marion have a very strong love-match; their relationship is clearly alive both physically and emotionally, and she is a beautiful woman. Ebertin connects Venus-Jupiter to artists. Simone worked in fashion, Christian in film, and Marion worked in the fashion part of film, before leaving that to write.

AUDIENCE: I remember reading that this is a lucky combination.

LYNN: In traditional astrology, Venus and Jupiter are the two benefics. The conjunction should certainly bring the good things in life, in abundance. Christian and Marion met during a film shoot in Tahiti, and feel quickly and deeply in love. It's hard to imagine a more idyllic environment. Both are well travelled true Sagittarians in that respect. Everyone in the family shakes their head at Simone's luck. She's always stumbling onto houses that she buys for half their value and sells extremely well. Even now, when she is wild and unpredictable, money comes through for her. She has a kind of protection in this respect.

AUDIENCE: Is Christian good-looking?

LYNN: He is not handsome in a classical sense. He has inherited Simone's dark looks, high cheekbones, and slightly slanted eyes. People often think he's North African. Some people find him very attractive and others wonder what his gorgeous wife is doing with a guy like him. Venus conjunct Sun doesn't always give physical beauty.

AUDIENCE: I would expect Jupiter and Venus together to be concerned with appearance, but I wonder if it doesn't have more to do with a cer-

---

11 Reinhold Ebertin, *The Combination of Stellar Influences*, 1960.

tain kind of receptivity. It isn't just externals, but also an awareness of loving, of a quality of heart. Her Venus is connected to both Saturn's realm and Jupiter's, so she has very precise requirements.

LYNN: You're right. Jupiter-Venus gives a soul deeply concerned with beauty and love, one that resonates particularly strongly to these things. However, it doesn't describe a specific system of values, and even though their mother's Capricorn planets may sound conservative, that isn't how this couple would look to most people. The children will inherit an artistic sensibility and a cultured environment with artistic friends, but their parents avoid convention, and combine objects of value and folk culture with furniture found on the street. But they are not adverse to luxury.

Almost all the Jupiter-Venus people I know "follow their bliss." They believe that doing what you love will bring abundance, that if your heart isn't in something it won't really work for you. Marion feels that happiness comes when each person in the family can follow what matters to them. The members of this family really like each other. They enjoy being together much of the time, with crises and anxieties and moments of frustration, but on the whole they find life pleasurable. Luck has been shown to be linked to our belief systems, and Jupiter-Venus people, more than others, believe the goddess is on their side. They see no reason to deny themselves, and enjoy what she has to offer. It would be a mistake to consider this aspect superficial, since much depends on the core values that a person has chosen. They can be seduced by loveliness, occasionally charmed by the surface appearance of things, but they hold firmly to what they really care about.

AUDIENCE: I have Venus-Jupiter in the 12th Does that make a difference?

LYNN: Does it give you a basically happy nature? No? It's worth trying to tap into that, because there will always be an area of well-being with the conjunction, an island of beauty in the psyche, even tucked away in the 12th house.

Among the negative manifestations of this combination, Ebertin lists "laziness, negligence, wastefulness and an excessive expression of feeling." I get the impression that was written by someone with a strong Saturn! However, these individuals often make decisions without thinking about the bottom line; they won't help you balance your check book. Given the amorous impulses of both Jupiter and Venus in mythology, we might imagine aspects between these planets to run to a certain hedonism, but I haven't often found that to be the case. These individuals are motivated by love or pleasure or beauty. Following these as a touchstone brings wonder into their life. They may love literature or children or healing or flowers, but they flourish when their heart is fed.

The Moon-Pluto thread

This family functions really well, so far—there is a lot of love. Of course there is also more in these patterns than Venus-Jupiter. Both children have Moon square Pluto. Since they are young, I'm reluctant to speculate on what that might mean, but I can guarantee that their mother doesn't slide over things without deep reflection. I like to think that the Moon-Mars pattern from the father's side has become Moon Pluto—a more deeply mined emotional vein. Their mother has suffered from depression and creative paralysis, and is in the middle of analysis; this may be part of what the aspects reflect. She hesitated a long time before having the second child, and had a difficult pregnancy, despite her husband's enthusiasm.

AUDIENCE: From what I've seen of Moon-Pluto, it tends to hold emotion in for long periods, whereas Mars will bring it out. The atmosphere can be weighed down. There's a kind of pressure to introversion, but to the extent that somebody is working on it, it can facilitate consciousness. I wonder if, with all that Capricorn, she's not trying to be a perfect mother. That might explain why it was difficult to have a second child—the stakes get higher. The children feel this as Moon-Pluto, and learn to keep their own feelings inside.

LYNN: That's very perceptive. Marion does approach parenting with vigilant reflection, and a great deal of thoughtfulness and attention to what the children might be feeling underneath. She has said that she thinks she's put them under pressure in some ways, and wishes she'd been a bit more relaxed about things. In this case it doesn't take an outwardly structured form of rules and time schedules. Quite the contrary, she has trouble getting books back to the library, filling in medical forms, balancing a check book. The tension she carries is internal, and perhaps the children feel this as Moon-Pluto.

AUDIENCE: I have Moon conjunct Pluto, and find it can make it difficult to reconnect to feelings. It's square Mercury, and as soon as I speak, I feel a certain relief—I become more aware of what's going on underneath. Maybe it's the 10th house Mercury, but I feel both compelled to put things into words, and anxiety about doing so, as if I might get it wrong. It means that when you open the door, all kinds of unsavory things might come rushing out. So sometimes it's locked, and then you have to go round and find another way in.

LYNN: I think it depends on the Moon-Pluto, whether you hold it in or whether you let it out, but usually part of what's inside is kept back, held in reserve. This aspect means a mother has a connection with a deep and mysterious inner world, and this can feel threatening to a child, but it can also nurture an inner connection to self. Not all Moon-Pluto mothers are devouring and destructive, but most of them ride a psychological edge.

I remember one woman who came to see me. She had the Moon on the MC opposite Pluto, but her mother seemed to carry no whiff of Pluto whatsoever. She spoke of this mother in idealized terms; her mother was sensitive, artistic, beautiful, wistful—a classic Moon in Pisces image. However, this woman worked in the art business, and had had terrible "luck" with her women employers, all of whom were scheming, manipulative, and domineering. She was on the verge of quitting a desirable position, but with a sense of desperation, because she couldn't recognize this problem as having to do with her. And yet it kept repeating. She and her mother had "perfect communication"—they always understood each other even without words, and she was perplexed that I would assimilate her soft-hearted mother with these hard-as-nails monsters. The astrology already gave a kind of explanation (Moon opposition Pluto = power struggles), but it seemed clear to me that there was something from her past that was involved. I checked her mother's birth data, and her mother also had Moon-Pluto. Of course, we could argue that her mother was so idealized that the daughter somehow drew the opposite—the shadow side of the feminine in her work life.

Several years later she came back in great emotional turmoil, with an incredible story. She'd fallen deeply in love with a man and had moved in with him, but eight months later he was diagnosed with a brain tumor, and she watched, utterly shattered, as he wasted away and eventually died. It was during his illness that her mother revealed a similar experience; before meeting and marrying her husband (my client's father), she had been engaged to a wonderful man, who she loved wholeheartedly. They'd known each other eight months when he was killed in a plane crash. She had never, never spoken of this to her husband, let alone her daughter. It was a secret tucked deeply away in the mother's own emotional life. Can you see how that Pluto on the 4th house cusp pointed to a family secret of some kind? And how its opposition to the Moon described a hidden side of the mother? The daughter lived this shock in her mother's history as a kind of fate, irrevocably drawn to painful situations that eventually brought her mother's secret out into the open. This kind of story evokes a great deal of reflection—on karma, on our ability to read another's unconscious, on the mysterious links that tie parents and children to similar fates.

The Anniversary Syndrome

During the break Evelyn asked a question which reminded me of something quite important. Both her children have Moon-Pluto conjunct with a 9° orb, and she has a 9° degree orb between the Sun and Pluto. Her question was whether this might be significant in some way. When

I see an aspect like this in an individual chart, I am inclined to ask what happened when the person was nine years old. Using symbolic progression, a system where 1° equals one year, we would look for a Sun-Pluto or Moon-Pluto event at the age of nine. In a family, the repetition of orb can be significant, pointing to the kind of coincidences we spoke of earlier—the anniversary syndrome.

This process, that sets up a traumatic repetition in the next generation, is quite mysterious, and yet very powerful. It's been commented on at length in the psychological literature. You've probably run across it in your own lives on a more personal scale, when an accident or depression comes almost exactly a year after a traumatic loss. There seem to be shock waves that move out at regular intervals, six weeks, three months, six months, nine months, or a year after an event. These experiences are often at least partly conscious, or make some sense in retrospect, but it is harder to understand the underlying mechanism for repetitions between the generations.

AUDIENCE: I have a friend whose father committed suicide when she was six. When her own daughter was six, she and her husband split up, and he left to live in another country.

LYNN: Yes, that would definitely fall into the category of the anniversary syndrome. I like to think of it as a wave of resonance, an after-effect that provokes change of some kind, although not necessarily the same kind of event. Imagine that an important emotional event took place when you were nine years old. It could be the loss of a beloved grandparent, or the death of your first pet, or perhaps your father had an operation and spent some time in the hospital. You may have even forgotten completely about it, or neatly packaged it away in your memory with a nice ribbon tied round it.

When your own child reaches the age of nine, that experience somehow reawakens inside you, even if you are completely unaware of it. This can create feelings of sadness or unfocused anxiety, and these sometimes affect your relationship with the child in question. In Evelyn's case, if something happened when she was nine, linked to Sun-Pluto, her children would then enter a powerful emotional field when they got to the same age, and perhaps this is reflected by their own Moon-Pluto aspects. Something Plutonian begins to wake up; they feel this wave of intensity coming from their mother.

We're not describing a causal mechanism here, but part of the triggering system. All this could be simply a question of atmosphere, because Pluto is hidden out of sight and mind and often plays beneath the field of conscious awareness. But things could get very sticky in the family psyche, and we would probably find a trigger in Evelyn's childhood. The tighter the orb, the earlier an event is activated by symbolic progression, and the more powerful its impact. Wide orbs between planets will be activated at a later age, but these still have impact, especially when the Moon is involved. I have seen cases where aspects I would normally consider too wide reflect an event of major importance.

AUDIENCE: Would you go through the charts and look at all the orbs between planets among different family members?

LYNN: Perhaps, but it wouldn't be first on my list of priorities. It is hard to keep things simple, even with the planetary genograms. So today we will concentrate on pulling threads out of families, and acknowledge how much more can be done with family charts. This subject covers so much territory it really is inexhaustible, and I have to watch my Gemini nature and its tendency to get excited by all kinds of peripheral details. I want to give you something you can use, and this is the technique I've found that reveals patterns most quickly. It's a starting point. You can spend years going on from there. You can immediately go home and pull the Mercury pattern out of the charts in your family. If it doesn't speak clearly, go to Venus or Saturn, until you find one that does. Then take it further by looking at orbs, or if you're so inclined, look at the midpoints. I understand that Bernadette Brady has developed a programme called Jigsaw, that does just that.

GENEALOGY AND IDENTITY

LYNN: During the break, many of you have been coming up to me saying, "It's too difficult to show this example to the group." I understand that some of the material is very charged and can't simply be casually shared. Usually, when I work on family material, we create a space where people can go deeply and feel safe doing so, where the rest of the group focuses on one person's story and holds some of the emotional energy in that way.

I presented some of this in a seminar at UAC. Sophia Young was there, and she commented that people began to treat her like a long-lost sister. She said she had the feeling that just talking about the material activated family dynamics for people in the group. It's something you might want to watch for as the day goes on.

AUDIENCE: How about the royal family? What kind of patterns turn up in their charts over generations?

LYNN: The royal family's charts have been commented on at great length. They seem to have a strong resonance to the Saturn-Neptune cycle. Like Princess Grace of Monaco or the Kennedy family, these charts are well known and fascinating. You can find the data and work through them yourselves. An external example is easier to start with, because we can always see other people's patterns more accurately than our own.

AUDIENCE: How many generations do they go back?

LYNN: I'm not sure, but the point is not necessarily to go back hundreds of years, simply far enough to find significant patterns, and that's something that happens quickly enough. There may be people here who have a whole family tree. Others have much less to work with.

AUDIENCE: I have a whole family tree here.

LYNN: You do? What an impressive map! What luck to have all that investigative work done. Someone has given you a fantastic tool to begin weaving in and out of the family history, and see what has come down to you over generations. Some people scour their family tree for famous ancestors, the life force of an exceptional person coursing through their DNA and giving direction or hope to their own sense of identity. In the eastern religions, a stream of vitality and support was seen to come from the spirit world via your ancestors, and regular offerings and prayer in their memory maintained your own good luck. We are particularly concerned here with the inner inheritance that coalesces into fate, the family complexes and psychological tasks that link us to these ancestors. Blood relations are not ordinary, and all our instincts tell us this.

Who you are in society's eyes becomes less important once you have embarked on a conscious path, but most of us move in and out of external and internal notions of identity. Being born into a successful family can give solid material support, but if the family's focus is on outer development at the expense of inner growth, the pressure can be crushing and the wealth debilitating, producing wastrel sons and wild daughters. Later this afternoon I'll put up the pattern of a man who comes from an aristocratic family with a famous ancestor. He said, "Up until now, I haven't been interested in this material, especially as family is such a big deal. It has so much weight. It is like a burden. Why think about it?" He got quite excited at seeing his inheritance from another point of view, free from the pressure to live up to the past, or fit into a particular mold. It's essential to look at a family tree psychologically, and to see that everyone is carrying some kind of inheritance with them. As an American, I probably have a very different take on this than most of you, since I come from a culture built on breaking with the past. Don't confuse genealogy with identity. We are looking to find how the past may continue to be alive inside us, but I don't think it will magically reveal who we are. The family material contains important information, but the work of self discovery, in the deepest sense, lies outside the family paradigm.

Transforming the models

Not long ago, one of my students, whom I will call Tina, presented her family's charts, saying there were huge communication problems. I drew a map of all the Mercury positions in the family, but they didn't strike me as particularly significant, so I probed a little, wondering exactly how the communication problem showed itself. She has Mercury conjunct Venus in Aries, opposition Saturn in the birth chart. They are all square Chiron in Capricorn and Uranus in Cancer, which oppose each other. The issue of communication is clearly fundamental for her, but the pattern doesn't show up in the same way in the charts of other family members, and this suggests that the communication issue may belong more to her than to the family in general. As it turned out, there were three generations of teachers in her family, giving a tremendous importance to the possession of knowledge. What drove her round the bend was a pompous professorial style, exemplified in its most acute form by her father. What do you think turned out to be important in the family map?

AUDIENCE: Could it have been Jupiter? A particular kind of self-satisfaction often seems to accompany an unevolved Jupiter. I immediately associate this with the word "pompous."

LYNN: You are probably onto something there. In Hindi the word *guru* means "teacher," and it is also the name of the planet Jupiter. The Jupiter coloring is quite strong on the father's side, with many contacts between Jupiter and the Sun. Tina herself has Jupiter conjunct Sun, which she lives out through travel and many foreign friends—though the "guru" part of Jupiter seems to be carried by her father and other men. In Tina's generation, only one of the five siblings became a teacher, and that brother has a very strong Jupiter. But there is another pattern running through the charts of the paternal side of the family—many squares, conjunctions, and oppositions between Saturn and Venus. Does anyone have an idea what that may be describing?

The Saturn-Venus thread

AUDIENCE: I always think of Saturn-Venus combinations as a fear of not being good enough. Somehow the person can't connect to their own sense of worth. But I'm not sure how it would work if everybody had the same aspect.

AUDIENCE: There must be a huge lack of self-esteem. It might make things terribly awkward, or formal.

LYNN: Both of you are probably picking up on important issues in the family, but how would they correlate with Tina's own description of congratulatory self-satisfaction? It may be interesting for you to know that, on the paternal side, her grandmother, grandfather, father, mother, uncles, and aunts are all teachers, as well as her eldest brother. The great-grandparents were also teachers.

AUDIENCE: I can't get my thinking around it exactly, but with Saturn and Venus there's something about living up to a specific standard. Perhaps the Jupiter gives high expectations, and with Saturn-Venus, the person feels they can't live up to them.

AUDIENCE: Isn't Saturn-Venus a crystallized value system?

LYNN: That's exactly it. There is tremendous pressure to conform to a particular system of values in order to be good enough. In this case they are the values of the patriarch, the paternal grandfather, who had a genuine love of learning—Saturn conjunct Venus in Sagittarius in the 9th house. This was so strong in him that each of his children became teachers in turn. We could speculate that being good at book learning was the only way to feel loved in this family. Interestingly enough, Tina describes her father as being terrified of his own father. Can you hear Saturn-Venus there? Fear and love go together.

AUDIENCE: I would have thought that Saturn-Venus would indicate a problem around beauty, perhaps even some downgrading of femininity—a family where women are undervalued.

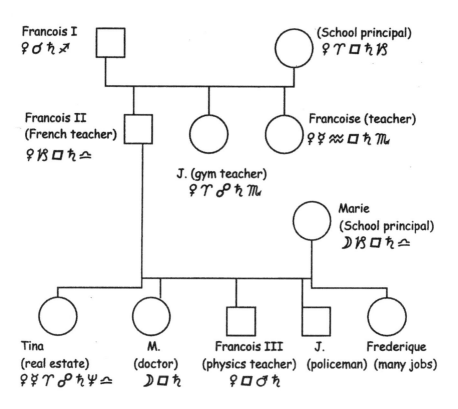

LYNN: Tina certainly feels some frustration around how she is valued by her family, but it isn't even feminine versus masculine. One of her brothers is a policeman, daring, physically courageous, but not particularly head-smart; he suffers from the same issues around self-esteem. She has always been able to draw men to her easily, but she doesn't know how to communicate with them. Remember, she's the one with Mercury-Venus opposition Saturn. This planetary combination tends to narrow one's sense of self-worth, because the perception is that love and appreciation come only when certain requirements are fulfilled.

In another family, beauty might very well be the primary issue. Much will depend on what Venus represents in the family system. With this combination there are rules (Saturn) about what really matters (Venus). Tracing the thread to its source, in this case the paternal grandfather, we can begin to understand how something comes into being. If we went a little further back we might even find a story in preceding generations about a thwarted desire for education, or an unrecognized illegitimate child whose father came from an educated class. Tina's Venus-Mercury conjunction is in Aries and square Uranus, which makes it virtually impossible for her to follow someone else's rules, but her interest in astrology means that she is working towards the acquisition of a body of knowledge, much as the teachers in the family might do.

The Uranus opposition to its natal place, which as you know occurs between the ages of thirty-eight and forty-two, often coincides with a turnaround in our way of being in the world. After years of working successfully but soullessly in real estate, she decided to move to the United States and commit herself to a particular form of spiritual training with a well-known alternative teacher. Her subject matter is in complete opposition to her family's vision of the world, and virtually guaranteed to remain unrecognized by her father, but she is now using the family model of specialized knowledge towards a path she values for herself.

On a personal level, she felt that dialogue with her father was painfully impossible; she could never hold his attention. This frustration carried over to many of her relationships, and although she is quite articulate, she has an acute sense of blocked communication. In classes she would often take the floor for long stretches of time, causing eye-rolling and impatient responses from some of the other students. The family style leaked through. In order to be listened to, Tina would have to have a whole litany of facts and citations at her fingertips, and she would have to be able to wield them objectively, marking points and underlining ideas. Can you see this? There is a confusion of sorts between style and content, ideas and delivery.

During a session with me, Tina commented several times on how "lazy" she was; she found it difficult to read for more than twenty minutes, even when she had a passionate love of the subject. This "bad habit" carried over from childhood. Given the amount of stressful aspects to Mercury in her birth chart, it seemed clear to me that she might have a vision problem of some kind. A few months later, she did indeed discover a problem of convergence, an inability to bring the vision of both eyes together, and this often gives reading difficulties. Since her vision is otherwise normal, no one had ever thought to look for a possible problem. Of course, this kind of visual difficulty has a perfect fit symbolically with a strong opposition structure in the chart. It's interesting to note that Tina's mother's family are earthy and affectionate without intellectual pretension, even if they also have rather strong Saturn aspects.

Tina's issue is much bigger than a feeling that her father (and therefore most men) won't listen to her. Even if she had a diploma, she would still feel unacknowledged for her own deeper values. Unless she shared her father's value system, nothing she could say could really touch him, while he probably experienced this early on in relation to his own father. In her family it wasn't so much what you said as what you knew that was important. Family dialogues tended to revolve around the recitation of facts: "In 1847 that bridge was built, and the plans for the observatory were approved." It's doubtful that issues of sentiment got much air-play, since global Saturn-Venus aspects probably describe an atmosphere of squashed personal feelings. Her work has to do with claiming what is truly important to her, and perhaps accepting that her kin will not be able to understand this.

AUDIENCE: Are you saying that it isn't about communication after all?

LYNN: That would probably be excessive. Consciously she has been aware of the stresses in communication for a long time, without being able to do much to change things, because the root issue is fuelled by something else: self-worth. Mercury and Venus are conjunct, remember, and they need to be healed together. But it can be quite difficult to differentiate between the two.

Those of you who come from teaching families may have noticed similar dynamics. I see some heads nodding in the group! Families build unconscious pressure around certain values. For teachers, knowledge is both power and grace, and it can be tough to live up to this one. Although we might expect teachers to be well-spoken, they are often used to one-way communication, and to having an answer for every question. The French call this a *deformation professionelle*, a bias or quirk in behavior created by skills you develop professionally and over-use in your personal life. Come to think of it, astrologers may fit into this same category!

Few parents feel good about a child with difficulty in school, but for the child of a teacher, an inability to understand or learn quickly can be wounding for both. It's easy to envisage any number of scenarios involving failure as rebellion, where a learning difficulty is a pointed cry for help; most of us have probably observed this kind of thing. It extends to many professions. I remember a friend who developed a rare illness as a child. His father was a successful doctor, with a specialty in the very same field, but incapable of curing him. Children need to dis-cover a parent's limits in order to move away. It can be a costly process, especially when a parent clings to fantasies of omnipotence.

AUDIENCE: What about the mother's side of Tina's family?

The Moon-Saturn thread

LYNN: Interesting that you should ask. I don't want to go into too much detail with this, but there is a Saturn-Moon pattern that goes back to the maternal grandfather, the youngest child in a very poor family. He began working in a factory when he was fourteen, and most of his brothers died in the First World War. In this case Saturn-Moon describes difficult material and emotional conditions in the very begin-ning of life, and Tina and her siblings have either Saturn-Venus or Sat-urn-Moon hard aspects which point to different sides of the family. Tina's mother came from a humbler social background than her father, which may be part of the issue.

AUDIENCE: It sounds as though the restriction described by Saturn-Venus concerns a different level of experience from aspects with the Moon. I wonder, does love exist at all in a family with so much of this?

LYNN: That may be an existential question! Love is often frustrated or tested with this pattern, but that doesn't mean it doesn't exist. What is perhaps most difficult with Saturn-Venus concerns a narrowness of range, a difficulty in receiving love unless it comes in a particular form. You could say that each member of the family who has inherited a Saturn-Venus aspect is working on love. As we know, Saturn demands effort, and gives little gratuitously. Does love exist? The Greeks believed Eros was the unifying force that brought the world into being, but they also saw it as an irresistible force. Even the gods, with the exception of the virgin goddesses, were powerless to resist the erotic impulse. Now, Saturn, as we know, hates to lose control, so part of the problem could lie there. Since Tina has Uranus square Venus as well, her role may be to break out of the narrow confines of her family's values. But she cannot feel the love with her father, and this is a source of suffering, not helped by the fact that his Saturn is also opposed to her Venus. In a Saturn-Venus family there are rules about how to be loved, and about who or what is lovable.

Great expectations

Since those who have these aspects feel worthwhile only when they have fulfilled certain conditions, and then only for a brief period of time, they need to find an antidote. Love will either become very focused, very central to their lives, or they will be acutely aware of its importance through its absence. Does anyone here have a Saturn-Venus aspect? And do you have an idea about what the dominant values or rules were in your family?

AUDIENCE: We had to be excellent at everything, but I would say the highest value in my family was music. I have the conjunction in Cancer.

LYNN: I imagine, with Saturn, that means classical music in particular! Yes? So, in order to be worthy, you had to be excellent in everything, but you may have felt inadequate if you were less musical than the others.

AUDIENCE: Yes, I can relate to that. I don't have the same gifts as other family members do, though I certainly have an ear for it. I was more interested in dance, but somehow, whenever I gave a performance, my family never came. All the other mothers and fathers would be there, but not mine. I remember my mother saying, "All music is great music." Her attention was usually on my sister, who was a gifted pianist.

LYNN: This is a telling illustration of Saturn-Venus. Your family placed a lot of importance on musical creativity, to the point that nothing else could compensate for the lack of it. Presumably, your mother gave up a career in order to raise her family, so there is a story of artistic frustration?

AUDIENCE: That's right.

LYNN: Saturn-Venus can sometimes mean that there's a story in the family where someone was held back from what they love. This can create unconscious pressure to make similar choices, or to support what has been chosen at great cost. If you follow your heart, it can cause pain for those who didn't, and there may be a great deal of internal or external pressure. Saturn-Venus aspects place conditions, usually difficult ones, on your ability to feel good about what you do. Haven't you noticed that individuals with these aspects don't enjoy things that come too easily?

It can be very hard to offer some treasured part of yourself and find a total lack of response from other family members. You pour your heart and soul out and are met with an indifferent response: "That's nice, dear," or someone says, "No, we don't want any of that, thank you." If you persist and stay true to what you love, you may often end up treading a lonely road. On the other hand, if you give up and try to please someone else, the issues of self-doubt and an acute sense of emptiness can become overwhelming. It becomes easy to slide into a no-man's land of worthlessness and lack of self-love. In extreme cases, the more difficult aspects between Saturn and Venus can give a climate where the people close to you consider your most cherished desires to be dangerous rubbish.

Saturn-Venus in the birth chart has very rigorous requirements. It will frustrate you, it will augment your doubts, it will test your ability to hold true to what you love. You may be tested through time, you may be tested through someone's lack of interest, through feeling unac-knowledged and unrecognized. It can be like buying a wonderful bou-quet of flowers for someone that you've chosen with great care; they thank you absentmindedly and then lay them down somewhere, forget-ting to put your bouquet in water. Your hopes for connection wilt along with the flowers. What you offer with your whole heart may not touch them at all, and this is even harder when you offer your talent, as Susan did, and no one comes to see. It can be easy to doubt it all, whether it was good, or worthwhile, or interesting, or whether you have the tiniest shred of ability. Some people close back up and hide their heart away. Then it can be very difficult to find a way in to them.

Now, imagine a family where everyone functions in the same way. Either you're all in lockstep over what is important, or everyone feels frustrated and misunderstood. One of the most interesting issues in this work is looking at your chart to see whether something belongs to you alone, or is shared with other family members. Ask yourself what you have that is new, since each person brings something in, a new piece to be fitted to the family pattern or to take things in a totally new direction.

There is an enormous difference between being a member of a family where everyone shares an aspect like Saturn-Venus, and being on your own with it. If you are the only one with Saturn-Venus, it probably means that you treasure something your tribe does not understand, or they may be missing an ability that would allow them to appreciate what you love. Then you are tested about whether or not you will hold true to that inner direction. It can be a source of tre-mendous strength if you do. Very early in life some people say, "Well, nobody else seems to think this is important, so I guess it must not be." Then you "let your magic turtle go," as the *I Ching* would have it, and go around feeling, "Where is my Joy? What is it that really matters to me? Why can't I feel anything strongly enough?" You can get cut off from what you love, and become lost to your heart's desire. The consequences of this are enormous in later relationships because it becomes terribly difficult to feel enough, or in the right way. Much depends on the decision you make about that early experience of frus-tration. If you let go of what you love because others do not understand it, you can become a prisoner of the feeling that they (or you) don't love enough or in the right way. Does that make sense?

Tina used to be caught in a particularly painful interaction with her father. She would struggle to find the right words, convinced from the beginning that she'd never manage to get through to him, and she felt that communication was a real stumbling block in all her relationships. However, her work in real estate meant she had a lot of specialized knowledge, easy contacts with people, and a great ability to bargain. She slowly came to realize that the issue was not so much what she said or how she said it, but her father's inability to acknowledge anything outside his own value system. Her desire to be recognized by him perpetuated a relationship of frustrated, unrecognized love, and a lack of self-esteem. Once she understood the mechanism, she could stop and say, "It is just too hard for them to appreciate the world the way I do, so I have to pull back. Saturn-Venus needs to acknowledge other people's limitations, without cutting off from their loving feelings once they recognize their need will not be met. They can then begin to think about satisfying themselves, even if this feels very unfair.

AUDIENCE: I always think of Venus-Saturn aspects as indicating a possible relationship with someone older. How would that fit into the family issues? Would it be a way of resolving earlier frustrations?

LYNN: That's probably a good guess, since Saturn can often symbolize the father. In an older cultural model, the Venus-Saturn combination might indicate a lack of choice, the combination of duty and love so frequently associated with this pairing. A marriage might serve the prevailing structure or consolidate the father's interests. Since most of us in this culture are free to choose our partners, the Saturn signature will get more subtle. I have often seen this in the charts of women or men who work out an early wound by finding an older partner to replace the unsatisfactory parent. This can be healing up to a point, but it can also lead to getting stuck in rather rigid roles, and giving up a great deal in exchange for the material and psychological comfort of a strong substitute parent.

If you'll think back to the example we used earlier, Marion, Christian's wife, has Venus conjunct both Saturn and Jupiter in Capricorn. Her maternal grandmother was a concert pianist and came from a whole line of singers and musicians. She began to play the violin at the age of three, and by seven she played concertos with a small group once a month. She was being groomed for a career as a concert musician. At age eleven she announced that she didn't want to play any more, and she never picked up the violin again. She is still trying to figure out whether she stopped playing the violin because she had been forced to play and never had any real choice in the matter, or whether the decision to stop was a genuine choice not to follow that path. She played the violin all those years out of duty, to please the grandmother and the rest of the family. She suffered from depression later, when she found herself blocked in her chosen creative path, writing, and that led to analysis and a long exploration of her motivation and desires.

With the dissonant aspects in particular, it becomes urgent to ask the following question: "Am I doing this because I really want to, or because I feel I must?" All of us have obligations, things we must do, and sometimes there is no way around them. But Saturn-Venus individuals need to learn to recognize what they really want, and not only what they *must* do.

Family values

AUDIENCE: I have Saturn-Venus, but I am the only one in the family with it. The midpoint happens to fall exactly on my father's Sun.

LYNN: So there's some connection with him. I wonder if that points to an allegiance to the father's values? Earlier we saw an example where Moon-Mercury meant that the child spoke to the mother. It's the same kind of resonance. Sometimes Saturn-Venus can mean, "I value what my father values."

AUDIENCE: Yes, that's true for me. I valued his originality but rejected my mother's manipulation. I have Pluto-Moon as well.

LYNN: It might be interesting to trace both of those aspects back in the family. You may find that one comes from your mother's side and another from your father's—but not necessarily the side you expect! It also seems clear that Moon-Pluto can be quite overwhelming, and might welcome the more contained energy of Saturn-Venus.

AUDIENCE (CHRIS): Saturn-Venus is clearly a pattern in my family. All three children have it, and on top of that either my mother's or my father's Saturn sits on the Sun or Venus of all the children.

LYNN: Have you an idea of what was most important in your family?

CHRIS: I have been trying to think, but I can't quite work it out. I remember not feeling valued as a person. I have Venus-Saturn and Mercury conjunct in Sagittarius.

LYNN: Didn't you mention travelling around a great deal as a child ?

CHRIS: I love travel, but it's true we had to be able to pack our bags on twenty-four-hour notice.

LYNN: It sounds like a Sagittarian value system to me! You basically had to be ready to see the world, to go anywhere and talk to anybody about anything. Isn't that the dominant family value?

CHRIS: It seems far too natural to make sense. I loved picking up and going to a new place. Isn't Saturn-Venus supposed to be difficult?

AUDIENCE: But wouldn't it be difficult to constantly leave people and places?

CHRIS: You're right. The departure was often quite difficult emotionally, but then again, it was mitigated by excitement. I suppose it's a family tradition to be on the move, since my mother left her country of birth when she was twelve, and we regularly changed countries.

LYNN: The conjunction falls in the 9th house, which often corresponds to our notion of the highest good. The ancients called it the House of God. It's quite possible to adhere to a family value system without suffering, though in your case I suspect there are drawbacks. The nomadic lifestyle can be hard on relationships.

CHRIS: As soon as I made friends, it was time to leave again, and I tend to repeat that pattern by uprooting myself over and over again.

LYNN: It sounds as though you don't give yourself enough time, and this creates a lack of continuity. With Saturn-Venus, a narrowing often occurs in certain areas of your life.

CHRIS: I often have the feeling that when someone begins to love me, they pull away out of fear of rejection, and my relationships never seem to get beyond a certain point. That's how I perceive it. I once lived with someone for a year; that was the longest one.

LYNN: Let's go over this again. As a child, you got close to somebody for, say, two or three years, but you were always the one to say good-bye. You may carry within you this cut-off, the Saturn-Venus experience encoded in the way you relate to other people. Somehow you're sending unconscious signals that you will not be staying very long. It seems to me that you carry within you the experience of love ending. There isn't ever enough time for love, and Saturn in Sagittarius says, "Pull yourself together, time to move on." I know you have Moon conjunct Neptune in Scorpio, though, and that combination can mourn a loss for a whole lifetime. Saturn-Mercury may very well judge your feelings rather harshly.

CHRIS: I know we moved when I was four, but I don't remember much about that. Then, at six, we moved again, and I really suffered. The next time, I was nine, and I didn't really think about it much.

LYNN: It sounds as though you had already pulled back. You protected yourself from connecting as deeply in order not to suffer, but that must have been terribly frustrating for your Scorpio Moon, a Moon that thrives on passionate intensity. Venus-Saturn is afraid because Venus-Saturn's experience is, "When I love, I will be cut off. I won't have enough time to go deeply before the love is lost." We can see how this comes from the family experience, and since all your siblings share the Saturn-Venus aspect pattern, they must have built a similar internal response. I wonder if your parents had a similar issue? I could imagine that you send very mixed signals in relationship—the strong fusion-seeking demands of Moon-Neptune, coupled to Venus Saturn's coolness. Although the initial barrier to relationship came from external circumstances, you most likely internalized that barrier without being aware of it. Relationships can be cut for many reasons, but if you leave, it can be very hard to go back and maintain a tie. Sometimes a pattern like this gets accelerated. You meet someone and they push you away It used to take six months, then it was six weeks, and now the whole thing happens in forty-eight hours. The intensity of the repetition means you are getting closer and closer to the core wound.

CHRIS: I really feel that so strongly. Until two years ago I was reluctant to connect, and I never felt loved, not really. About four weeks after I hit town, I met someone and fell deeply in love. I was not rejecting, quite the opposite, and it was wonderful. But oddly enough, I was about to travel back to Chile and connect with my long-lost childhood friend—the one I had suffered so much in leaving when I was six. It turned out to be an anti-climactic reunion because he had grown to be a nice but ordinary fellow, and couldn't work out why the whole thing was so important to me. I really felt the fool. Then, when I came back to London, my lover had pulled away, and we weren't able to find that initial magic.

LYNN: You could have cancelled your trip.

CHRIS: In retrospect, yes.

LYNN: Perhaps, at some point, you will need to choose to stay rather than leave in order to break the pattern. You know how to go somewhere new, and you still enjoy that, but the emotional frustration remains. I'm thinking of a man I know who has Venus in the 9th opposition Pluto. He travels a great deal for his work, and uses the discontinuity as a protection in relationship—work would always come first. For the first time he was with someone he really cared for, and he turned down a job in order to be with her when she had to go into the hospital. Fear of emotional manipulation was a big one for him, and that decision allowed something else to open up in his relationship.

This is such a major issue for you that it's rather obvious we are not going to resolve it here today. But it would be interesting to look back and see what Saturn-Venus says about your parents' choices in life.

CHRIS: I am convinced that if we hadn't constantly moved around, they would be divorced.

LYNN: Moving was their way of staying together, but it hasn't helped you to develop relationships. It's had the opposite effect.

CHRIS: I am only anywhere for a limited period of time.

LYNN: We are all here for just a limited period of time. I wonder, with that conjunction in Sagittarius, if there isn't a story about running away to get married? Did your parents do that?

CHRIS: I am convinced that my mother married my father because her father rejected him. The story goes that my grandfather told my mother, "If you marry this man, you are no longer my daughter." She took the keys off her ring, put them on the table, and walked out the door. It took three years for him to recognize their marriage.

LYNN: It may be that your Saturn-Venus heritage began with saying no to the patriarch's law, but there are consequences to such a decision. Your mother sent herself into voluntary exile. She cut herself off by refusing to be bound by her father's values. She had to break a relationship in order to begin one. Somehow this pattern of brusque endings and emotional distance has continued in your own life, a kind of loyalty to the choice she made. Further back in the family, there could be a story of a marriage made under pressure. Sometimes a really radical break needs to be made in order to get rid of the accumulated frustration, even at the risk of major disagreement. You may want to find out whether the maternal great-grandfather was forced to marry someone against his will. As I said earlier, often we are asked to remain loyal to painful decisions made in the past. Many generations later, a conflict erupts, and your mother says, "No one is going to tell me what to do!" Unresolved issues go underground for a while, but if they haven't been dealt with, they'll come back around, taking different guises, variations on a theme, until someone in the family manages to break the pattern. One of the reasons that working with the family inheritance can be so fruitful lies in revealing the unconscious power of these stories running through our lives, seeing how they get passed on and take on a life of their own, and wrestling with them until the curse becomes a blessing.

Family curses and family ghosts

AUDIENCE: Oddly enough, there is a story on my father's side concerning my grandfather, or maybe my great-grandfather, in Hungary He got married, but sent the bride back because she was no good in bed.

LYNN: Imagine the rejected woman! A Venus-Saturn figure, who pronounces a curse: "I hope their toenails all fall off for seven generations!" Well, it may have been another part of the body; euphemisms are necessary in polite company. But family curses are no joke because they ride the psyche unforgivingly, and take on a relentless repetitive quality, as we saw earlier in the myths connected to the house of Atreus.

Some events loom too large to be healed in the span of an individual lifetime. I was talking to a friend whose parents were both Holocaust survivors, and she described how reading a book about the children of those who'd been in the camps had helped her enormously. It described how the second generation often had more physical symptoms, more emotional disruption on a conscious level, than those who experienced the actual event. Her mother, now in her eighties, is adamant in maintaining that none of that had any effect on her whatsoever. Both daughters find this mother very difficult to deal with, and Mona has out-of-kilter, larger-than-life emotional responses that ripple disruptively through her daily life. In large part, these have been fuelled by her parents' experience; as the watery child, she absorbed the emotional shock waves in her family history. Understanding that she wasn't alone in carrying this kind of experience, that other children of Holocaust survivors shared much of her inner turmoil, helped her accept the power of this force within her life, a power she has tried to channel through creativity. And she has become increasingly aware of how fundamental it is to give voice to her experience. Being born into a family that has suffered from great social upheavals of this kind means that you are asked to participate in the healing of the collective. It can give a special gift in this regard.

Liz Greene writes with great eloquence about these kinds of issues in *The Astrology of Fate*:

> The process of development of complexes within families has a feeling both of teleology—movement towards a goal—and an inevitability, just as the curse of the House of Atreus has an inevitability. If one looks backwards from the conflicts and compulsions of one's own drama, one may glimpse the family myth, twisting and winding through father and mother, grandparents and great-grandparents, endlessly uncoiling like the Stoic's vision of *Heimarmene*, into the racial collective unconscious. The myth of Orestes and his family seems to suggest that whatever we are as individuals, part and parcel of that personal identity is our inheritance, which sits upon us like fate and must met and be grappled with in an individual way. It cannot be repudiated nor run away from; it is not enough to model one's life on "anything but mother and father," for in so doing we are as surely dominated by them as if we tried to be exactly like

them. One may do what one can do, or wishes to do with an inheritance; but the inheritance itself cannot be ignored or given away, for our families are our allotment, our Moira.[12]

Liz gives the example of a family with an autistic child, and traces the planetary patterns back through the generations. A child may be born handicapped, or come into a family with a terrible physical problem, as if something has constellated in this child, a blind and fettered energy that had been building and building, getting tenser and tighter with each generation, finally erupting as a kind of fate. In retrospect, an initial life-denying choice in an earlier generation may seem quite minor, much less dramatic than murdered children or collective suffering; but it slowly grows in importance within the collective psyche of the family.

Freud's skeletons in the cupboard

A family secret can act in such a way that it blooms into a powerful, often unacknowledged motive force. Some years ago, a book on Freud appeared, with the thesis that much of his life and work had been unconsciously determined by a family secret. Here is Freud's genogram (on page 133).

Freud's father Jacob was considerably older than his mother. He had been married a first time and had two nearly grown sons by the time Sigmund was born. But there was a mysterious second wife in between the death of his first wife and his marriage to Amelia, Freud's mother. She was never mentioned, and no one knew what had become of her. The author of this book hypothesized that Freud's obsessive need to uncover secrets had his own family story as a root cause—an interesting idea from an astrological point of view, since Freud had an 8th house Gemini Moon square to Neptune. It's also interesting to note that Sigmund was his father's third son, but his mother's first child, and this may go a long way to explain his need to be "first" at any cost.

---

12 Op. cit.

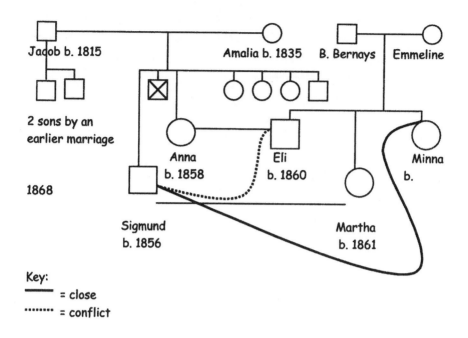

Key:
——— = close
········ = conflict

AUDIENCE: Would Neptune describe the presence of a family ghost?

LYNN: Neptune's lack of boundaries makes it a good candidate as carrier of the family unconscious, and it is almost certainly involved, along with the watery houses, in leaking content from psyche to psyche within a family. However, I would hesitate to give such an attribution to only one factor in the horoscope.

AUDIENCE: How would you differentiate between the 8th and 12th in terms of secrets? I can sense a difference, but can't put words to it.

LYNN: To my way of thinking, the 12th house contains secrets that have been lost to awareness through time, death or negligence. Nonetheless, they remain alive in the family psyche, taking the form of strange recurrences, disturbing dreams, and even "hauntings." In many cases, an 8th house secret is kept by one or more family members, creating a very different kind of atmosphere—one of brooding tension, locked drawers, and mislaid papers. In some ways, then, the 8th house is more conscious than the 12th, but one person in a family takes power by withholding knowledge. This is true even if something is hidden "for your own good." Inheritance issues, revenge, betrayal, and other "shameful" family secrets, especially involving sexuality, are the special predilection of this house, and Erin Sullivan associates it with the family complex. An 8th house secret can feel heavy and tortured, full of foreboding, while a 12th house "ghost" carries a sense of longing and sadness, a resigned, lost feeling, that takes an individual away from life into a mournful realm.

AUDIENCE: In Germany, a lot of work on the family constellation has been done by a therapist named Bert Hellinger. He puts people on stage, and they choose surrogates to represent all the different family members. He believes this reveals a deep inner structure to feeling relationships. It sounds quite similar to some of the things you are talking about.

LYNN: That sounds fascinating! I'm not familiar with that approach, but there has been a great deal written in English on family systems work; Erin Sullivan gives a good beginner's bibliography in her book. To go further, some of the top names in the field are Murray Bowen, Carl Whitaker, Jay Haley and Chloe Madones, Virginia Satir, Mara Selvini, Minuchkin, and Böszörményi-Nagy.

INHERITING A NOTION OF SELF

We will now look at the charts of another family, that of someone I met recently, who has kindly agreed to let me use these charts. Let's begin with the genogram, shown on page 135.

As you can see, three children were born very close together: a girl in February 1963, a boy in May 1964, and another son in October 1965. My information comes from the second child, whose name is Fred—short for Siegfried.

The Saturn-Sun thread

There is a very powerful Saturn influence running through the family, but this time the Sun is involved. Almost everyone has Saturn conjunct, opposition, or square the Sun, and Saturn is often conjunct the Ascendant or MC. Do any of you have ideas about what this kind of pattern could mean?

AUDIENCE: The first thing that comes to mind is some kind of pressure between the individual and society—a strong awareness of what the world expects from you.

LYNN: That's one way of looking at it. An individual's sense of self is determined by how the world outside responds. That might be a pattern.

AUDIENCE: There would be a sense of the weight of things, perhaps a burden of responsibility, being pushed to take on more than others.

AUDIENCE: I would expect a feeling of specialness, based on the recognition of responsibility. They can handle whatever is thrown their way.

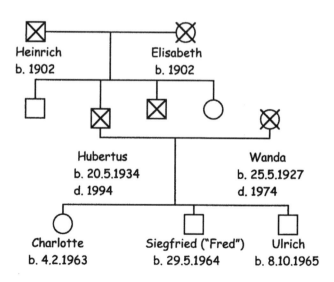

But I could imagine a stiff sort of pride, too, a pride based on what has been accomplished in the past.

AUDIENCE: If Saturn represents the rules, as you said earlier, then this combination might describe an incredibly rule-bound family, and I could imagine it feeling very narrow and restrictive.

LYNN: You've given a number of very pertinent themes associated with the Saturn-Sun combination. I find it fascinating how quickly some of you talked about the positive side of the combination, because when I've presented this material in the States, there was a much greater focus on the difficulties and restrictions of Saturn. I suspect this might be a reflection of differences in the two cultures. After all, the chart for the United Kingdom has a Saturn-friendly Capricorn Sun, and the United States chart has a strong Jupiter.

Like any aspect, Saturn-Sun can work out in a number of different ways. It almost always describes a great deal of pressure to measure up to certain standards, but whatever the origin of that pressure, these individuals seem to internalize and even identify with it later in life. Since Saturn and the Sun are both symbols for the father, this combination often comes with echoes of Cronos, who, as you know, swallowed his children in order to stay on top. Sometimes the shade of Cronos inhabits the family patriarch, who crushes any spark of individuality, but the energy can also be more diffuse, giving an atmosphere heavy with tradition, and portraits of dour ancestors guarding the hallways. The less tangible ghosts of accomplishment (or failure) weight an individual's path toward certain pre-ordained choices or roles.

It's fascinating to reflect on the differences between Jupiter and Saturn squaring or opposing the Sun. In both cases there seems to be difficulty judging one's abilities realistically, with the Jupiter-Sun person often taking on more than they can reasonably manage. Saturn-Sun people do the same, but feel they have no choice, doubt themselves, and fret about getting it right. Often the individual with a Jupiter dissonance feels good when they are stretched and slightly off center, but they rarely indulge in doubt on the wing.

AUDIENCE: I've met people with Saturn-Sun who constantly doubt their ability; they limit themselves. I don't see them as taking risks; it's almost the opposite. They operate within very narrow boundaries, and seem to be fearful of life.

LYNN: Yes, the fearful Saturnian is quite a common species, but it's important to ask where this timorous attitude originates. Too much or too little of something are classic Saturn expressions, and the hard aspects often correspond to frustration involving the father. As we have seen, an overwhelming father is one of the possibilities. All of you will have run across examples where these aspects describe the opposite—an absent or terribly weak father—and this creates a sense of lack deep within the individual. When this is the case, the limitation can come from an internalized sense of inadequacy, of not being good enough, or not having done enough, or not being ready. A self-imposed narrowness can inhibit the individual's range of accomplishment, through fear, self-protection, or unrealistically high demands. It's not infrequent for the Saturn-Sun person to cling to external rules that shore up that inner uncertainty, the missing structure.

It must be said that those with Saturn-Sun aspects are irrevocably drawn to difficulty, although this may be only partly conscious. They may push to overcome it, giving a driven, high-achievement personality, capable of great accomplishment, but often bound to struggle. Other Saturn-Sun people feel constantly thwarted by circumstances or other people, and nurture a classic inferiority complex, while still others "marry" the rules and elect themselves guardians of the system. The identity of a Saturn-Sun individual is carved out through their relationship to obstacles, and they tend to see obstacles or difficulty even when these are invisible to others. They will hone in on difficulty as a testing ground, interpreting success or failure as proof of their worthiness.

Aspects between Sun and Saturn seem to correspond to very specific inner parameters. Saturn represents some kind of barrier to expression that must be acknowledged for a time and later integrated, and the life force is held back accordingly, contained within bounds which may not have been chosen initially. A habit of introversion, or order and discipline, can take root in the individual, who no longer feels comfortable without it. Having built their own containing walls and limited their own possibilities, the real work of Saturn-Sun often has to do with acknowledging how and when they stop themselves, as well as learning how to open up their boundaries. Now, what happens when a whole family has a pattern of this kind?

AUDIENCE: It doesn't strike me as a big party signature. I don't get a sense of fun and laughter. The image that comes to me is this severe farm couple posing for their portrait with a pitchfork and a frown.

LYNN: Oh, the Grant Wood painting, "American Gothic"—that's a famous portrait from the 1930's. You're right, there's a decidedly Saturnian overtone, and Saturn does have general rulership over the agricultural world. So one possibility is a hard-working, serious family with very little time for play.

AUDIENCE: In my own family there's a strong Saturn imprint, and things were very difficult, financially and otherwise. My father worked very hard, ten hours a day, with little to show for it, and he died relatively young, leaving my mother with five children to raise. All of us had to work and help out. That doesn't mean we didn't laugh or enjoy each other, but my mother was often tired and drawn.

LYNN: It's not unusual for a Saturnian pattern to describe harsh external circumstances. The barrier represented by Saturn can be internal or external, and sometimes both. Occasionally conditions are so difficult that it literally wears people out, resulting in diminished hope or vitality—a pattern of struggle and ill health. This signature can be found in families where the parents work very hard to pay for a child's education, accepting their own limitations but piling up energy and savings for the future. You can imagine the pressure to succeed contained in this kind of family system, falling squarely on the shoulders of a Saturn-Sun child. Saturn asks us to build our solar energy strongly enough to move through whatever limitations we encounter, and to use them to make something of ourselves. Saturn-Sun is obstacle prone, in part because these individuals welcome difficulty as a way to achieve growth. Over a lifetime, they use obstacles to build a sense of identity. This may come through overcoming an external barrier, or wrestling with inner doubt.

When poverty crushes the spirit of a family, it can also reduce a family's capacity to choose another future. Take the example of children who have had their growth and mental development damaged by ingesting lead from old paint. Recent studies have shown that lead is stored permanently within the bones, but released from a woman's body when she is pregnant, where it enters the bloodstream of the fetus, and the cycle of damage continues. The external constraint of poverty becomes internalized, not just psychologically, but on a biological level an encoded physical fate. Conditions this severe may require many generations to finally ease the cycle of limitation, so sometimes Saturn asks us learn to live with what cannot be changed. Often Saturn individuals feel responsible for everything and bound by guilt, and wear themselves out trying to undo difficulties that stretch beyond their possibilities.

AUDIENCE: That doesn't sound very hopeful! Are you saying that we should simply give up and accept our fate?

LYNN: Not exactly. I suspect that Saturn bars the route in certain areas, but not in all, so that even in the most difficult conditions, a path opens that will offer less hardship, less resistance. A child who stays to work in the mine, beaten down by physical exhaustion and a structure of injustice, may have less chance of overcoming Saturn's conditions than one who leaves the village for the insecurity of a larger world. In either case things are difficult, but these difficulties bear fruit of different kinds. Part of Saturn's wisdom is knowing when we are ready to take something on, or recognizing that we aren't yet strong enough to tackle the system.

Let's go back to our example. I'm going to put up the Saturn pattern of the parents and their three children (see page 140).

Saturn has an undeniably powerful role in this family. In the case of the parents and the eldest daughter, its aspect to the Sun is extremely close, under 1° degree of orb. Now, we know that such a precise relationship to Saturn will demand that an individual, and a family, integrate certain external rules, or perhaps confront very real limits in the outside world.

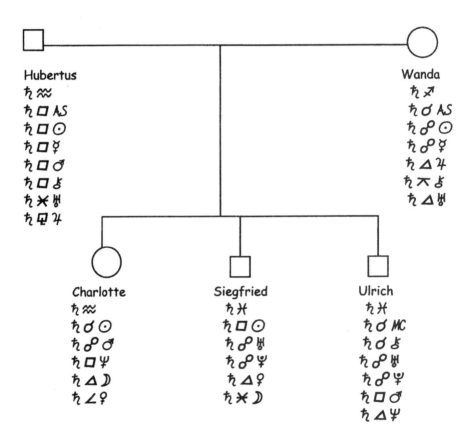

- Wanda has the Ascendant at 27° Scorpio conjunct Saturn at 4° 26' Sagittarius. Saturn also opposes her Sun at 3° 32' Gemini and Mercury at 10° Gemini.

- Hubertus, the father, has the Sun at 28° 24' Taurus, conjunct the Ascendant at 25° Taurus and Mars at 20° Taurus. They are all square Saturn in the 11th house at 27°54' Aquarius.

- Charlotte, the eldest child, has the Sun at 14° 32' Aquarius in the 3rd house, in a tight conjunction to Saturn at 13° 54' Both oppose Mars at 15° 7' Leo, and both square Neptune at 15°37' Scorpio.

- Fred, the second child, has the Sun at 7°53' Gemini, square Saturn in the 9th at 4° 48' Pisces. Saturn opposes Uranus at 6° 01' Virgo and Pluto at 11° 36' Virgo, so we have a T-square involving Sun, Saturn, Uranus and Pluto.

- Ulrich, the younger son, has Saturn in Pisces at 11°34', conjunct the MC at 15° 41' Pisces and Chiron at 19° 05' Pisces, and all are opposed to a Uranus-Pluto conjunction in the 4th house at 17° Virgo. Although Saturn is angular, it doesn't aspect the Sun unless we count a wide bi-quintile, or an even wider quincunx.

AUDIENCE: The diagram you've just put up seems to describe a group of people with a very strong sense of purpose. But something else just jumped out at me. All the children have Saturn in hard aspect to outer planets. I'm sure this is significant. Perhaps it suggests a generational shift in their experience, maybe some kind of evolution in the social patterns, since Uranus and Pluto mark a whole generation.

LYNN: That's very well observed, and I think you're on to something important. The children will not be able to maintain the same relationship to whatever Saturn represents, even if they should wish to.

As we saw earlier, Sun-Saturn often comes with strong rules and a sense of tradition. I've seen this in cases where the family has had a central role in the community for generations. Social history becomes entwined with the story of the family; individual identity emerges out of the past. In this particular example, the family is not only noble, but also counts a well-known ancestor in their family tree, a great-uncle who was a famous military commander. This kind of past success may boost our sense of self, but also turns the screws; we have no choice other than to live up to that past. The pressure of living in a family that needs to embody a particular image can result in spectacular inhibition, or self-sabotaging incompetence. For those individuals who "fit" the successful pattern, this kind of heritage is indeed a gift, a fast track to outer mastery. However genius can also engender famously inept or simply ordinary offspring, The hopes of those who have recourse to sperm banks are not always realized. Here, the outer planet involvement with Saturn in the charts of the three children will most likely act to change the relationship to their inheritance, or perhaps that pattern had already changed by the time they were born.

Although most of us do not come from aristocratic backgrounds, we often have something to live up to. It could be having an older brother or sister who was the school genius—the teacher's eyes light up, and if you turn out to be merely ordinary, their disappointment is palpable, and your sense of self takes a dousing. Those with Sun-Saturn aspects have a particular sensitivity to the judgment of the outside world. They feel pressured to hold to a successful outer pattern, no matter what is inside. So they worry about being good enough, smart enough, rich enough, having the right mettle. Not so long ago, a son was expected to follow his father's calling, whatever it was. Sun-Saturn people typically put themselves under tremendous pressure. Whatever they do, they should be doing more, or better; the inner critic is never satisfied for very long.

To begin with, I'd like to look more closely at the father's chart. Let's put it up. Saturn in this chart is the most elevated planet, and it has dignity in Aquarius. I've always felt there's a good fit between Aquarius and aristocrats—a special group of individuals, clearly differentiated from the rest of society, and free to develop individual quirks and talents. Have you noticed this kind of thing? Even when Aquarians come from ordinary backgrounds, they often set themselves apart, quickly assuming that the usual rules do not apply to them. They carry an inner

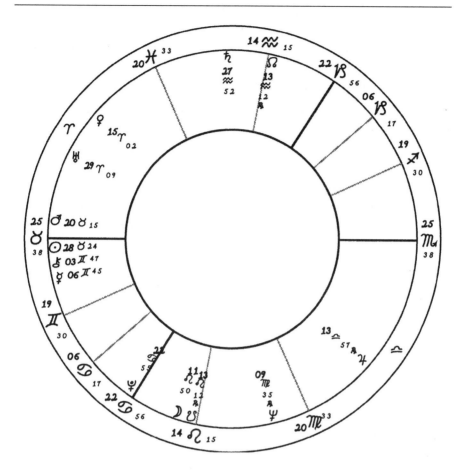

Hubertus, 20 May 1934, 4:00 AM CET, 53N57, 12E41

attitude that says, "We are different from other people!" (And sometimes, unconsciously, better, than other people.)

AUDIENCE: I would think that strong Saturn in the 11th gives a powerful outward push to accomplishment, and yet it feels ambivalent somehow, as if he wasn't in the right place. Perhaps the father put all his
energy into outer things, into living up to the aristocratic image at a
cost to his personal fulfillment. His wife's chart suggests he may have
neglected his marriage. She has Saturn conjunct the Ascendant and
opposing the Sun in the 7th. An opposition falling across the 1st and
7th houses like that must be quite frustrating for relationship.

LYNN: Yes, Saturn seems to push each of them to act in particular spheres; it plays different chords for each family member, so that the same aspect creates very different conditions. The father has Sun and Mars conjunct the Ascendant, and the mother has Saturn there. These probably describe quite opposite personal styles, and a considerable difference in self-confidence and physical vitality.

AUDIENCE: I always thought that Saturn in the 11th meant some kind of difficulty with the group. I know someone with this placement who only has friends who are much older than he is, or who are from a very different background socially. But he feels he doesn't fit in with people his own age. Could the father have taken on a role that met with the disapproval of the aristocratic world he came from?

LYNN: There is something like that in his story, although it has more to do with social convulsions than personal choices. The 11th house shows how we fit into society as a whole, and Saturn may indicate an experience of exclusion, or a voluntary distancing from one's "normal" peer group. I have also seen it activated in the charts of children from immigrant families who live in a world apart. They grow up speaking another language, following their parents' cultural practices, feeling unable to be part of the world "out there." Since Saturn is square the Sun and Ascendant, the relationship with society will greatly affect Hubertus' sense of self. We already know that the strong family tradition is involved, but there is something more, a loss of social position and wealth following the war. Look at the strong Pluto in this chart. It is at 22° 55' Cancer, one minute away from the IC—an exact conjunction. What could that be?

Pluto in the 4th house

AUDIENCE: Pluto in the 4th house indicates some kind of decay of the roots. It means that the past will not provide a solid base to build on; it will be rotten in some way. Perhaps the father was killed in the war, or his reputation was blackened or dishonored. So on the one hand there is that strong tradition, Sun square Saturn, the pressure from the outside group to be a certain kind of person, and on the other hand, Pluto on the IC, undermining that.

AUDIENCE: Pluto points to secrets, unsavory things in the family past. With Pluto in Cancer, there could be a murder of the feminine principle. The Moon rules the 4th, and is also posited there, conjunct the south Node. This looks like some very heavy cleansing of the past is required.

AUDIENCE: Maybe Pluto on the IC describes the destruction of the family home. The father was born in 1934, so the war must have played a major role in his childhood. I would imagine that the past was wiped out on a certain level.

LYNN: In fact, the family castle burned to the ground![13] We are looking at the planetary genogram of an aristocratic Prussian military family, and the grandfather must have been very involved in the war. Hubertus, the father, was about ten when the ancestral home was lost, in 1944 or 1945. Everything was wiped out, the entire heritage destroyed except for the title.

AUDIENCE: This period in Germany, after the war, was marked by so many losses, so much upheaval, that it's also a collective event, a complete change in the fabric of society. Many people of that generation, with Pluto in Cancer, lived terrible things and experienced great poverty, but they speak little of this time.

---

13 When Fred first told me the story of his family, certain details were not strictly correct. This is very common in this work, and it's important to verify your memory of stories told by a parent with the memory of the older generations where possible. As it turns out, the family castle was sold in 1929, probably for financial reasons, and Heinrich and his wife Elisabeth—Fred's grandparents—raised their children in a farmhouse some twenty kilometres from the castle, a farmhouse that belonged to her family So the castle did burn down, but they weren't living in it at the time! Heinrich supervised work on the land, both in agriculture and forestry, later taking jobs as a forest warden and gamekeeper. The loss of the family inheritance began before the war. Only recently was the grandfather's active role in the Nazi Party documented. He was a member of the SS and worked in the regional Office for Racial Politics, which was in charge of implementing Nazi policy toward Jews—a good reason to choose low-key posts in the countryside after the war.

LYNN: That's a good point, and it's also worth considering another. Even if the castle hadn't burned to the ground, it was in the eastern part of Germany and would have soon come under communist rule. One way or another, things would have come to an end. The parents left everything and ended up in the West, where they eventually found lodging in a cheap, modern high-rise building. It's hard to imagine a more complete break with one's roots, from neo-gothic castle to faceless skyscraper. Perhaps we can see this family as a particularly clear illustration of a transformation that touched the whole of society. That, too, is Pluto in the 4th.

Pluto in a family pattern has to do with finding the impulse to rise up out of the ashes. On the 4th house cusp, in particular, it often bars access to the past, or renders the family inheritance so heavy that one is better advised to leave it behind. One of the first times I gave a workshop on the family, I remember stating this rather dramatically. A woman in the group, visibly shaken, raised her hand to say that she had Pluto on the IC and was still close to her family. As it turned out, a brother had been killed in a car accident when she was young, and she had stayed close to support her parents in their loss. Then her own teenage son was killed in a motorcycle accident, and a long cycle of self-examination was set in motion. It's impossible to say whether the same thing would have happened if she'd lived far away, but the toxicity of the root, that energy of deep mourning and loss, was repeated in her own experience.

Another woman with this placement had been labeled by her family as "the unlucky one." She was the child who would fall ill, lose her schoolbags, break her arm, and various gloomy predictions were made about her ability to amount to something. As an adult she suffered from inexplicable depressions. It was only after leaving home, and moving to another town, that she began to emerge from the family spell, and after much psychological work realized that she had been the designated patient, the carrier of the family shadow. It is likely that she was the only child with Pluto placed on the IC, and her story is an illustration of how we can be captured by the family unconscious, particularly with this kind of signature in the 4th house.

Fred's father inherited a broken root, snapped off at the base. He went from an expectation of material comfort and status to the hard scrabble of earning a living, and as a teenager took a job in the docks, lifting and hoisting loads, working as a physical laborer in order to support the family. The image of a young Count, sweating and dirty, is like a scene from the underworld—the prince grappling with the earthy, the ordinary. Perhaps it speaks to the Saturn square Sun work of cutting the ego down to size, but in Hubertus' case, it is the family ego, the proud history that swallows dust and starts from the bottom, much like the game of snakes and ladders, where you step on the wrong square, and go "Whoosh!" all the way down. Although an older brother followed the family tradition of a military career, it was Hubertus, the second son, who took responsibility for his parents and younger siblings, growing down into the world, in Hillman's terms, earning enough to put them through school.

AUDIENCE: I wonder why the older son didn't take on that role? This story strikes me as quite extraordinary, like a fairy tale, as if Hubertus is working out a debt for the sins of his forefathers. I notice that he has the Moon conjunct the south node in Leo, and this surely points to old issues around pride of place, or even a soul memory of comfort and luxury.

LYNN: It is very tempting to fall into ideas of karmic reward and retribution, but we cannot really know the truth of these things. All we can say for sure is that something was irrevocably coming to an end. Just as an empire or civilization runs its course, or a species becomes extinct, sometimes a family winds down and the name dies out; the memory is lost. At its worst, attempting to build on tradition with Pluto on the 4th house cusp is like building on a cemetery or a toxic waste dump. In Jane Smiley's chilling novel, *A Thousand Acres*, her character describes memories of life on the farm she lost:

> Let us say that each vanished person left me something, and that I feel my inheritance when I am reminded of one of them. When I am reminded of Jess I think of the loop of poison we drank from, the water running down through the soil, into the drainage wells, into the lightless mysterious underground chemical sea, then being drawn up, cold and appetizing, from the drink-

ing well into Rose's faucet, my faucet. I am reminded of Jess when I drive in the country, and see the anhydrous trucks in the distance, or the herbicide incorporators, or the farmers plowing their fields in the fall, or hills that are ringed with black earth and crowned with soil so pale that the corn only stands in it, as in gravel, because there are no nutrients to draw from it.[14]

In her novel, Smiley describes an environment that can no longer nourish those that live there. With a history of incest and death and the agro-chemical poisoning of the land, one sister dies of cancer, the other walks away; when the farm is sold, only debt is left. Pluto can describe this kind of extreme impasse. Read this novel if you want to plunge into the destructive power of a family inheritance.

Fortunately for Hubertus, he had an opportunity to rebuild the family's fortunes on new ground, and with his strong Taurean Sun and Ascendant he met the difficulty of the Saturn square head on, eventually entering a bank on the clerical level and, over time, working his way up to become bank director. Hubertus must have had the sense of redeeming the past in some way by bringing security to the lives of his family, a reflection of that strong 4th house Moon/south Node conjunction. Yet the Moon squares Venus in the 12th, suggestive of a sacrifice of some kind. With both Venus and Uranus in Aries intercepted in the 12th, we need to ask questions about his relationship to love and pleasure, and to personal freedom. On a certain level, Hubertus found a successful response to the family crisis and the destruction of the past. Yet there must be more to the story, because both his sons have Pluto conjunct the IC.

AUDIENCE: So you are saying that that it might somehow be dangerous for his sons to go work in the bank?

LYNN: In a way, yes. Hubertus used the obstacle of Saturn square the Sun and the energy of an angular Pluto to climb back up out of the ruins of the castle. The pressure of the family background gave a boost by

---

14 Jane Smiley, *A Thousand Acres*, Ballantine Books, NY, 1991

---

saying, "Show you are one of us. Show that our kind does not stay sunk in the mud. Rise out of your condition." In keeping with the strong Taurus signature and that 4th house Moon, he made money and financial security his goals, taking it upon himself to pull the rest of the family back up with him. I would suggest that Fred and Ulrich will need to find other motivations, and Venus may offer a particularly important clue. However, they carry a new energy as well, a new archetype which might be stated something like this: "We are not ordinary people, and we have had to rise from the ashes. We can overcome extreme difficulty." On the 4th house cusp, Pluto demands transformation of the past. It is both the after-image of the castle in flames and a powerful inheritance coming via the father—the indomitable personal will of Mars sextile Pluto with its phoenix-like capacity for new life.

Here you see the weaving together of two patterns, the Saturn-Sun thread describing a tradition going back over generations, hundreds of years, and a Pluto theme coming in like a fireburst, breaking that past apart. Now, in the younger generation, Pluto is conjunct Uranus as well—an even more explosive combination, particularly in the charts of the sons. But even the daughter, Charlotte, has the ruler of the 4th house, Neptune, in Scorpio, adding a Plutonian flavor to the 12th house longings. Fred describes her as a "Lady Di type," always perfectly coiffed and made up, and very conventional, looking as if she needs to keep her less predictable Aquarian side hidden from view.

The artist and the military man

Look at his chart (on page 150). The Gemini Sun forms the handle of a T-square, with a 90° orb to both Saturn in Pisces and the Uranus-Pluto conjunction in Virgo. Like his father, Fred has Sun square Saturn, but with an extra twist added by the transpersonals. How do you think this might be expressed?

AUDIENCE: This structure feels full of tension, charged with an overwhelming desire to break out of the family pattern and the father's rules. I can't imagine this would be an easy relationship.

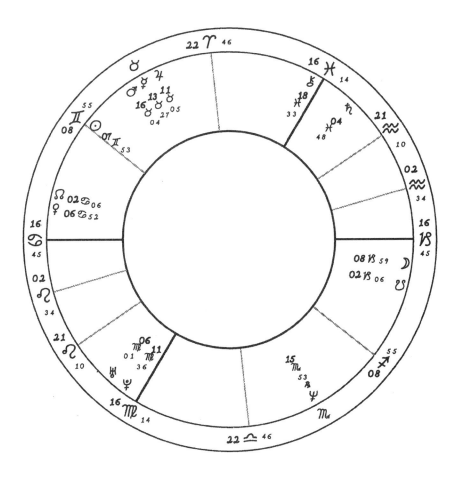

Siegfried, or Fred, 29 May 1964, 7:15 am CET, 51N12 6E47

LYNN: Yes, Uranus makes the tightest aspect to the Sun and demands to break free. It will react absolutely to the inherited pattern represented by Saturn. The tension is dual, however, because there is a need to both break the rules and live up to the standards of Saturn. It might be that he simply replaces one set of rules with another, radically different in appearance but rules nonetheless. The T-square also describes how Fred "received" his father, and shows the father's own tension between the need to be responsible and the desire to break free of the past. If you look closely, you'll see that they have much in common astrologically besides Saturn-Sun and Pluto-IC: Moon conjunct south Node, Venus in the 12th, and Mars in Taurus in trine to Pluto. Their charts show deep structural connections. The famous great uncle, a military genius, had an exact Mars-Pluto sextile, so both Fred and his father inherited versions of this incredibly potent will.

AUDIENCE: I find the contrast between the Sun's tense aspects and the rest of the chart quite startling. Almost everything else forms a giant trine and sextile pattern. It looks like the chart of someone with tremendous gifts. And yet, underneath, at the core, the energy is very uncomfortable, very driven.

LYNN: Yes, this chart has an extraordinary amount of energy funneling into the grand trine and interlinked sextiles. Your comment goes to the heart of Fred's nature. He is handsome, charming, gifted, and internally very driven, at times devoured by ambition. When he was younger, he wanted to be a musician and would practice guitar compulsively for hours, determined to be the fastest in the world; if his playing wasn't good enough, he would smash his room to pieces. He is the first artist in a military family, and you can imagine the shock wave that choice of profession sent through the family. He plotted his artistic career like a military strategist, using consummate social and intellectual skills to win people over, and he has been quite successful, winning an important prize and having shows, and has been noticed by major collectors. The only problem is that, with transiting Pluto opposing his Sun, he has lost his motivation to do art. Anyone who has a transpersonal planet right on the IC of the chart can become an agent for change—change within the family or outside it, sometimes affecting an entire group. Whether this impulse is unconscious or willed is not necessarily indicated by the planets alone, and we cannot know on which level the impulse for change will play out. The unconscious saboteur, the unhappy black sheep and the wild original have a great deal in common. Fred has Pluto in the 3rd house, 5° from the cusp of the 4th, close enough to consider the conjunction, but it will act a bit differently here, seeking change through communication or a conscious elaboration of ideas. Perhaps this Pluto will be partly carried by a sibling. But it is likely that Fred's role will be to give voice to what has been kept quiet until now.

It is impossible to say at this point whether this marks a permanent change in direction, but the transit tests one's motivation on the deepest possible level. It may be that Fred's artistic identity was essentially a way to differentiate himself from his father, and now he is itching to squeeze out of it, as a serpent sheds its skin. The choice of art as a profession may not have been motivated by Venus (although Venus is clearly very strong in this chart) as much as by the hard aspects to the Sun. Do you see that? I have also noticed that those born with the Uranus-Pluto conjunction in opposition to Saturn often feel an inner compulsion to knock down what they have built just as they are about to reach the top, perhaps to protect themselves from watching it fall to pieces otherwise. But for Fred, the shift in direction began at the Saturn return. A celebration had been planned around his thirtieth birthday and his father's sixtieth, but it never happened; his father had a sudden, fatal heart attack while walking in the street.

Fred had also had a professional setback of sorts. He was one of ten finalists in an important artistic competition, but wasn't chosen in the end. Up until then he had poured all his energy into getting famous, being recognized as an important artist. Again, one of his paintings was bought by a major museum in Germany, hugely important for his reputation, but fate intervened when a museum patron insisted on having it in his private collection instead. Many people might have interpreted these near-misses as disappointing but encouraging. But for Fred, being "good" wasn't enough. He needed to be at the top of his profession, and he felt as though a door had been shut on his career.

A few years before, around the time of the progressed lunar return, Fred had encountered astrology—love at first sight, "heaven and earth kissing each other." He began to invest more and more energy into astrology, where he felt connected to music through celestial harmonies and visual patterns in a chart. Even more, he opened up to a larger understanding of himself and the people around him. This shift in vision and focus often occurs when such powerful planets form an opposition in the 3rd/9th house axis, an axis of awareness. And we can also hear echoes of the inspiration contained in Jupiter conjunct Mercury opposition Neptune.

AUDIENCE: I was wondering about whether those 3rd house planets describe the relationship with his siblings. In the seminar on the 3rd house, you spoke of the possibility of carrying the shadow, particularly with Pluto here.[15]

LYNN: I suspect that Fred was not easy for anyone in his family, and he and his brother fought wildly in adolescence, although they have a good relationship now. His sister always felt dwarfed and inadequate, and rather dull in comparison to Fred, who was always the "star." We'll look at these relationships in more depth later.

AUDIENCE: I was born in Prussia, and would like to say something about the cultural archetype. In the 18th century, Frederick the Great was a central figure. He was sensitive and cultured, interested in music and literature, and he was gay. His father was incredibly strict; he demanded absolute obedience. In Prussian culture you do not disobey authority, you do not break the rules, and your desire is subordinated to your obligation or your responsibility. It requires a lot of effort for someone from this background to break out, and that inner tension is probably always there. When Frederick the Great ran away, his father had him captured and killed his lover in front of his eyes; then he kept him in prison for a year to break his will, and forced him to accept his destiny as a military leader. I believe he had a Uranus-Pluto conjunction as well![16]

LYNN: That's a pretty harrowing story! I'm grateful you've mentioned it, because these kinds of larger cultural myths play an important role in family work. They are part of what a family uses to build its own identity. I had some notion of authority and obedience as central to that

---

15 This seminar forms Part Two of this book.
16 Frederick the Great was born "at noon" in Berlin on 24 January 1712, with Pluto-Uranus conjunct in Virgo. He had an exact Mars-Saturn opposition with Saturn conjunct the Moon and opposing the Sun.

tradition, but hadn't realized to what extreme point it could go. That's very helpful information. What happened to Frederick?

AUDIENCE: He became a very powerful ruler, an "enlightened despot" interested in philosophy, but incredibly disciplined and militaristic. I suppose you could say that the father's will won out.

LYNN: The story Katerina has evoked tells us that any son of a Prussian military family who becomes an artist has taken a highly charged decision. It helps us judge more precisely what is at stake. Of course, Germany in the 1980's had little in common with 18th century Prussia,

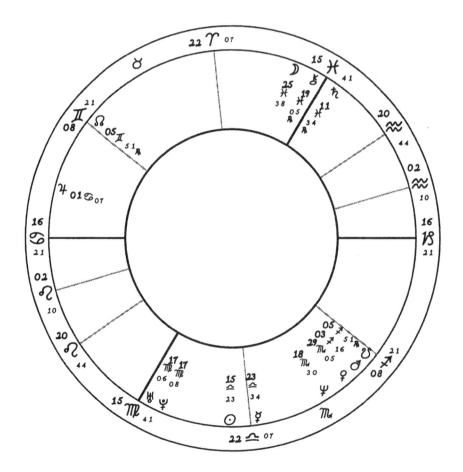

Ulrich, 8 October 1965, 10:31 pm CET, 51N12, 6E47

and the weight of Fred's family tradition had already been broken by the war and the loss of the ancestral home. His unconventional professional choice continues a process of change that began in the preceding generation. Unfortunately I don't have the birth times for his paternal grandparents, but Pluto is strong in both charts: opposition Uranus for both, square the grandmother's Sun and the grandfather's Venus.

AUDIENCE: The grandparents had their life turned upside down. I suppose that is a way of seeing the Pluto-Uranus opposition. This period after the war was so traumatic for the older generation that they almost never speak of it. The past was covered up, and if you're German it's very difficult to ask questions about it.

LYNN: Fred's grandfather, Heinrich, had to lie low after the war. He had been a Nazi, and might have been tried or punished if he had been caught, so he lived a rather quiet life. But you can clearly see the Pluto symbolism—the father hiding, keeping quiet about what may have happened. Fred found this grandfather rather brutal and stubborn, narrow-minded and limited, but he doubts he did anything particularly horrible during the war. As landowners (even though now landless), they were expelled from their village in 1945 by decrees passed by the new government, and they moved north, changing towns every five years or so, until they retired to Hanover and the dreary modern post-war apartment.

Ulrich, the younger son, has an even tighter Pluto-Uranus conjunction on the IC, so we can assume that the family story has a powerful resonance in his own life. His work has a powerful Plutonian theme: he is a criminal lawyer! Although Saturn is strong, conjunct the MC, it doesn't aspect the Sun, and he has a much more easy-going nature than his brother. But his family-pleasing choice of law studies veered into this rather unconventional specialty, and he rubs shoulders with the darker side of the human psyche on a daily basis. It may be that this choice, defending the accused, has something to do with the grandfather. There is something about an aristocratic family that looks down at the world from a height, distant from the lands around. Ulrich's choice of profession, with its secrets and digging underneath, has a feeling of coming back down to earth and scrabbling at the roots.

Chiron's threads

AUDIENCE: Two things leap out from his chart—that strong Moon in the 10th, and Chiron right on the MC. In fact, Chiron has been prominent in all these charts so far. But in the 10th house, and conjunct the Moon, it seems to point to the mother. We haven't really spoken of her yet.

LYNN: I wanted to explore the Saturn and Pluto issues first, and they clearly led us to the father's side of the family. But the story of the mother is very powerful, very painful, and tied into Chiron's themes.

Wanda was a dark-haired, transcendent beauty, sensitive and artistic, but very demanding emotionally, and her relationship with Hubertus was a stormy one, which is not surprising when we look at that Venus-Pluto-Mars conjunction in the 8th house. Her chart is very watery, dramatic and hypersensitive, with Scorpio rising and Moon in Pisces conjunct Jupiter. Fred remembers her always being ill. She seems to have been physically frail from childhood, and perhaps she never recovered from the pregnancies and births of three children so close together. As we might expect with that strong Pisces Moon, Wanda was extremely close to her own mother, who cared for the children during her frequent illnesses. Wanda died of heart failure in 1974. It was Fred's last day of primary school, and he was ten years old, roughly the same age his father had been when the family castle burned down. All three children experienced this devastating loss, the shattering of their emotional security. Both sons are understandably reluctant to commit to a family life, given the immense anxiety engendered by this kind of loss.

Each chart reflects the loss of the mother in very personal ways. Both Charlotte and Ulrich have Pluto in hard aspect to the Moon. But Fred, who was closest to her, has the Moon in that powerful grand trine, and opposing Venus in Cancer in the 12th house. Pluto on the 4th house cusp or ruling it means they literally must let go of the past; it makes any attempt at security doubtful. Thinking about this aspect,

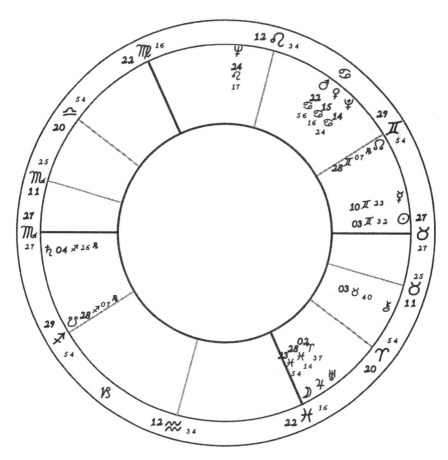

Wanda, 25 May 1927, 7:30 pm CET, 52N34, 32E24

I came across a passage in Thomas Wolfe's novel, *You Can't Go Home Again.*

> He saw now that you can't go home again—not ever. There was no road back. Ended now for him, with the sharp and clean finality of the closing of a door, was the time when his dark roots, like those of a pot-bound plant, could be left to feed upon their own substance, and nourish their little self absorbed designs. Henceforth they must spread outwards—away from the hidden, secret and unfathomed past that holds man's spirit

prisoner—outward, outward, towards the rich and life-giving soil of a new freedom in the wide world of all humanity.[17]

The work we are doing today goes beyond identifying patterns, to help us understand what it is we have to do. Family is one of the more fated areas in our lives; our debts and inheritances are often more structural, more psychological, than material. And certain tasks demand our attention. Often we grope our way towards some kind of completion, like the hero or heroine of a fairy tale who accidentally enters a strange and dangerous labyrinth, the only way through to one's heart's desire.

The Venus-Moon thread

Moon-Venus aspects are another signature found in this family, either in trine, square, or opposition in the charts of the parents and children. How would you describe a Moon-Venus climate?

AUDIENCE: Off the top of my head I would think this might be sweet and cozy, but perhaps a little too cloying, like the families in children's stories where everyone loves each other, oh so very much.

AUDIENCE: Perhaps the ones with Moon-Venus trines enjoy being close, more than the ones with the opposition? I would guess there's a great deal of caring, but also something about being overwhelmed by feeling. The hard aspects might indicate difficulty taking in love.

LYNN: Yes, that's probably a good way of looking at it. There is a great deal of feeling here, and with Moon-Venus there often seems to be confusion between love and dependency. Certain sign positions will exacerbate this. Venus-Pluto in Cancer trine the Moon conjunct Jupiter—what a tidal wave of passionate feeling in Wanda's chart! She probably had very little psychic separation from her loved ones, since the water trines are also in water houses. Boundless, big, full, and very emotional, easily

---

17 Thomas Wolfe, *You Can't Go Home Again*, HarperCollins, 1988.

wounded as well, she married a man with Venus in Aries trine Moon in Leo, widely square Pluto and opposed Jupiter. Both trines aspire to soaring, romantic love, but one could imagine a certain amount of misunderstanding once the initial fascination cooled. Fire needs air to burn, and Hubertus' Venus in the 12th will pull back into solitude at times, while water needs the feeling of connection and closeness.

This abundant maternal love might have been overwhelming for those close to her, who would be lifted up by it and then cut off by her illnesses, when she lay suffering in a darkened room. Later, of course, when she died, the suffering became a deeper pain, a more permanent separation. Ulrich has the same Venus-Moon trine as his mother, but the Moon opposes Pluto and Uranus and conjuncts Chiron. It isn't hard to imagine that a fundamentally kind temperament balks at too much closeness, runs away from the power of those feelings and the possibility of suffering through loving too much. Their father watched his wife suffer and die—powerful emotions with their swift currents run through the fabric of this family and seep into all the relationships, though they are disciplined and contained by the even more dominant Saturn structures.

In fact, Pluto is involved with the Moon-Venus structures in all the charts, intensifying the emotional patterns in the family. We know that the hard aspects often indicate difficulty integrating certain facets of the feminine, and that in a man's chart this can result in a "split anima." Loving more than one woman protects a man from becoming too dependent, from being swept back into a overly demanding maternal love. In this family it also offers protection from loss and devastation, and both sons and the father have tended to look for love elsewhere, as if a part of their emotional life must be channeled off. I think this is particularly clear in Fred's chart, with Venus in the 12th in Cancer opposing a Capricorn Moon, as well as Chiron in Pisces on the MC. Here we have a very clear signature for the suffering and illness of the mother, the soul's buffeting between exaltation and loss, and the conflicting need to contain feeling or to completely let go. The opposition contacts Saturn, Uranus, Neptune, and Pluto by trine and sextile, and one imagines this opening up and closing off to be of great power in his life. No wonder the pull of an artistic life was so compelling for him. Venus in the 12th aches for the impossible, brushes wings with the divine, but that Moon in Capricorn must have some illusion of control over the process.

The Moon in the 6th house needs to repair, and, in Capricorn, may feel responsible for the wounding or suffering of others. While Fred's father was alive, he armored himself with his ambition, refusing to take his father's path of material security and responsibility for others. But his father's death allowed him to open up more fully to his feeling nature, his sense of connection to others, and his generosity and interest in them through the astrological work. I have known many individuals with Moon in Capricorn who have held back their powerful feelings because of difficult external circumstances. My guess is that the artistic impulse dried up because it was constructed in such a way that it strengthened the ego and the will—the Sun-Saturn-Pluto-Uranus T-square—but barred part of his feeling nature. He might have feared that too much tenderness could lead to self-sacrifice, or that too much sensitivity leads to sickness and frailty. His father's death, always a powerful event for Sun-Saturn, allowed him to see that he was driven by something but gained no real satisfaction or happiness from it.

Darby [Costello] often speaks of the light and dark twin tucked away in every Gemini, and we can easily see where the split lies for Fred. Whether he enlarges the artistic impulse to include more of this feeling element, or takes the path of teaching and guiding, remains to be seen. He says that with astrology, for the first time, the outer structures in his life correspond to his inner experience. With Neptune ruling the MC and in the 5th house, he is asked to take the path of an open heart, and Venus in the 12th, conjunct the north Node, confirms love as his real teacher.

AUDIENCE: What about the sister? How does the Moon-Venus opposition work out for her?

LYNN: In a woman's chart, the hard aspects between Moon and Venus touch on fundamental issues of identity. With Venus in the 1st, there

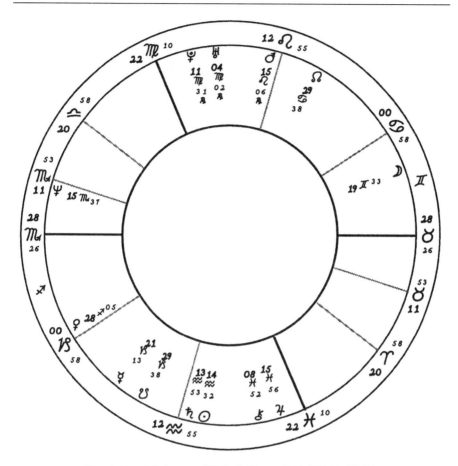

Charlotte, 4 February 1963, 3:10 am CET, 51N12, 6E47

may be an initial tendency to base identity on beauty, on appearance, and Fred says that Charlotte is always impeccably dressed, perfectly made up. She has struggled a great deal with her sense of self-worth, and the opposition with the Moon in the 7th house may make her particularly sensitive to others, and to how they see her. She has very few friends, and generally withdraws from contact with other people, and it is hard for her to reveal herself. The aspect is wide a 9° orb—so it may be less obvious than the tight Sun-Saturn conjunction in the 3rd house of learning.

She was considered the "dumb one"; learning was always difficult for her, and she suffered in comparison with her clever brothers. She has been married twice, and her eldest son has serious learning difficulties, which may have exacerbated her own sense of inferiority, but eventually served as a spur. In her desire to help him, she has gone back to school to study psychology, and is undergoing a radical change in her sense of self. But even in this environment she remains isolated, since she is much older than the other students and dresses differently, like someone from the older generation. Although Saturn in the 3rd is clearly the driving force, the shift in values is part of the Venus-Moon opposition, similar to the process Fred has experienced. She is becoming a very different kind of woman from the one she started out to be. The daughter she had with her second husband has a dazzling personality, with a powerful stellium in Scorpio in the 4th house, and a Sun-Pluto-Jupiter conjunction. If I were working with Charlotte, I would probably explore the Mercury pattern in the family, and everything connected to knowledge and communication.

AUDIENCE: I'm beginning to understand something, because there is a Moon-Venus pattern in my own family, which manifests as a great deal of covert pressure on everyone to agree with everyone else. This made it extremely difficult for me to stand up for myself, and I've always been something of a coward when it comes to conflict. It was hard to pull away and develop my own ideas, without losing the sense of being cared for or valued.

AUDIENCE: I'm curious to know what happened after Wanda, the mother, died. Did the father remarry?

LYNN: Yes, Hubertus married a widow, who had lost her own husband to a brain tumor. She had three children very close in age to Fred and his siblings, and the blending into a new family was quite an important event in their lives. One of the things I've noticed in this work is the strength of connection between adopted children and parents, and often between add-ons and an original family. Ursula, Hubertus' second wife, and her children, are all strongly Saturnian. She has Saturn conjunct the Ascendant in Capricorn, and her son Niklaus is a Capricorn

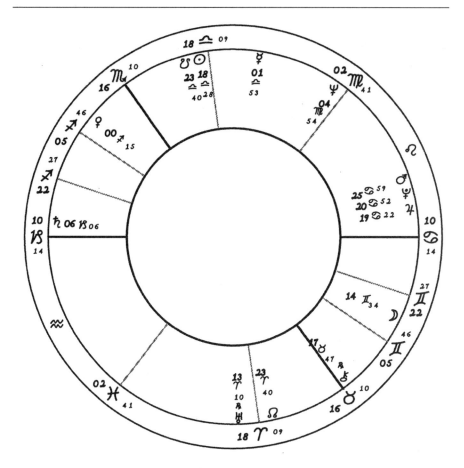

Ursula, 12 October 1930, 2:00 pm CET, 51N40, 8E20

with Sun conjunct Saturn. Their father had been quite successful in his field; he was brilliant and very authoritarian.

Ursula was a fine person, very organized and responsible, but absolutely incapable of intimacy or physical closeness. Her life revolved around rules and ideas rather than feelings. She couldn't have been more different from Wanda. Fred had a hard time understanding why his father married her; she seemed so distant, even cold, until his father explained, shortly before he died, that she gave him the space he needed, an immense relief after the emotionally exhausting relationship with Wanda. These two women also reflect Fred's Moon opposition Venus:

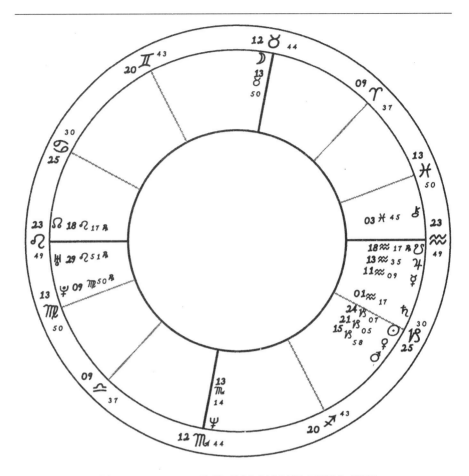

Niklaus, 14 January 1962, 7:30 PM CET, 48N30, 9E03

the sensitive, tender, suffering, beauty (Venus in Cancer in the 12th) and the organized, cold, efficient stepmother who embodies Moon in Capricorn.

The transition was fraught. Charlotte struggled with anorexia, Fred was turbulent and unmanageable. But the new family brought an important relationship for Fred: his stepbrother Niklaus, who became his admired and envied hero, both a friend and a rival. For the first time, Fred found himself in the shadow of a gifted sibling who seemed to get whatever he wanted, particularly girls. I want to put the chart up, because there are a remarkable number of similarities, from the grand trine in earth to Jupiter conjunct Mercury

The 11th house—which in horary symbolizes other people's children—is quite powerful in Fred's chart. I also see it as an antidote and resolution to difficult issues in the family, through the natural quincunx relationship to the 4th house. Niklaus's Moon falls right in the middle of Fred's Jupiter-Mercury-Mars conjunction, and while he ran the family, he also opened many doors for Fred, and they developed an intense friendship. As you have probably come to realize, Fred has an intensely competitive streak, and the feelings of inferiority engendered by comparison to this older stepbrother probably fuelled his need to succeed even more.

Sadly, Niklaus's strong solar energy—Leo rising—has been diminished by drugs and alcohol, and he is a bit lost, something of a recluse, scraping out a living for his family as a restorer. His sister has been diagnosed with multiple sclerosis, so we could say that Ursula's children have had a harder time dealing with the shock of a parent's death -perhaps because of the tight emotional boundaries in the family, and the Saturnian bind. I could go on, but I'm afraid you're all beginning to glaze over. I warned you in the beginning about the amount of detail, and I hope you've been able to follow the planetary threads through these charts in a way that will be fruitful for your own research. While doing this work, Fred's vision of his father has undergone a transformation of sorts. He's been able to get past the rigidity, past the ambition and the drivenness, to a sense of Hubertus' generosity, his steadiness and sensual enjoyment of life. Fred's ex-girlfriend wished she had had a father like Hubertus. Her comment was, "He made you feel that nothing could fall apart." This transformation of vision is typical of family work, and perhaps it's no coincidence that it was begun during Fred's transit of Pluto opposing his Sun.

In pursuit of a mystery

AUDIENCE: What happens when someone never knew their father? I have a friend who has Neptune on the 4th house cusp. He doesn't even know who his father was, so he can't explore the family past.

LYNN: We have already spoken about the power of the unknown working through the family unconscious. When there is really no possibility of uncovering the past, an individual must re-invent themselves with the material at hand, or use another source. Neptune can direct this quest for connection towards the spiritual or religious, or accentuate the disconnection. Gauguin lost his father as an infant, while the family was sailing from France to South America. The lost past, the willingness (or necessity) to leave everything and everyone behind, became a fundamental myth in his life, and eventually led him to Tahiti. Not knowing has a force to it as well. Even when the father is a complete phantom, when the past is a question mark, the questions can still lead to extraordinary places. Neptune is often involved when things are missing—the absent presence that leads to a vague, half-formed quest, and sometimes to answers, even when the questions have never been asked. And sometimes there are real mysteries. I read an incredible statistic somewhere that claimed that one out of seven children in France are not genetically linked to the person they call Papa!

AUDIENCE: I've noticed that my parents and siblings all have planets around the middle degrees of mutable signs. Is this significant?

LYNN: It is not uncommon for families to connect around certain points of the zodiac. In fact, it would probably be more surprising if they didn't. Perhaps certain degrees point to a very specific kind of trait in a family, but even more significantly, when a particular section of the zodiac links all the members of a family, a transit can ripple through the lives of everyone involved at around the same time, and change everything all at once. The entire family seems to be held together in that place, that pivot point. When a transit comes along, it is time for the whole structure, the system of the family, to move. If there are very tight connections like that, you can see ripples travelling through the family. as relations change and individuals re-arrange their lives. These shared astrological zones may also point to areas that need to be developed or worked on, talents or problems running through the fabric of the family The events that come with a common transit will generally push people to change in ways that affect everyone else.

I hope you'll continue thinking about this material, and begin to use it in your own work with astrology. Sometimes, far back in the family tapestry, an event has taken place, an episode that holds a key for your own life choices. Recently I worked with a woman who had been struggling with a career change. She's in her early forties, and she has gone back to school to become a midwife. She kept saying how she wasn't sure, but she felt pushed to do this despite her doubts. As we spoke, a story emerged. Her father was two when his mother died, and as it turned out, the grandmother had died in childbirth. As she saw the connection, her face lit up with wonder. We spoke of how she was healing something in her father's past, healing not personally, but structurally, by going back to learn about helping to give birth. An image comes to me: that of a mother lost in childbirth, the grief and mourning that settle over her family like a cloud, and another image, the granddaughter, almost past the age of childbearing herself, with her hands on a slippery newborn as he emerges fully healthy into this place, this time, safely into his mother's arms.

And that is the goal of this work: finding what part we can play in the process of healing the past, not only for ourselves, but for all those who share that past with us. Thank you.

PART TWO

Siblings & Friends

*This seminar was given on 19 October 1997
at Regents College, London, as part of the
Autumn Term of the seminar programme of the
Centre for Psychological Astrology.*

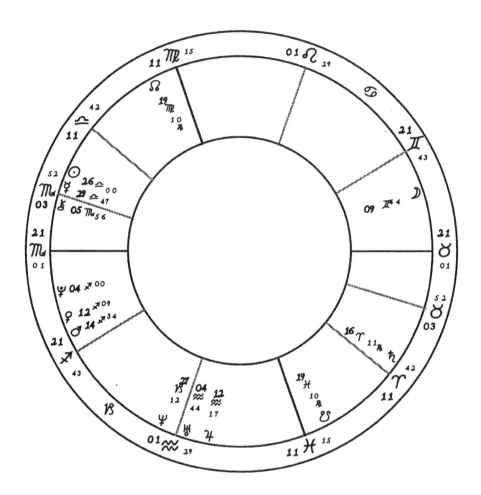

Chart of the seminar 19 October 1997, 10:00 am, London

CONNECTING WITH OTHERS

I have got the chart of the moment here, which I find wonderfully appropriate for this subject. It is, of course, an accident, because the subject was chosen a year and a half ago. I didn't look at the date to see what would work! First of all, there is the Moon in Gemini. One of the things we are talking about today is siblings. The Moon is opposing Pluto, this triplet in Sagittarius, and the twin Moon. Then there are Uranus and Jupiter in the 3rd house, and Sun and Mercury in the 11th.

Some of you might have wondered why we put the 3rd and 11th houses together. I am sure you have figured out that they have to do with non-romantic, non-sexual relationships. The other air house, the 7th, is clearly included by its absence in today's seminar, even if we won't spend much time talking about it. All of these houses concern how we move out into the world and make connections with other people. I am probably not going to talk about every aspect of the 3rd house and every aspect of the 11th house, because I have chosen to concentrate on certain kinds of relationships, but we are going to cover a bit more territory than just siblings. Remember, as the day goes on, the Moon is going to move into opposition with Venus and Mars, which is very charged energy, especially for those in the room with early/middle mutables. Mercury is probably going to change signs into Scorpio some time while we are together. So we can expect a change in focus.

Psychology has focused almost exclusively on the impact of our parents, and one of the things I'd like to explore today is how other people, both inside the family and out, play a role in our becoming.

Let's look at the 3rd/11th and their relationship to the 1st house. The Ascendant, the cusp of the 11th and the cusp of the 3rd are symbolically equidistant. Do you see that? In fact, their original meaning as friendly houses comes from their sextile relationship with the *horoskopos* (as the Greeks called the Ascendant), indicating areas in life where helpful people (friends and siblings) were to be found.

Another way of looking at these houses is that they represent two different paths out into the world, two different ways of emerging into relationship. One is related to the familiar, everyday environment, so ordinary that we take it for granted. We share this space automatically with siblings and neighbors, bakers and milkmen. Relationships just happen, or are already part of us through ties of kinship and coincidence. The other house, the 11th, has a different quality This is where we enter a room with our antennae, our feelers waving, looking for someone with that indefinable something. How do we choose? How do we recognize a possible friend? The 11th house connects us to a social group, or we meet through a common interest, but more importantly, there is an inner recognition—we meet through some fundamental quality of being.

If most textbooks are to be believed, the 3rd and the 11th are among the least interesting houses. It is very hard to feel juicy about descriptions like "the lower mind," "communication," neighbors, siblings, groups. Some of my students in France, who are trained in the humanist system, have learned that the 3rd house represents the automatic, unconscious mind. This has always struck me as terribly limiting for a house that has to do with speech, one of our greatest gifts. Yes, it can be pretty pedestrian, overly concrete, but like all the other air houses, it is a place where ideas and people circulate.

The 3rd house does contain a notion of the past, because it shoulders the 4th and holds the design or pattern for our earliest peer relationships. But it also rules our ability to learn, to move about, explore, and ask questions about anything we encounter in our environment. Planets here are lively and mobile, and will always color our interactions with others as well as the quality of our thinking. And whom do we meet first? Our brothers and sisters. These relationships bring our first learning about others, and these early contacts can leave a strong imprint on all our adult relationships. Parents play a role in determining just how close or how distant we may be to a sibling; they bring their own family experiences, their own vision of fairness and exchange, competition or helpfulness. More subtly, they also bring unresolved issues from their own families, and this unfinished business seeps imperceptibly into the family psyche, affecting relations between brother and sister. Undigested stories from the family past remain alive in the psyche of the present generation. We shall see more of this in the seminar on family patterns.[1]

One of the useful astrological models that many of us have learned has to do with thinking of the houses as an evolutionary spiral. We begin things in the 1st, solidify them in the 2nd, spread the word in the 3rd, put down roots in the 4th, and so on. It can give a tendency to see 3rd house relationships as immature, with the 7th and 11th as more complete stages of relating. Although there is a kind of truth to this, in actual practice, we do not live the houses in order. As an example, we usually build friendships well before we marry. The chart is both a wheel of experience and a map, alive and radiating outward in our lives with all the houses activated from the moment of birth.

An exercise

Here's an exercise which can help us see the difference between a 3rd and 7th house relationship. Stand face to face and take the hand of the other person, while looking into their eyes. Now pull away, then move forward, then pull away again. The tension and connectedness of the 7th house should be clear. We are very aware of the other person.

Next, stand side to side with your arm around the other, just like all those visual representations of Gemini. Look towards them and then away, off to the side. Notice that you are linked and at the same time have only a partial vision of the other. Your awareness of them is less complete, and cozier—very much like a sibling connection, where the biological linkage is taken for granted.

A 3rd house relationship is less differentiated than those in the 7th or the 11th. You don't have as wide an angle on the other person. One of the key questions for both Gemini and the 3rd house is, "What does this person have to do with me?" The question is self-referencing, and our desire

---

1   See Part One of this book.

is not to know exactly who the other person is, but rather, what information they feed back to us about ourselves. 3rd house people are simply there, part of the environment, to be brushed against, acknowledged or taken for granted. Of course this gets a bit more complicated when there are many planets or certain signs there, as we shall see later.

THE 3RD HOUSE

Twins

Let's play with the archetype of the twins, the archetype of Gemini—the only zodiacal sign where two people, and siblings at that, are represented. It is the first sign in which the notion of the other appears, although not entirely differentiated, for often in representations of the sign, the twins are joined at the hip or their arms may not be entirely separate. They look, not at each other, but outward towards the world, at once connected but dissimilar. Twins, of course, are a very special kind of sibling, and my own experience has been that they share 7th house connections more than 3rd, perhaps because they are partners in the truest sense. They activate in us the idea of the perfect mirror, the one who can show me who I truly am, because we are the same (this is especially true for identical twins). This idea that a brother or a sister holds a key to our identity is basic to all sibling relationships, and our hope extends outwards towards lovers and friends as well.

But twins can also be seen as the incarnation of opposites, opposites that together create a unity This is the deepest core of the Gemini archetype. An examination of some of the cultural beliefs about twins in different parts of the world may give us a clue to the underlying issues in ordinary sibling relationships. In West African culture (which has the highest rates of twin births in the world), twins are seen as proof of the existence of the spiritual world. Among the Yoruba of Nigeria, everyone is considered to have a celestial double whose life mirrors their own. The birth of twins is a powerful event because it offers evidence of this spiritual self, although no one can tell which is which. In all of West Africa, there are special ceremonies surrounding the birth of twins, carriers of this supernatural reality, and even a child that follows later is considered to carry some of this supernatural energy.

Twins mirror the duality inherent in each of us, and they are treated with awe as revelations of our other, more mysterious self. The first-born, who is considered the junior, is referred to as Taiwa, and he or she is "quick-witted, impatient, a risk-taker," while the second-born, Kehide (who is considered the elder of the two), moves more slowly and with wisdom. These special names and complementary personalities set them apart from other, ordinary children. For the Yoruba, the twin is at the center of spiritual notions of humanity. They see our nature as profoundly dual, and there is a mysterious link between the celestial and the earthly. Only part of us is fully revealed: there are mysteries that can only be explained by the presence of our spiritual twin.[2] This notion that we are all more than we appear to be, that a part of each of us is missing, colors all our relationships. We imagine that, if we meet the right person, we will feel whole and connected. It is with our siblings that we first scrutinize the other hoping to find ourselves.

According to Claude Levi-Strauss, the American Indians were also keenly aware of the dissimilarities of twins. For them, each person had an opposite with whom he/she co-existed in unresolved tension. In Pueblo mythology, the twins are sent into the world to place the Sun correctly in the sky—an interesting idea from an astrological point of view. The center is found through more than one point of view In the Judaic tradition, Jacob and Esau, the first twins, fought each other in the womb, and only one could win the blessing of the father. Both traditions assume that we are made up of conflicting forces, constantly pulling towards different ways of being. Will one way win out, or is there possibility of accommodation? In the Biblical myths, one brother is chosen. In the founding story of Rome, Romulus and Remus are both raised by the she-wolf, but Remus dies when it comes time to build the city. In these myths it seems one side must be eliminated; a choice must be made, from the multiple possibilities represented by twins.

---

2   James Elniski, "Finding One's Twin," in *Twins, Parabola*, Vol. XIX, May 1994, No. 2.

The twins in Greek myth

Most of you will be familiar with the myth of Castor and Pollux. Their mother Leda was impregnated by Zeus, who took the form of a swan when he came upon her. The same night, she lay with her husband Tyndareus, so that she conceived both mortal and immortal children. In one version of the myth she gave forth two eggs, one with Castor and Pollux, the other with Clytaemnestra and Helen. We can look at these twin/sibling pairs as representing different ways of connecting. Each of these "egg-twins" has inherited a different piece of fate, and yet their destinies are interwoven, inextricably linked throughout their lives.

Castor and Pollux were lively, athletic and inseparable, and when the mortal of the pair, Castor, was killed in battle, his brother pleaded with Zeus to bring him back to life. Instead, they were granted alternate periods in heaven and in the underworld, dying and coming back to life. They were placed in the sky as the twin stars of the constellation Gemini. Here we have a model of closeness and fidelity, a willingness to share whatever happens, good or bad. They enjoyed fighting, but their aggressive impulses were directed outwardly -towards strangers, not towards each other. They chose to stay connected.

AUDIENCE: But don't Castor and Pollux represent different aspects of ourselves?

LYNN: Yes. Usually we look at this myth to talk about the light and dark side of our own nature. Here I'm extending the idea to brothers and sisters, in part because we often project certain aspects of ourselves onto siblings and only reintegrate them later, if we have that consciousness.

The sisters

Leda's second egg contained Helen, whose great beauty set the Trojan war in motion; and her sister, Clytaemnestra, who killed her husband Agammemnon when he returned from that same war. In Yeat's powerful poem, "Leda and the Swan," he evokes the raw force of sexual possession by the god, and the consequences of that act:

...a shudder in the loins engenders there. The broken wall, the burning roof and tower. And Agammemnon dead.

Isn't it striking, how clearly he identifies this seed moment as the cause of so much destruction and suffering? Both of the sisters born from this coupling inherit a family pattern, a woman's fate, of being overwhelmed by men. Helen is first abducted by Theseus when she is barely twelve, on a dare, and spirited away until she is of marriageable age. Eventually she is rescued by her brothers. Later, of course, under Aphrodite's influence, she runs off with Paris, leaving her chosen husband and launching "a thousand ships." Her destiny is far from comfortable, but throughout her story she lights the lamp of love and desire in those who meet her. We could say that she carries all the Venus energy in the family.

Love is not part of her sister's marriage. Clytaemnestra watched as Agammemnon killed her first husband and the baby at her breast, in order to take her to wife and consolidate his political power. Later, he sacrifices their daughter Iphigeneia so that the winds will carry the fleet to Troy. Even the lover she takes is motivated by a desire for revenge on the House of Atreus. Together they plot to strike Agammemnon down; she weaves the net that binds him, and when she chops his head off with an axe, she feels no remorse. If there is Venus here at all, it is Venus-Pluto.

The sisters marry two brothers, Menelaus and Agammemnon, who go to war—one for love, the other for glory. It could be said that both sisters carry the vengeance of their mother's rape, but one evokes the power of love—a power that leads to the Trojan War, to both great deeds and destruction—while the other nurtures a dark, bitter hatred. She represents the frightening, unforgiving aspect of the feminine. A great war springs from that initial act of overpowering desire, carried out against the woman's will. In families, different individuals carry quite different "takes" on a traumatic family inheritance, and it can move through their lives in varied forms. Helen and Clytaemnestra embody feminine opposites—overwhelming desire and overwhelming rage, mirrors of their mother's ambivalence. They are rarely portrayed together in the myths, yet their lives unfold in counterpoint around the great stories of the Trojan War.

Love or war?

It seems, then, that twins speak to us of a split that contains the seed-desires of love and war. From the very beginning, it's as if the choice is always there, to say yes or no—to welcome or reject. And even if you say yes, will the other say no? How do we welcome each other into life in the same family, on the same planet? How do we open our eyes on the world? Largely because of new technology like ultra-sound, we now know that a very large percentage of conceptions are twinned at the beginning. In the majority of cases, one of the twins dies and is absorbed into the other's body. There has been much speculation on this idea of the lost other, and what effect it may have on our inner development.

According to the Yoruba, "Everyone has a spirit twin; when you meet yourself you will be happy all the time."[3] This idea is similar to Plato's story of the origin of the sexes, a being cut in half, and constantly in longing for the bit from which it's been separated. No happiness is possible without being whole. "Twinship is a mirror, and the gift of the twin is to reveal aspects of ourselves that have gone unseen."[4] Perhaps in an ordinary sibling relationship, we sense that a brother or sister also has clues to who we are, but they are harder to find, disguised in some way. After all, a twin has been with us in that most contained of spaces within the womb, there from the beginning, in the same time and place, their growth entwined with ours. Other siblings have shared the same place, the same mother's body, but at a different time, and, remembering that matrix, may have clues for us about things we have left or forgotten there.

Those who follow us may feel we took something they didn't have a chance to receive. When primogeniture was the rule, only the first-born son inherited title and lands from the father, so this was quite literally the case—it caused a great deal of bad blood between siblings. The Napoleonic Code abolished this system of inheritance in France, though it continues in England. In certain earlier cultures (the story of Beowulf is an illustration of this), inheritance passed through the moth-

---

3   *Op. cit.* (Note 2).
4   *Op. cit.* (Note 2).

er's side, to the father's sister's son. If you think about it, this system guarantees a blood relationship between uncle and nephew, because the link to the grandmother is undeniable—you can see a child emerge from its mother's body. A father, however, could never be absolutely sure that a child was his.

From these stories of twins, we can see that ambivalence is a central issue in sibling relationships. We seek connection, but resent being usurped. We feel lonely without them, but our uniqueness is questioned by their very existence. We may feel cheated by fate's distribution of talents or love; we admire or reject, fight and compete, offer comfort and support. We begin to learn about our ability to love and care for others. Perhaps that's partly why the ancients associated this house with the Moon.

The Moon's joy

Did you know that the Greeks connected the 3rd house to the Moon? I've been looking at the planetary joys for the past few years, and find them an extremely rich tool for adding to our understanding of planets in houses. Is there anyone who doesn't know about the joys? These are from the ancient Greek texts which have recently been translated by Project Hindsight and others. Whereas we, modern astrologers, would tend to assimilate the 3rd house with Mercury, the ruler of Gemini, and the 3rd sign of the zodiac, for the ancients the houses were not connected to the twelve signs. Mercury had its joy in the 1st, Moon in the 3rd, Venus in the 5th, Mars in the 6th, the Sun in the 9th, Jupiter in the 11th, and Saturn in the 12th. We don't need to throw out the idea that Mercury has a strong connection to the 3rd house, but it's worth exploring this other model. In the ancient texts, the 3rd house was called the House of the Goddess, and it opposed the 9th House of God.

The Planetary Joys	
Planet	**House**
☉	9th
☽	3rd
☿	1st
♀	5th
♂	6th
♃	11th
♄	12th

Does anyone have an idea why the Moon would have its joy in the 3rd? After all, we tend to think of it as a mental house and not particularly associated with feeling.

AUDIENCE: The Moon changes and likes changing. The 3rd house is so elastic. It likes being social, meeting and even changing people.

LYNN: That's good, because you're talking about change on a lunar level of variation, the kind of movement to and fro that has a particularly fluid quality. Lunar change doesn't shatter and break; it maintains flow and fecundation in our lives. There is a rhythm and regularity that brings us back to the point of departure. In the same way, our casual conversations and encounters keep a healthy connectedness to the world around us.

The Moon also rules memory. Before pencil and paper were readily available, the ability to hold knowledge in the mind was absolutely essential for learning. In the ancient world, you couldn't go and look at the index in your book to get information about, say, friendship. Your knowledge depended a great deal on your ability to retain what you had heard in the past, to memorize poems or texts. We might even say that the whole notion of the mind was more eidetic, image-filled. The mind as a logic machine and tool of abstraction is a relatively recent idea. Of course, the planet most connected to memory and image is the Moon.

AUDIENCE: But why would the 3rd house be connected to the Goddess?

LYNN: I'm not sure anyone really knows, but we could say that 3rd house consciousness is more lunar, more impressionistic and feeling-based, while 9th house awareness is solar, with a direct link to the divine plan. So many writers, from Robert Graves to Jung and his disciples, have explored the Moon/triple goddess connection. The Goddess represents a constantly unfolding, rhythmic and cyclical relationship to the world, rather than an absolute truth. Lunar truths change as the light changes, with shifting landscapes and points of view.. They are much more subjective and personal. It is an interesting way of looking at the 3rd house.

In her book on the Moon, Darby talks about how it represents the natural mind, the natural intelligence. Here is something she said that connects in a very interesting way with this notion of the 3rd house and the Moon's joy:

> Learning that does not include your Moon does not nourish you. It is through Mercury that you gather information, but it is the ebb and flow of your Moon which absorbs it and assimilates it and makes it your own.[5]

Let's explore the connection between communication and siblings. How do you see this?

AUDIENCE: I have the Moon in the 3rd, and I often translated my younger brother to my parents. Maybe the 3rd is about siblings speaking the same language?

LYNN: Two interesting things there. An older brother or sister may be the one who opens up our connection to the world through language. Once again, to go back to twins, a large number invent a private language that no one else ever learns or shares. But the sense of similarity and communion in your case is probably linked more to the Moon's placement than the 3rd house per se. Much is going to depend on what planets are tenanting the house.

AUDIENCE: I would almost say the 3rd house would be you and your siblings speaking alike.

LYNN: But you don't, necessarily. That depends on what you have in the 3rd house.

AUDIENCE: Could the Moon in the 3rd have its joy because of that family connection?

---

5 Darby Costello, *The Astrological Moon*, CPA Press, London, 1996.

LYNN: Maybe. I think, if you have a difficult Moon in the 3rd, that's not necessarily going to be the case. You might have the Moon square Mars, opposition Pluto. Then you will have part of the Moon's energy of connectedness, but it's clearly going to be a lot less cozy! In such a case, someone in the environment may be trying to control others through words, or there could be such strong emotions flying around that communication is lost to the more theatrical interchange of family life. Perhaps all the emotions in your family need to be said out loud. And in some cases, the person with the Moon here will become the spokesperson for the emotional undercurrents of family life. Since Moon often describes the mother, at least in part, a child with the Moon in the 3rd may be strongly influenced by the mother's patterns of thinking and communication, for good or bad.

Without language, and barring the existence of some extraordinary telepathic capacity, we would have no way of connecting what happens inside us to the world around us. Language carries our inner experience outside, however inadequately. Remember, the 3rd house is always a place of exchange between you and others. It is the place where you breathe in and out, and describes the quality of "air." The Moon would give a "wetter" environment than Saturn, which might feel like living out in the desert.

I was re-reading Rob Hand's book, *Horoscope Symbols*,[6] written at a time when he gave very little weight to houses. He describes the 3rd house as "containing a great number of seemingly unrelated ideas," but found an unconscious element, a lack of choosing, as the one link tying 3rd house attributes together. He speaks of automatic pilot and habit patterns, and this too sounds as though it could be linked to the Moon.

Past and future

The 3rd house does have the flavor of the past. One of the unique things about brothers and sisters is that they share our past in a way no-one else can do. They are our connection to the most subjective part of the

---

6   Robert Hand, *Horoscope Symbols*, Schiffer Publishing Ltd, 1987.

chart, the 4th, and through them, we remember who we are and where we have come from, especially after our parents are no longer alive. Early on, a sibling relationship can open up the world for us, or keep us bound to family patterns and secrets. Many of us move on as we grow older, and no longer share the same life path as our brothers and sisters; meeting up with them can feel like being pulled back into an old self. Sometimes this is uncomfortable and binding, but it can also be comforting. Much will depend on how much family members have been able to accept each other's growth.

The 3rd can be lived on a level of repetitive stories and phrases, ritual conversations without meaning, endless gossip about people from the past.

On the other hand, the 11th house has a distinctly future quality. Is there anybody who doesn't think that's true, that notion of future with the 11th? No? There's this idea of something evolving or emerging in the 11th that doesn't belong to the 3rd in the same way, even though there is plenty of curiosity and openness and often a keen desire to learn with 3rd house planets. The 3rd house connects very much to the present moment, to our way of seeing the world in the here and now. The 11th speaks much more to where we are going and what we wish for in the longer term. While the 10th shows our impact on the world, and possible professional success, the 11th has a wider field of potential—the potential to be a human being in the fullest sense of the word. We act this out through our friendships, the people we choose and the people we leave behind.

I remember reading somewhere in Hindu astrology that the 5th house, its pleasures or lack of them, were rewards from your previous incarnation. The 11th house, as the "fruit" of the 10th in this life, had to do with what you would take with you into the next life, your upcoming incarnation. It's a fascinating thought. In certain cases, a strong 11th house corresponds to an ability to influence people long after the person has actually died. Van Gogh had a charged 11th house (Saturn, Pluto, and Uranus), and great difficulties with friendship while he was alive. "Friends" of his work only began to really appear after his death.

Saturn in the 3rd house

AUDIENCE: I have Saturn in the 3rd, and I was one of these people who didn't speak, almost to the point of autism.

LYNN: Saturn here often indicates some kind of initial barrier to communication, whether through absence or blockage. In general, planets and signs in the 3rd color your first attempts at contact, and the responses you get to them. Your first connections will be through the planet, sign, and house ruler, generally in that order. Clearly, Saturn is going to indicate more difficulty than other planets in the 3rd.

AUDIENCE: Same for Capricorn?

LYNN: Often Scorpio rising people will have Capricorn on the 3rd house cusp, and these individuals have a reputation for being careful about what they reveal. One woman with this configuration said there was no one to talk to in her family environment. Her older sister kept her at a distance, was closed down, uncommunicative, and serious, much like the mother. She felt all her attempts to break through to others were inadequate in some way At seven, this woman began to speak to mirrors, use a pendulum, and conduct séances: "Since all the people in my family were the living dead, I sought out the dead to speak to." It isn't as morbid as it sounds, because her naturally lively personality (air Sun and Moon) found an outlet in friendship, and she has Mercury and Venus conjunct in the 11th house.

Of course, whenever you look at a house, you need to take the ruler into account, to flesh out the information given by signs and planets. In her case, Saturn is square Venus, the Sun's ruler, which connects the 3rd house issues to her sense of self-worth and identity. It may tell us that she will only feel "good enough" when she has found the right way to communicate. Saturn is also square Mercury, which will exacerbate the issues around communication. But she is a talkative, fun-loving person, and often didn't feel as if she were taken seriously by others. She lived the other side of the Saturn square. This may explain why she went back to school in her mid-thirties to get a diploma in a highly technical subject.

Sometimes Saturn in the 3rd means having no one to speak to, as in the case of only children. It may be more correct to say that they have people to speak "up" to, because their parents always know more than they do. Saturn in air houses often describes situations of inequality or hierarchy in relationship, which is the case when siblings are born many years apart. All of us have seen the classic pattern of an older sibling who takes on the role of one of the parents, the co-mother or co-father. In these cases Saturn can speak "down" to the younger sibling. In later years, this Saturn placement can continue to speak to others with the language of authority.

Of course, not all only children have Saturn in the 3rd, but when it is present it can indicate a heightened sense of isolation, and an awkwardness about entering into a spontaneous exchange with others. Early experience of difficulty here, from whatever source, can push an individual into a deep relationship with a private world of thought. On the other hand, the lack of "oxygen" can create a disconnection and habit of solitude which, taken far enough, becomes depression or even a kind of mental asphyxiation. Oddly, Saturn here is just as likely to pop up in large families where a more introverted child can have difficulty finding someone to listen.

Children of approximately the same age share a process of discovery. They map the world together through language, and explore those parts of the world that escape the parents' watchful eye. The larger the difference in age, the less likely this kind of *camaraderie* becomes. But at the same time, siblings are never peers in the sense that 11th house relationships can be. They have an intensely acute awareness of small differences in age and accomplishment. Saturn will tend to exacerbate the distinctions in a family and distribute rather rigid roles. A sibling, say, seven years older, will orbit in a different universe from yours.

Siblings are a peculiar kind of peer. They are special. You can have a friendship with a sibling, but a friend will never be a brother or a sister in the true sense of those words. That's not possible. There's a lack of choice in this relationship, and the biological connection is permanent, even if one day you completely sever relations with a brother or sister. For a time, at least, siblings are there whether you want them to be or not, and they test you in certain ways.

AN EXAMPLE CHART: LORNA

Now let's look at an example chart.

This woman has a strong 9th house, with Sun-Mercury in Aries near the MC and conjunct Jupiter in the 10th. They oppose Saturn in Libra in the 3rd, as well as Neptune, which is right on the 4th house cusp. There are two T-squares, one involving Uranus, the other with the Moon, both in Cancer in the 12th house, though not conjunct.

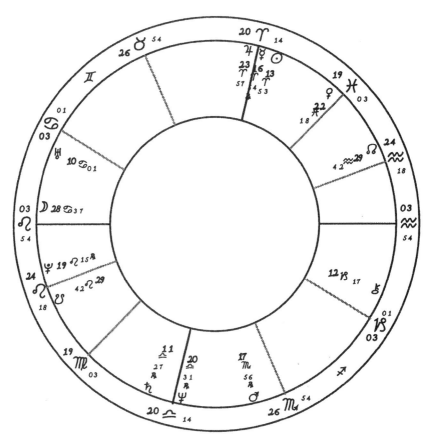

Lorna 3 April 1952, 12:23 pm EST, Hoboken, New Jersey, 40N42 74W13

AUDIENCE: If you include Chiron at 12° Capricorn, there's a grand cardinal cross. Don't you use Chiron?

LYNN: I've been observing Chiron more and more, but I tend to be shy about giving it equal weight with other factors in a chart. We'll have to bring Melanie [Reinhart] to Paris to give a full immersion course in Chiron. Some people do use it in France, but it is not so common. They are much more likely to use the *Lune Noire* than Chiron.

La Lune Noire

AUDIENCE: What is the *Lune Noire*?

LYNN: As you know, the Moon has an elliptical orbit, rendered irregular by the pull of the earth's gravity and the other planets in the solar system. The Moon approaches the earth in perigee, then pulls away from the earth until it reaches apogee, the most distant point of its orbit. Joelle De Graveleine was a wonderful astrologer, the most eloquent proponent of the *Lune Noire* in France, but she had a kind of indifference to math, and never seemed to be able to explain just what the Black Moon was. So bear with me here. Unlike a circle, every ellipse has two centers. In the case of an astronomical body, one of these centers, or focal points, is occupied, the other is empty. The Earth is one of the centers of the Moon's orbit; the *Lune Noire* is the other, invisible center, and symbolically represents something that is left out or unaccounted for. Jean Carteret spoke of the *Soleil Noir*, which is in fact the invisible other center in the Earth's elliptical movement around the Sun, and we could postulate this kind of point for any astronomical object whose path follows an ellipse. The Greek word *elleipsis* means to "leave out or to fall short of," and we use the word "elliptical" to describe a "deliberately obscure conversational style." An ellipsis is something that is left out in a text: sometimes a word, sometimes a logical connection. I think you can begin to imagine where to take this information symbolically.

For me, the major difficulty lies in knowing exactly where this point is. The Moon is so small that its movement is affected by many different gravitational fields; it wobbles, and so this center isn't constant. Until recently its position was only approximate, and even though we now have accurate tables for the Black Moon, many astrologers still use the older calculations—the mean or corrected position, much as we used the mean Node rather than the true Node until the tables were available. The difference between the mean *Lune Noire* and the true Black Moon can be enormous, as much as twelve degrees, so this skews interpretation considerably. Many students have solved this problem by putting several different Black Moons in a chart, each with a slightly different interpretation. I have a little trouble with this kind of imprecision.

AUDIENCE: I always though that the Black Moon concerned the dark side of sexuality, and the darker aspect of the goddess. What else does it signify?

LYNN: The *Lune Noire* has a central position, but is impossible to see, so you can understand why it has been assimilated to the unknown or dark side of the feminine. Lilith, whom Joelle de Gravelaine identified with the *Lune Noire,* was supposedly the first wife of Adam, and was later erased from the story because of her refusal to let him be on top. The *Lune Noire* speaks of feminine energy that resides in the shadows, denied and cut off from consciousness.

AUDIENCE: Was she made out of another rib?

LYNN: No, she was made out of dust, like Adam. You only find Lilith in alternative versions of the myth.

AUDIENCE: Does that mean she represents a feminine energy equal to the masculine?

LYNN: Yes, or rather demanding equality and in rebellion—outcast, she became the demonic feminine. A key word for the Black Moon is ambivalence. The interpretation swings from the more destructive and compulsive aspects of desire, through refusal, cutting off, sacrifice, and a powerful urge to consciousness. Much of the symbolism associated with the *Lune Noire* in France is what we would consider a feminine version of Plutonian themes. I do look at it when students ask me to, and it can give a very interesting gloss on a chart. In this chart the "mean" *Lune Noire* would be around 0° of Leo, conjunct the Ascendant, and so we would want to explore themes around denial or cutting off. It is also conjunct the Moon, so you might want to listen for Lilithian themes as we tell the story of this woman. As you can see, this is a vast subject and not really on the agenda for today's seminar. To some extent, the use of the *Lune Noire* reflects cultural preferences. It might be interesting to speculate on why Chiron, who symbolizes an area of woundedness, has been taken up so enthusiastically in Britain, in contrast with French passion for the Black Moon.

It seems we are in tune with today's Moon in Gemini, following its curious and wandering path, sidetracking to interesting topics. I have a natural tendency to do this, so we may want to make an extra effort to hold to the topic at hand!

How Saturn affects communication

Back to our example chart. Not only is Saturn in the 3rd *and* opposition Mercury; they are both square a planet in the 12th, Uranus, *and* Chiron in the 6th. Mercury is retrograde. In fact, there are a tremendous number of retrograde planets: Pluto, Saturn, Mars, Neptune, and Mercury, five in all. This leaves little doubt that there is major work to be done, some kind of barrier around communication or contact with others.

AUDIENCE: She may have had had a lot of responsibility early on, which made it difficult to enter into contact lightly. I have the impression of someone being pulled inward by all those retrogrades.

AUDIENCE: There is either suffering from a lack of free flowing communicative ability, or suffering from a highly developed one. Maybe there is a disadvantage, like dyslexia, which creates a motivation to improve communication?

AUDIENCE: Someone in the seminar last week had Saturn in the 3rd and he was perfectly able to read and write at the age of four. He got kicked out of school because he was so bored that he was misbehaving.

LYNN: Perhaps the fundamental issue with Saturn in the 3rd is that, instead of finding a mirror, one finds a barrier, like a wall. A wall may be a weight-bearing structure; it can perhaps offer support; but it generally does not have reflective power. With a difficult sibling (or one perceived as difficult), an individual may recoil from contact, and the refusal can set up a inner barrier which extends to the world in general. This will often force an individual inward, and leave a trace of inhibition, but also encourage the development of an inner voice. Work is required if an individual is to break through this sense of loneliness. I have seen Saturn in the 3rd in families with many siblings, where it can be hard to get anyone to listen to you. Everyone else can say it better or faster, or interpret for you, and at some point a surface communication replaces the child's genuine need.

AUDIENCE: At the bottom of the chart is a lack of ground, from Neptune. The 4th house usually represents the past, and I imagine an obscure or misty background. There's a need to shine light on the past through understanding.

LYNN: Yes, interesting. On the other hand, the zone around the MC, the 9th and 10th houses, is a very pleasant area in this chart. Jupiter is up there, near the MC, and the Sun is exalted in Aries and in its joy in the 9th house. Venus, also in the 9th, is exalted in Pisces. These planets are all up at the top of the chart. Don't you think this encourages her outwards, in the direction of the light, rather than keeping her at home?

AUDIENCE: Aries gets pushed out or pushes out.

LYNN: Right. There's a feeling of being pushed out of the nest, isn't there, with Aries up on top?

AUDIENCE: Look at Saturn in the 3rd and the Uranus square scientific planets that would tend to find expression in the life of the mind. Both are in aspect to Mercury, and with all that 9th house stuff, there could be a very investigative intelligence.

AUDIENCE: But the 12th house is also strong, with Moon in Cancer—and those retrogrades would represent a process of internalizing. Wouldn't the person feel connected with their inner life, with all that emphasis in the 12th house?

LYNN: It is true, there is an interesting contradiction between all the retrogrades, the 12th house, and that emergent Aries energy on the MC. The Cancer Moon is angular, in the 12th but conjunct the Ascendant. Remember, last time we talked about the Moon in the 12th as someone whose own emotional needs were not noticed, or rendered invisible to the environment. Saturn in the 3rd could increase a sense of isolation, and also has to do with assuming responsibility for siblings. The Moon here could indicate very powerful emotions that go unacknowledged. The Moon is in a T-square to Jupiter and Neptune, and, as you said, there is a lack of ground from Neptune on the 4th house cusp. These aspects could all go towards creating a very powerful inner world. At the same time, Saturn opposes the Sun and demands a confrontation with reality.

It is worth noting that many planets in this chart—Moon, Mars, Venus, Sun, and Saturn—have dignity through rulership or exaltation, a traditional indicator of great strength. We could say that this increases the range of possibilities available to an individual.

AUDIENCE: The Moon in this T-square is also very sensitive to the collective level. Could it indicate a family who are in contact with something that becomes useful for her personal development?

AUDIENCE: Won't there be strong spiritual energy, with Moon in the 12th house aspecting Neptune and Jupiter ?

LYNN: These aspects give a longing for connection, which may or may not translate as spirituality. The Moon-Neptune, on a collective level, gives fine tuning and receptivity, but in terms of personal needs being met, there can be a feeling of tremendous hunger or emptiness. I often use the image of a pitcher with a nearly invisible crack in it that slowly leaks its contents, however much you fill it up.

AUDIENCE: Lack of boundaries.

LYNN: Yes. And Saturn has to do with boundaries. Opposing the Sun, opposing Mercury, it acts as an obstacle to Moon-Neptune's desire to let go completely.

AUDIENCE: I would think that Saturn would give rise to something very precise, an interest in the material world, maybe a collector of some kind.

LYNN: Even with no earth in the chart?

AUDIENCE: Saturn often is more comfortable with controlling things, limiting them in some way.

LYNN: The image that comes to mind is her tiny, exquisite handwriting, which can fit several perfectly legible pages on a postcard. She is quite a good writer, but freer in that form, like many people with Saturn in the 3rd, than in verbal communication. She has collected things, but her basic impulse isn't really towards material accumulation.

A handicapped sister

I think I should tell you the story. This is someone who has a handi-capped sister I brought you some brother-sister charts that we are going to look at, but here we'll explore it in her chart alone. Lorna (not her real name) is the second child, and her "problem" sister Janet arrived two years later, in March 1954. Then there is a big gap of seven years, followed by the birth of another sister in February 1961, a brother in March 1962 (the first boy), and one more girl in September 1963. It's almost as if there were two families here, and the space was needed to absorb the arrival of an abnormal child. The handicapped sister was deprived of oxygen at birth in a difficult labor, resulting in brain and motor damage, and she's not a particularly pleasant person to be around. My friend is now forty-five years old and she still dislikes this sister intensely, which is not a "politically correct" position. Society says we should have compassion for a handicapped sibling, and there is a lot of romanticism about the suffering and discomfort that can be engendered in this kind of situation.

The birth of a handicapped child sends a shock wave through a family, and for Lorna, it came when she was just two, the age of language acquisition. Even more striking, in terms of that 3rd house Saturn, is a total absence of communication from the parents about the sister's condition. They never told the children that there was anything wrong with their new sister. It simply wasn't mentioned. The normal feelings of jealousy and displacement that often follow the birth of a sibling were compounded by the fact that something was wrong, but she and her older sister had no means to speak about it. Imagine you have a little sister who arrives, who bugs you and grabs your toys and hits and bites, but on top of it this little sister is weird. She has both speech difficulty and learning disability, and tends to be a bit violent. She is not a nice, cuddly handicapped person.

Recently Lorna has started to get in touch with memories of looking in the mirror as a child to check that her head wasn't misshapen. She worried there might be some sign, something secretly wrong with her that others could see but that remained invisible to her. The school environment mirrored this fear, and Lorna and her sister were taunted as "retards." And this worry, tucked away very deeply under an apparent confidence, ate away at her for a long time. Siblings play an important role in speech acquisition, and in this case her efforts at speech would have been quickly frustrated by a baby sister who could not respond or understand "normally." A feeling of incomprehension, of the impossibility of conveying her inner feelings, has been one of the key issues in her life. Her nun-ruled Catholic education offered little to help in dealing with this powerful inner anxiety. What happened with her parents? The mother went into an emotional shutdown and withdrew from the two older children. She says she has no memory of her mother holding her, caring for her, no memory of affection or physical warmth. The mother fled to her religion for comfort, and that desire for spiritual sustenance, as well as the renunciation of her mothering, are well described by that 12th house Moon square Neptune. As so often with this aspect, there is a profound experience of abandonment. With the idealized 9th house Sun, she had a very privileged relationship with the father. For a long while she only spoke of her father in glowing terms—his openness, his humor, all in contrast to the mother's coldness.

If we think of the 3rd house as the door that opens out into the world, Saturn here represents an obstacle of some kind, perhaps a difficult response, or the lack of one. Things do not flow easily between you and the world outside, and something must be worked on, turned over in the mind, or this feeling of blockage will remain. This woman carries a sense that, as she moves towards others, she will not be able to say what she means, or make herself understood. Early in life, she found a non-verbal form of communication, which is often the case with Saturn placed here. Lorna is a gifted artist with a particular talent for drawing from life, but she had been blocked for about fifteen years. She could pick up a pencil and create anything, but was unable to do so, because what she drew seemed disconnected from what she felt, and therefore pointless. Notice that in this chart, Mercury is so powerful, and at the same time Gemini is intercepted. Again, you get this notion of, "How do you get access to communication? How are you able to show what is going on inside your mind and consciousness?"

Past patterns and the 3rd house

Sometimes a planet in the 3rd house conjuncts the 4th house cusp, and then a story involving siblings has a central place in the family myths. This may not originate with your own brothers and sisters; it could reach back to the grandparents' generation, or involve aunts and uncles.

Banished or abandoned children, inheritance squabbles, betrayal or too much love, are among the kinds of stories I've seen with this signature, stories that continue to echo powerfully in the family psyche, or set up repetitions in the following generation. Sibling relationships are the first place where we learn about sharing. When they go wrong, a warp can be set up in relationships that follow.

I personally believe that when the 3rd and 4th are difficult, people will go to the 11th house, because it is another doorway out to connecting with people, and most of us cannot function without connection. They will need to find connection elsewhere, in what is less familiar, a tendency that becomes stronger when planets occupy the 11th house. With Gemini intercepted in the 11th in Lorna's chart, she will look for people who are very eloquent and can communicate easily That's where she is going to go for friendship. All of you look perplexed. I am deliberately talking about these houses in a non-traditional way, so you can think about them and use them differently

AUDIENCE: Could you say more about a planet conjunct the 4th house cusp from the 3rd house?

LYNN: It will often indicate an unresolved issue in the family that concerns brothers and sisters. Let's say that you are an only child with Pluto in the 3rd It may be that, in a previous generation, a sibling has disappeared—either gone and lived in another country and isn't seen for twenty years, or died in the war, or perhaps even stole the inheritance, when the 8th house is involved by aspect. This will then set up a field of energy that is somehow activated in the person who has Pluto in the 3rd, and will particularly concern issues around trust. Remember, in the system of derived houses, the 2nd is the 12th house of the 3rd, and money is often a huge shadow issue among brothers and sisters, as evidenced by the inheritance tales we have probably all heard. You will often find that indicated by a planet in the 3rd with squares or quincunxes to the 8th. Childhood feelings of unfairness are often resurrected around money much later in life. Here Neptune is on the cusp of the 4th, activating issues of faith or the loss of it. For an Irish Catholic mother, the birth of a handicapped child raises some serious questions about God, and this is probably a factor in her emotional shutdown.

The mother's disconnection from her belief that life would be benevolent subtly permeated the psychic environment of the family. For Lorna, it manifested in an acute restlessness around her living situation, and an inner drive to find the "right" place. She changed schools many times, each time feeling things weren't quite right. Until recently she has spent much of her adult life wandering from place to place, living in Scotland for a time, England, the east coast, the southwest. She would move to the city and then long for a connection to nature, but once there, all the virtues of the city would again seem infinitely more appealing. It was as if she couldn't find herself echoed in her connections with the people around her, and the urge to find another, better place would slowly assert itself.

AUDIENCE: Surely Neptune, as part of that T-square, would reflect that difficulty in feeling at home.

AUDIENCE: But isn't what you're describing more a function of the Aries energy square Uranus?

LYNN: You're both right, of course, but we're looking here for an underlying mechanism, one that seems to be at the core of her responses. Perhaps someone with less fire would have stayed close to home and tried to repair things. Neptune conjunct the IC very often conjures up the myth of "Paradise Lost," a powerful dream of a place that will finally hold and sustain us.

AUDIENCE: Does that mean she would also feel very connected?

LYNN: That's an interesting point. Usually the connection would happen for a brief time, and then it would fall away She would begin to feel different, and become more and more conscious of all the things she disagreed with or disliked in a given environment. This is a woman who lived for a time in a spiritual community and then became anti-spiritual.

She would say, "All these people are always talking about things that have no meaning for me. I can't relate to this language." And so she would have to leave. But, of course, the connection she's seeking can only be made inside. It's a fascinating expression of a 12th house Cancer Moon square Neptune on the IC.

AUDIENCE: I would think that there is a lot of anger here, with all that Aries, and Mars in Scorpio.

LYNN: Yes, you could say that she has less trouble than many of us in expressing anger! There was a period during the Reagan years where she would engage in long political tirades. She continues to feel outrage, with good reason, at her first husband. More recently, she's expressed a lot of her discomfort around mothers and children, or "rug-rats" as she called them. She would talk about the social pressure to ooh and ah over babies, whom she found basically uninteresting as a genre. As you can see, she isn't afraid to express socially controversial ideas. It is pretty clear, if you know the story, that the anger about mothers and children is quite personal, and comes from her own experience. At one point it was so strong that it created a rift in a long-standing friendship when the other woman became a new and attentive mother. However, through therapy she has started to get in touch with her feelings of abandonment, which are the real issue here, and this has released some very powerful creative energy

As always when a "problem" child arrives in a family, the parents focused much of their available energy there. The mother's "coldness," her depression, meant she was unavailable on other levels, and perhaps no longer believed in her ability to be a good mother because she had produced a misfit child. Remember, nobody ever talked about this. At school, with this weirdo sister in tow, people would taunt her-"You're just like your sister! Retard!" She had no information from the adult world to help her deal with that, so she created an inner world of the imagination, which is one of the gifts of the 12th house. She was a bright student, very good at school, which helped her develop a powerful relationship with her father, whom she describes as fun, open and interesting. For a long time that held the whole structure in place. But suddenly, when she was twenty-one, her father died in a helicopter crash. That moment may be the beginning of a disconnection from her creative energy, since this event made it very difficult to have faith in the future.

AUDIENCE: What changed things for her? A particular transit?

LYNN: Therapy. She works with a therapist whom she really likes, and who pointed out that her urgent desire to leave her New England home after three years to go back to New York City probably wouldn't be a constructive change, just as they were getting to a very deep place. She stayed with it, and I find this fascinating—she started to do very big black and white drawings of dreams that she remembers from her childhood. For several years she'd been working in decorating, wall painting and *trompe l'oeil,* but as she touched the feelings and percep-tions of the past, she started to do these huge drawings like "a child's nightmare book." They took her by surprise. She found them very emo-tional, almost frightening to work on, and yet impelling and exciting at the same time.

If we look at this in terms of Saturn in the 3rd, we can see that there were emotional memories barred from conscious perception, cut off from expression until she could find access to them. The two transits involved were Uranus opposition the Moon, releasing uncon-scious material and changing emotional structures, and Saturn transit-ing the 9th house Sun, which has turned out to be very positive. She was awarded an important commission for a wall mural in the state capitol, and decided to go back to school for a Masters of Fine Arts Degree. Recently she had a one-woman show of her work. It's very interesting to note that, as you get older, Saturn often becomes quite constructive, quite friendly. She bought a house, and has stayed in the same place for the longest she has ever done in her adult life. In this case, staying in place means not using the 3rd/9th escape mechanism. Can you see this?

AUDIENCE: I was thinking of the long passage of Pluto transiting her 4th house. She started to come out of that when Pluto went into Sagittarius and the 5th house.

LYNN: Pluto often works under the surface for a long time, but it didn't emerge immediately when it entered the 5th. The change has been going on for about two years, so it would be more accurate to ascribe it to Pluto's entry into fire. Pluto in Sagittarius trines her early Leo Ascendant and wakes up the fiery energy in her chart. Before, her creativity was alive in the decorative work, but it wasn't really expressing her deepest feelings. Early on, Saturn in the 3rd says, "Don't say it. Don't talk about it. Don't ask." It can take a long time to get beyond this. Does anybody here have Saturn in the 3rd?

AUDIENCE: I do. In Capricorn.

LYNN: Can you relate to what we are talking about?

AUDIENCE: Yes.

LYNN: It's important to stress that Saturn in this house isn't about having a sibling who is mentally deficient. I find this example striking because of the powerful effect it has had on this woman's sense of identity. I have the charts of siblings in three different families with handicapped children. It doesn't always take this form. A child who isn't normal can mean very different things in a different family. In one example, every member of the family has Sagittarius rising, and they all have Pisces on the 3rd house cusp. Can anybody guess how the handicapped sister was perceived?

AUDIENCE: Perhaps she was more idealized?

AUDIENCE: Could she have been an inspiration in some way? Helping the rest of the family contact their intuition?

LYNN: Yes, it does seem to go more in that direction. I'm thinking of a family with a Down's Syndrome child who was loving, funny, and extremely affectionate. Despite the rather positive image they portray, the other children in the family have chosen not to have children, and this suggests the experience was probably more traumatic than they like to admit. Pisces on the 3rd can indicate a sacrifice of some kind, and sometimes a sibling carries suffering for the rest of the family. It is also one of the signatures for very fusion-oriented sibling relationships, where there is a great deal of confusion about who is who and who does what.

Kenzeburo Oe, the Nobel Prize-winning Japanese novelist, has written a simple, powerful book about his severely handicapped son and the immense patience needed to deal with daily frustration, anger and suffering. Their son was born with a brain deformity, and yet had a special acuity for music, for the sounds of birds and later music of any kind. With attentive parents and teachers, he even learned to compose. Although the family is not religious, the father writes that it is difficult for him to deny the presence of something greater, something close to grace, while listening to the music of his son, a music that reveals a life otherwise entirely hidden and unknown. He entitles this book, *A Healing Family.*

Unfortunately for Lorna, her family was unable to find a way to heal, and her frustration is perfectly described by Saturn. The initial barrier to communication has remained a major stumbling block in her adult life. Until she can find a way to express what is behind the barrier, she cannot really live out her 10th house. I don't know if it is because of all the retrogrades, or because the nature of Saturn is to take time, but it has taken her many years to get to this point. She now feels she is in touch with something that she hadn't been able to contact for a very long time. With Saturn making the opposition to its natal place, she has finally found a channel for her own expression.

AUDIENCE: Is that Moon at 28°? With aspects from transiting Neptune?

LYNN: Yes. Neptune has been there most of the year, and will continue to be. The Uranus and Neptune transits to the Moon are taking the lid off things, opening up access to unconscious material.

AUDIENCE: I was wondering about the big age gap between her and the next child. Perhaps they said, "We might not have any more children at all." Tied into Mercury?

LYNN: It is very tied in. With an age gap like this in a family, you know that something has happened. The mother said, "Disaster! I am not going to take a risk again." The younger children in the family don't identify with that sister in the same way. By the time the parents decided to begin having children again, they must have digested something. Lorna is the sibling who had the most difficult position, because her mother became frozen emotionally when she was quite small. It was her older sister who played the maternal role for her. Her older sister is responsible, practical, so she also has another typical Saturn in the 3rd house pattern—a sibling who plays a parental role. In families where there is a child who is ill or disabled, this issue of parentification is very common. She felt justifiably angry at being deprived of maternal affection, and having to put up with this awful, retarded sister. But she must have also felt guilt about these feelings.

AUDIENCE: Mars is in Scorpio, square Pluto, and this seems very violent to me.

LYNN: And she is an Aries. So we can imagine the power of her anger, and why having it acknowledged has been absolutely necessary. There is an underground river of rage here, and with Mercury ruling her 3rd house and on the MC, she must find a way to give voice to this.

Learning a new language

If you have Saturn in the 3rd and don't have a means to talk about whatever the experience was, you will continue to feel shut off or isolated from other people. Those of you with Saturn in the 3rd probably can't even talk about this.

AUDIENCE: I have Saturn in the 3rd, and I have twelve siblings!

LYNN: Well, I think we understand what your Saturn in the 3rd is. Older brothers?

AUDIENCE: They were always explaining what I really meant to say, so I stopped speaking for myself.

LYNN: You can see there is no echo in the sibling relationships for something that is inside her. You are laughing.

AUDIENCE: It is just the way it is.

AUDIENCE: I have Saturn and Jupiter in the 3rd house. I'm close to my brothers. I'm often trying to get them to understand things differently. But when I was younger, they wanted to play teacher and impose their knowledge on me. I had this feeling I had to be perfect.

LYNN: The family transmitted a message that, when you speak, you had better know what you're talking about.

AUDIENCE: Yes. I wanted to be taken seriously, and it sounded stupid, so they laughed at what I said. It's hard to be the smallest, because you can't be intellectually up to their level.

LYNN: For you, did that create tremendous pressure to learn?

AUDIENCE: I was a very bad student. I loved reading, but I also had this feeling that I could never catch up.

LYNN: Anyone else?

AUDIENCE: My parents were immigrants, and I had to learn another language at school. I was often the interpreter for my mother.

LYNN: That's with Saturn as the ruler of the 3rd. Isn't it fascinating that all of you who have Saturn coloring the 3rd house have had to learn other languages? If the first language or the first pattern of communication you get doesn't work for you, you will have to make an extra effort to meet the world. But that Saturnine difficulty can set up a situation that forces you to develop your talents as a communicator, that gives you tremendous ability. It is not only a barrier. It is a barrier that you are meant to get over, and in doing so, you may develop mastery in your contact with other people.

AUDIENCE: If there are any other languages, astrology is one of them.

LYNN: We have been looking at a vivid 3rd house story where a sibling relationship has had tremendous impact. Besides the issues around communication, it created a perceptual filter of the world. Much of what Lorna has done or not been able to do has turned around this problem of the disabled sister, the lack of nurturing engendered by it, and the repercussions for her sense of self. What she has started to realize is that her mother didn't take care of her, but wasn't really capable of taking care of anyone, including her disabled daughter. They live together, but the mother doesn't pay much attention to the future, and has made no provisions for what will happen after she dies. Did this event create permanent damage in the mother, or was her difficulty already present before? We don't really know.

AUDIENCE: I work with special needs children, and this is ringing a lot of bells for me.

LYNN: You're in a wonderful position to pursue these ideas—you have all those case studies to work with. It would be fascinating to explore the charts of the siblings and see what impact a brother or sister in difficulty has on how they view the world. That's one of the key points I am making here about the 3rd house.

AUDIENCE: Is Lorna aware that she has to take care of her sister when her mother dies?

LYNN: I'm not sure that's the case. When the father died, there was a lot of money that was divided among the siblings, so there is no financial problem per se. The older sister is the trustee, the technical trustee for the family. I believe there is a trust fund for the handicapped sister, and the brother and sisters will probably make those decisions collectively

AUDIENCE: Would the inheritance be Venus in Pisces near the 8th house cusp?

LYNN: Probably, along with Sun and Jupiter strongly placed, traditional indicators of protection. Notice there is no earth in this chart, and it is a very interesting example because the earth element seems to be taken care of. Living in the material world isn't the major area of work or attention, and I have seen this fairly frequently with missing earth.

AUDIENCE: I wish it were always expressed like that!

LYNN: I think most people with no earth would agree with you! When she was younger, Lorna would say that it was a real problem for her .She didn't have to earn a living, and in some ways it kept her from having to go inside and develop all her talents. I think in her case it was true, although it wasn't a huge sum of money. But ultimately finding her path in life has to do with her willingness to let all these blocked feelings come out, to find a channel of expression, whether it's acceptable or not.

TWO BROTHERS

Interpreting the Moon in the 3rd house

I'd like to do something a bit more complex now. We are going to look at some synastry between siblings. I have brought transparencies of the charts of two brothers, and we will look at them one at a time. The first chart has the Moon in the 3rd. You will notice that he was born in 1843, which means that it isn't the chart of a personal acquaintance! The data comes from the Lois Rodden collection,[7] and since they are from biographical material rather than birth certificates, there could be some slight doubt about the times. We find an early degree of Virgo rising, with the ruler, Mercury, in the 8th house, conjunct Pluto and the Sun, and a Scorpio Moon. What kind of personality are we dealing with here?

AUDIENCE: Intense.

AUDIENCE: Hiding their emotions.

LYNN: Yes. It's pretty clear that this is not somebody who is transparent or easy to get to know. This kind of Pluto/8th house combination gives density and defensiveness to the psyche. It may be necessary to pass a series of tests to get close to someone with a configuration of this kind, and very often you will end up revealing more of yourself than they ever do. Lately I've been thinking about this house as Manilius describes it, as the entrance way to the underworld. Someone with strong placements here can function as a gatekeeper, facilitating the passage from one world to another. Freud, who had Moon and Saturn in the 8th, is a classic example of this. There is a need to live near that edge, but, more often than not, such an individual prefers to control the opening and closing of the door, rather than plunge down into the underworld themselves. And who are we to say which is more appropriate?

---

7 Lois Rodden, *AstroData II*, 1988, revised edition: "Dirty Data."

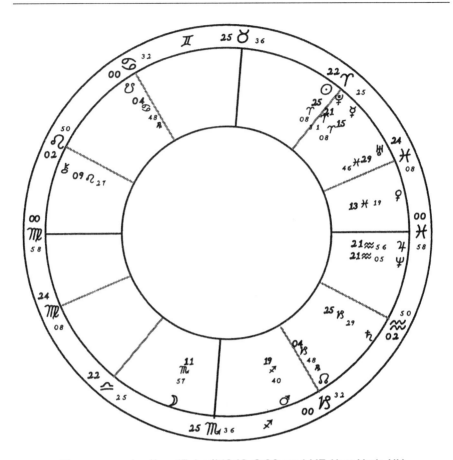

The younger brother, 15 April 1843, 2:00 pm LMT, New York, NY

In this case the 3rd house ruler is quite different in character from all that 8th house emphasis. Venus tenants Pisces, where she is exalted, and Venus is in the 7th trine Moon in the 3rd. So, what would that suggest about sibling relationships, or about his initial contacts with the world?

AUDIENCE: My feeling is that it's someone who isn't very easily understood by the world. The intense Moon in Scorpio, trine Venus in Pisces, may describe someone, the brother perhaps, as the only person who understands and supports him emotionally.

Pluto-Sun aspects

AUDIENCE: With Pluto and the Sun, there is the image of something which could be overwhelming. Maybe the brother and sister are too powerful, or there was a death in the family that brought the siblings together.

LYNN: Yes, it's almost as if there is too much feeling. For good or bad, the feeling response will be very strong.

AUDIENCE: Could you say the siblings manipulate, with the Sun-Pluto?

LYNN: Sun conjunct Pluto will certainly bring up issues around power, and with a strong 8th house, that power may be subterranean or hidden in some way. From there to manipulative siblings may be a bit of a leap, though we would certainly want to look at how the men in this family see themselves, particularly in relation to the father. Here the Sun is still in the 9th house, so he will be idealized to some degree. Because the Moon in the 3rd in Scorpio is linked to Pluto through rulership, this individual is likely to have an extreme sensitivity to all the undercurrents in the family. A planet in the 3rd weaves a pattern of connection with the environment, a daily moving in and out of relationship. It also embodies the kind of "oxygen" you will be bringing to other people, and the Moon here demands, and brings, emotional connection.

AUDIENCE: There seems to be a strong link to the houses of relationship, with the Moon ruling the 11th.

AUDIENCE: Maybe this man gets other people to make the first contact, and then he follows; it would be a way to feel safe. Besides the strong lunar influence, Jupiter is, after all, not so far from the 7th house.

LYNN: That's an interesting idea.

AUDIENCE: Could the siblings be sensitive and artistic?

LYNN: If you are not able to use a planet in the 3rd yourself, you may actually let a sibling carry it for you, and this is particularly true with transpersonals in the 3rd. But "good" planets can also be projected, or seem to belong to a sibling who already lives them out better than you do. As Liz is fond of saying, any planet in the chart can be projected. The house will tell us where and what kind of people would be good "carriers."

One of the underlying questions in this seminar is the relationship between siblings and how we see the world. What you can see in the 3rd is something the person carries within as an inner image. Remember, the ancients called this the House of the Goddess, and the goddess speaks to us through dreams and symbols. She connects us to a deep inner knowing. Even if modern consciousness seems more abstract and logical, that is probably not the true nature of this house. We first perceive what corresponds to our inner picture of the world, and interactions with others tend to confirm or challenge this internal model. Siblings are in a key position and can activate or frustrate what we carry within.

We could say that this man has the world on a lunar channel, so that he will be aware of all the nuances of feeling going on around him. In this case, the Moon in Scorpio feelings are also deeply connected to the underside of things through Pluto's rulership of Scorpio and position in the 8th house. It is not a comfortable chart, is it? He may be subject to powerful inner turbulence, and feel overwhelmed by his sensitivity to things and people. Astrological tradition considers the Moon in Scorpio a difficult placement, and that seems to be borne out by observation. But we need to factor in Venus in the 7th, often indicative of a powerful need to please. The Scorpio Moon is the only planet in the eastern hemisphere, and its more difficult emotional territory could be what this man most identifies with. Combine that with Venus in the 7th, and he may be more generous to other people than he is to himself.

AUDIENCE: With Moon in Scorpio, there is a real tendency to push emotional boundaries. There will be a compulsive quality in sibling relationships. There's a deep emotional necessity, and being nice or pleasant or civilized doesn't really come into it. We don't have much of a choice about it.

LYNN: I think you are right. It means that emotions are out in front in any exchange, at least on a certain level. The Moon in the 3rd may call out for protection, activating a maternal response in a sibling, or incarnating the role of caretaker. Which do you think is more likely? Hard call.

AUDIENCE: I think Moon in the 3rd will get the nurturing.

LYNN: Let's try to see if we can describe the family a little through looking at the chart, and then we'll go more deeply into the sibling relationships. Scorpio is on the cusp of the 4th, and the Sun is conjunct Pluto in the 9th. What might that tell us about the father and the family?

AUDIENCE: Powerful. Dogmatic. Possibly violent.

LYNN: I hear Mars in the 4th in that description. Other ideas?

AUDIENCE: The anti-Brady Bunch.

LYNN: I think that is probably accurate for this particular family.

AUDIENCE: The father finds his identity through fighting, and perhaps there is a war connection of some kind. With Mars in Sagittarius, he can give an element of fight to something involving another culture.

AUDIENCE: Could he be a fanatical preacher?

LYNN: From all descriptions, the father was a brilliant yet impractical thinker and philosopher, impassioned by Utopias, very much at odds with society, who felt the need to go elsewhere to escape the normative standards of 19th century American life. By the time this man was eighteen, he had crossed the Atlantic Ocean six times with his "purposely rootless" parents, and this long before there were airplanes. They had lived in France, England, Switzerland, Germany, and New England, and studied literature and languages, always with private tutors.

The Sun is both exalted in Aries and has its joy in the 9th house. For many years, I had noticed a consistently positive masculine image associated with this placement, so that when someone sent me an article about the planetary joys, I felt an immediate affinity with the idea. It was called the House of Deus, or God, by the Greeks, and has always retained its association with religion, morals, and ethics. Clearly, Mars in Sagittarius in the 4th feeds into this same archetype, and one gets the sense of a father with powerful dynamic energy, moving his family about, and battling with belief systems, fighting for a particular philosophy of life. The family had what is called a willfully eccentric education. Although they had a certain amount of wealth and social position, the father's writing and ideas never had the impact he wished them to. Now, we can see that Sun-Pluto-Mercury and the Moon in Scorpio in the 3rd all speak to the power of the intellect, the ability to impress and influence other people's thinking. You can imagine that in this family it was very important to think deeply, and to be able to defend your ideas. It is important to note that the Sun is also exactly square Saturn, which can only increase the pressure.

Sometimes Mars in the 4th describes a family where "only the strong survive." There can be overriding issues around strength and weakness, and an atmosphere of competition that leaves some members of the family exhausted and depleted. As it turns out, the members of this family have been described as "either geniuses or invalids." The two older brothers were both immensely successful, though in quite different fields, and their personalities could hardly have been more different.

When the ruler of the 4th is in the 8th, as we see here, there are often secrets in the family It has been suggested that this family carried a hereditary pattern of manic depressive illness, and that the father's nomadic tendencies and sudden enthusiasms were products of this pattern, so there is a darker side to this family hidden under the brilliance of two famous brothers.

Sibling synastry: the James family

We have been looking at the chart of Henry James, who idealized his older brother William all his life. We are fortunate to have one of the great biographies of the century by Leon Edel, as well as his own work, *Notes of a Son and Brother* an extremely evocative title! He never felt emotionally equal either to the powerful but ineffectual father or the incredibly likable, charming, multi-talented brother

Henry was sixty-seven years old when William died, and he wrote: "I sit heavily stricken and in darkness. His extinction changes the face of life for me." He began writing his autobiography soon after, intending it to be a homage to his brother, but it soon became more personal and wide-ranging. As his biographer said, he had an incredible faculty to remember the past, to remember very early events, and this talent "distracted him from his purpose." We could interpret that differently, but it gives us a clue to the power of the Moon in the 3rd.

Here are some of the ways he describes William: "The ideal elder brother," he says in the autobiography. "Whatever he might happen to be doing made him so interesting that I picked up the crumbs of his feast and the echoes of his life. I might live by the imagination in my brother's so adaptive skin." He also says, "Our brother moved in the higher plane of light, air and ease, and above all enjoyed easy social contact with others." Doesn't this sound as though William carries that 7th house Venus for Henry?

Henry James never married, and as far as anyone knows, never had a sexual relationship. It seems clear that he felt Venus as something belonging to the "other." However, he lived through the power of that imaginative Moon as an extremely perceptive writer of the human psyche.

In one telling incident, he recalls seeing what his brother had done during a figure drawing lesson: "I recall the crash of my emulation," he writes, flooded by a sense of the impossibility of even approaching the same level of expression. It was as if William already embodied all that Henry aspired to. All that he loved was projected onto this older brother, and he felt unable to compete. If we look at the Pluto-Saturn-Sun configuration, it may have been too dangerous for Henry to reveal himself. Rather than expressing his deepest inner feelings, he learned as a writer to express what he perceived and imagined inside others.

Notice how strongly this chart occupies the western hemisphere, which normally brings a strong awareness of others. He recounts that, as a child, his friends and relatives, the people around him, seemed quite alien. He struggled with bridging the gap between himself and other people, and as an attentive observer, he developed a subtle and refined perception of human interaction. Though he could move towards others, they could not so easily move towards him, and he was left with the "crumbs and echoes"—a fascinating image.

The external reality was quite different, because Henry James was one of the most prolific and successful writers of his time. His first publication was at age twenty-one, with transiting Saturn square the Sun, right on target with his Saturn cycle. *Daisy Miller,* written when he was around thirty-five, brought international acclaim, and that is the age of the Saturn square that follows the Saturn return.

The older brother

William James had a renaissance scope to his talents; a gifted artist, he began a career as a portrait painter, studying with the best painters. But he suddenly abandoned this path to study chemistry, then anatomy, then medicine. There are masterful drawings and paintings that he did as a young man. After a period of depression, he taught all these things at Harvard and eventually became a psychologist and, later, a philosopher, celebrated for *The Principles of Psychology* and, later, *The Varieties of Religious Experience*. It isn't hard to see how Henry could feel himself in the shadow of such a brother, though in fact Henry was the first to be successful. But William's perceptions of Henry are in a radically different vein, as we shall see. "Henry is a queer boy So good and yet so limited, as if he had taken an oath not to let himself out to more than half his humanhood in order to keep the other half from suffering."

Look at William's chart.[8] It's one of those astonishing Capricorn stelliums, with six planets conjuncting in the sign across the 1st and

---

8   Data from Lois Rodden, *Astrodata II*, 1988, revised edition: "Dirty Data"

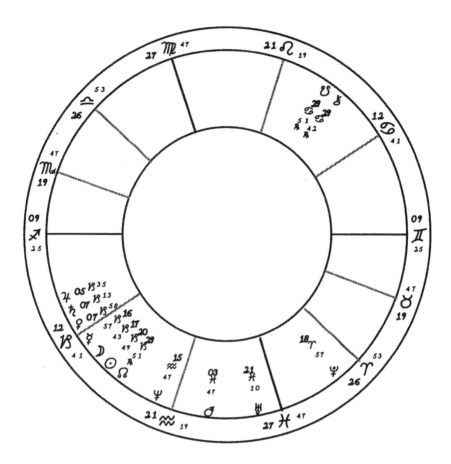

William James, 11 January 1842, 4:30 am LMT, New York, NY

2nd houses, and Jupiter, the first of these planets, rules the Sagittarian Ascendant. Here we have a strong sense of self and a positive, extravert personality—at least, at first glance. Capricorn is never such a straight-forward sign, with its horns and twisted tail, even when superbly structured and confident. Looking more closely, we see that Mercury, Sun, and Moon all square Pluto, and we know that anxiety and struggle are not unfamiliar for this man. He was born within hours of a solar eclipse, which can mean a struggle to maintain identity and connect with the deeper light of the self, as well as a need to be a path-breaker, rather than a follower.

Isn't it interesting that all the planets here, except Pluto, are in the first quadrant of self identity, quite the opposite from Henry's pattern? William James was a philosopher and a traveler, with Sagittarius rising and Jupiter in the first; and he codified, and systematized the nature of the mystical experience, which is a very Capricorn thing to do. Notice the strength of the New Moon doing something that has not been done before. He is also the originator of the idea of stream of consciousness. This is not the chart of a follower, and there is a confident approach to the world which is very different from Henry—even if both are strongly Plutonian.

Although they maintained a long correspondence, there was a time in their fifties when the brothers hadn't seen each other for seven years. After his return from Europe, William describes meeting his brother in a letter, "He has covered himself, like some marine crustacean, with all sorts of material growths, rich sea-weeds and rigid barnacles and things, and lives hidden in the midst of his strange, heavy, alien manner and custom; but ... under which [he is] still the same dear, old, good, innocent, powerless-feeling Henry." At this time Henry was a world famous author, well liked, highly regarded, generally socially at ease, and people enjoyed being around him. But with his brother he could not be himself, or rather, he became an older, inferior version of himself. Notice that William chooses these strongly lunar (and Saturnian) metaphors to describe his brother. He seems to have consistently felt his vulnerability, writing elsewhere that "there is always a feeling of helplessness about him," as if he could only see Henry's strongly defended Moon. Both men have Pluto-Sun aspects, connected to the 4th house, and these would heighten a perception of power issues around the father and in the family generally. Chiron is also in aspect to the Sun in both charts, and besides his frustration at not being recognized socially, their father had lost a leg in a childhood accident and limped noticeably.

Mars in the 3rd house

William has Mars and Uranus in the 3rd house—a forceful, original mind and he quickly stepped into the role of a dominant older brother. In his later work he explored the differences between "tough-minded" and "tender-minded" thinkers, which might be an interesting way of describing the differences between Mars and Moon in the 3rd! Mars in the 3rd will tend to come out on top in family discussions, and have a natural bent for competition and rivalry, needing to test itself against the environment. One can see how this could easily turn to conflict or bullying, or even fear, because Mars almost always needs confrontation to define itself. It might be an easier placement for an eldest child, because he or she begins life with some natural authority, but much will depend on whether Mars shows the civilized face of the athlete or hero, or the wanton brutality of an angry barbarian.

It's interesting to think of the mobility expressed by both Moon and Mars in the 3rd, a mobility intended to open the mind and stimulate reflection. The family regularly pulled up roots, and this tends to strengthen bonds among siblings, who are thrown back upon themselves. From Henry's description, we know that William successfully made new friends, easily stepping out into new worlds. But Henry's lunar 3rd house temperament constructed more intimate links based on reassurance, familiarity, and intimacy, so that his brother said of him, "Henry is a native of the James family and knows no other country." Underlying this, Henry's Moon in Scorpio and Sun conjunct Pluto give an almost theological position in life that does not allow denial of darker human impulses. He is all too aware of what may be wrong, either inside himself or in others, a dichotomy between innocence and evil often played out in his novels. Add Virgo rising, with its tendency to erode the self through constant questioning—"What's wrong with me? Why don't I do it better?"—and you have a recipe for self-mortification. Virgo rising has a habit of worrying away at things, as well as giving away its generosity to others. With Mercury in the 8th, there is great difficulty in finding a simple, straightforward confidence in oneself.

AUDIENCE: Venus is in the 7th house, and he has Saturn in Capricorn squaring Sun-Pluto.

LYNN: That exact Sun-Saturn square plays a crucial role, and here, combined with Pluto, it gives a sense of enormous inner tension and pressure. Can you feel how difficult it must be for someone with this configuration to allow their solar energy out? What's interesting is that Henry James' books are brilliant, but he always saw himself as inferior to his brother, and appears to have become psychologically overshadowed in his presence. Even as an adult, William made him all too aware of all he lacked, and the Moon, which elsewhere conferred an extraordinary sensitivity to others, here disarms him emotionally and invades his ability to communicate. Leon Edel wrote, "Although William seemed to have an enormous range of choice, Henry's only choice was between literature, devotion to literature, and neurosis."

It appears that William James was indeed an exceptional man, seen by many of his contemporaries as a genius. If you've read *The Varieties of Religious Experience,* you'll know that it has a breadth and clarity of exposition that's quite remarkable, and still very modern. Henry's admiration and idealization were based on something quite real. William, however, consistently described his brother's powerlessness, and this is a fascinating reflection on his own chart. Mars in the 3rd seeks a vigorous response, and instead, William found the Moon in Henry— tender, sensitive, withdrawn.

AUDIENCE: How would this connect with the Moon having its joy in the 3rd house?

LYNN: Henry James had an ability to enter into the inner workings of his characters' psyches and souls in a particularly subtle way. Remember that he "lived by his imagination," writing twenty-two novels and over 15,000 letters, as well as travel writings, journals and critical works. He must have written constantly. There is a flow of information, of impressions, between the psyche, the feeling nature, and the outside world, that is necessary with the Moon here. His writing concerns the emotional and psychological states of his characters, revealing unconscious elements in choices people make, choices that become fate. Moon in the 3rd, at its best, gives voice to the inner life, to the subjective experience of things. This Moon did not necessarily help him in his personal communication with his brother, but it gave access to the "otherness" around him.

In *The Astrological Moon,* Darby Costello writes about the connection between mind and the Moon. "The mind of the Moon is the heart as a place of knowing, and the soul as the container of all that ever happens to you. To learn, you have to be able to remember what you have absorbed."[9] The Moon's joy is the ability to make what you learn a part of the soul's knowing. The Moon can also carry soul content for the whole culture. The 3rd house has more to do with memory and personal impressions, while the 9th seeks an objective "sunlit" truth that comes from God. It's interesting that, with Moon-Pluto in the 3rd, Jung "discovered" the archetypes, deep structures of the psyche around which images form.

AUDIENCE: Could we say that Moon in Scorpio actually helps to go deeply?

LYNN: Yes, but that doesn't mean that the difficult side of Scorpio wasn't lived out—it was probably introjected. If we look closely at Henry James' 3rd house, we see the exalted Venus as ruler, and it seems that Henry chose to see his brother in those terms. There is no sense of the worst side of a Scorpio Moon—suspicion, betrayal or paranoia—when he writes about William. He had a choice between the easy and the difficult planet, and most of us will choose the easier of two energies when we can. Still, when he writes about his brother there is always a sense of self-denigration, and the admiration of unattainable heights. And his brother agrees, always seeing Henry as incomplete, missing something, an odd duck, however talented. We certainly know who is on top in the scheme of things.

AUDIENCE: I was thinking of his sexuality.

LYNN: It doesn't appear that he lived his sexuality out. Henry assiduously burned his journals and a certain number of his letters and correspondence, because he decided that he didn't want to make it easy for a biographer. He was one of the few Americans of that period to write

---

9 *Op. cit.* (Note 6).

an autobiography, an interesting impulse from someone who took care to hide himself. He wrote in order to shape and conceal, not to reveal. But he had a particular connection to women, perhaps expressed by his Moon-Venus trine—a capacity to put himself inside the skin of his characters, to identify with the feminine. Daisy Miller and Isabelle Archer in Portrait of a Lady are both considered remarkable portraits of woman's psyche. And speaking of women, it may be time to talk about little sister Alice.

Unable to compete: an unhealthy sibling

Alice was very bright. She had a sharp, acerbic intellect and cutting humor But from a very early age she was diagnosed with neurasthenia. Does anybody know what that is?

AUDIENCE: You are in a perpetual state of living on your nerves, and you push yourself to such an extent that you cross a borderline and get out of balance.

LYNN: The dictionary defines it as "a psychic disorder that is characterized by easy fatiguability, and often by lack of motivation, feelings of inadequacy, and psychosomatic symptoms." So she would sometimes be very lively and bright, but she suffered a great deal, and there were long periods where she couldn't get out of bed. Remember that William, the wonderful older brother, was a doctor and a professor at Harvard. Alice was constantly having examinations from the great specialists, who could never find a material cause for her symptoms. Notice how William is put into a position of powerlessness when confronted by his sister's invalidity. Alice's symptoms began when she was fifteen; they included fainting dead away, night terrors, and suicidal impulses. She wrote that she wanted to blast apart the white-haired head of her benevolent father.

I have an idea about siblings and the way they unconsciously find a niche in a family. All brothers and sisters share a common experience for a time, but their talents and abilities are rarely evenly distributed. It may happen that one child carries more of the light than the others,

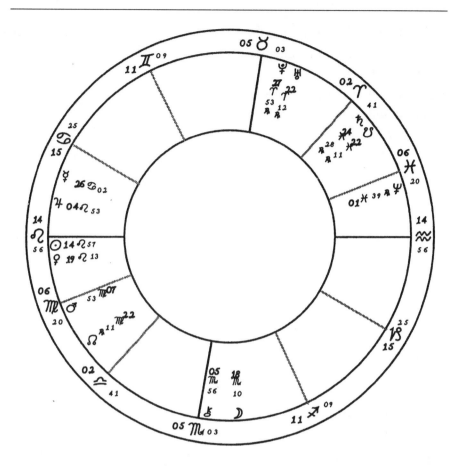

Alice James, 7 August 1848, time unknown, New York, NY [Chart is set for sunrise]

even without seeking to, and for a sibling that follows, it is hard not to be left a larger portion of shadow. At best, each child will look for a space where he or she can hold their own. With a first child like William, a "divine" child, what is left over for the others? What effect does he have on them?

William James was always in a position of strength *vis a vis* his siblings; he generated so much brilliance that the other children may have felt they had to make do with the "crumbs." Mars in the 3rd can dominate through the mind and through verbal ability, and it seems as if William wasn't entirely aware of just how much he ate up center stage. Interestingly enough, only Neptune is in air in his chart, and this can indicate awkwardness in the exchange of ideas and circulation of energy with others. In some ways it's not surprising that he saw Henry as repressed and powerless. You will notice that William's Mars at 3° Pisces is conjunct Henry's Descendant and not far from his Venus, so Henry couldn't help being receptive to his brother. They are not quite conjunct, but there is a fit between Mars and Venus. We could say that William James was the energizer for his brothers and sisters, but it also feels as though he got most of the energy in this family

Now, Alice James had quite a strong chart, although we don't have a birth time for her.[10] Jupiter, Sun, and Venus are conjunct in Leo. What a powerful solar image there, carried, no doubt, by her two famous brothers. But how does someone with such a strong impulse to be at the center of things find their place in this kind of company? Invalids have great power in a family, because so much turns around them, even if they pay a price for all that attention. She was the only daughter in a family of very brilliant men, but she wasn't treated differently—she received the same eccentric private education. Like Henry, Alice has the Moon in Scorpio, which can easily turn its energy against the self, and when Scorpio cannot touch the heights, it will rarely hesitate to bottom-feed. Mars opposition Neptune can give a thirst for the impossible, but also a terrible sense of futility if the exaltation sought for is seen as forever out of reach. A sick sibling is not dominated by her brothers only by her own unconscious.

Alice had a very close friend in later years—Catherine, who nursed her own ailing sister when she wasn't looking after Alice. Henry observed that whenever Catherine took care of this sick sister rather than Alice, Alice's symptoms would worsen dramatically. There is some suggestion that they had a lesbian relationship; it was certainly a very powerful attachment, but it's not clear whether it was lived out or not. Henry saw that his sister was only happy when this woman was there taking care of her. After the death of their parents, Alice was financially independent, and came to England to visit Henry. She arrived in such a state of nervous exhaustion that she had to be carried off the boat in a stretcher. It would be fascinating to have more information about

10 From Leon Edel, *Henry James. A Life*. Lippincott, Philadelphia.

the mother in this family, given the children's experience. Leon Edel describes her as prosaic to the point of dullness. I suppose someone had better be boring in a family like this. Does anybody here have Mars in the 3rd, or siblings with this position?

AUDIENCE: I have Mars in the 3rd, and my relationship with my sister used to be quite difficult.

LYNN: With this placement, it may not always be easy to be aware of your effect on other people. Mars will tend to focus on getting people moving, on activating their thinking and communication and shaking them up. Can you relate to that with Mars in the 3rd? Were you trying to get her to express herself more?

AUDIENCE: When we lived together when I was about twenty, I was always frustrated, trying to get her to go out, say things. It was only when she got married and I didn't see her for a year that she really blossomed. But I had never seen myself getting in the way of her growth—it was a shock.

LYNN: In other words, you were robbing her life by doing it for her?

AUDIENCE: Exactly, yes.

LYNN: You could say that a person with Mars in the 3rd is a pathbreaker for the other siblings, but there is a danger of breaking the other's will. It is when a sibling resists Mars that conflict patterns arise.

AUDIENCE: I talk too much.

LYNN: So there was no room for her to speak, was there? I have the charts of a family where almost everyone has Mars in the 3rd or Mars ruling this house, and they are rather wicked wordsmiths. There is a need to hold your own with this placement, but imagine what happens when everybody has it! At its worst, Mars in the 3rd can indicate such a competitive environment that there is rarely a feeling of being able to lay down your arms. It can create an atmosphere where weakness is seized upon as an enemy, and when an individual is in difficulty there may be nowhere to go. On the father's side of the family I have mentioned, both grandfathers committed suicide. If your first contacts are Martial, you have to affirm yourself or take the lead, but there can be an overly developed aggressive streak. We'd need to look at the 4th house and the Moon to see if there is a safe haven somewhere.

Uranus in the 3rd house: I'm different!

We haven't yet spoken of Uranus in the 3rd house of William James' chart. Does anybody have any ideas about this, especially as ruler of the sign on the cusp? There are those who count Saturn as ruler of Aquarius, in which case Saturn's conjunction with Jupiter would activate the archetype of the hierophant—one who possesses special knowledge and holds the key to understanding. William James studied at Harvard, and later taught five different subjects there, including anatomy, medicine, psychology, and philosophy. He shifted careers and became an expert in each one. But is that Uranus in the 3rd?

AUDIENCE: There would be more unconventionality—wanting to break laws.

AUDIENCE: Wouldn't there be something of Prometheus there?

LYNN: Usually this has the potential for intellectual brilliance, a mind which breaks boundaries and moves very quickly. I have noticed that those who have Uranus in the 3rd or 4th house often feel quite apart from other family members. If you go back to the original myth, you'll remember that Ouranos refused his "imperfect" offspring. Uranus often exists in reference to an idea of things, and is not truly relational. There is a powerful creative impulse that overwhelms, and carries others with it, but Uranus rarely seeks exchange. The fundamental relationship is with higher principles, with the life of the mind, and this will be accentuated in the 3rd house. Einstein, for example, had Uranus here and he didn't speak until he was nearly three, perhaps because his inner life was stimulation enough. Of course, when Uranian impulses are unintegrated, this can result in a disconnection somewhere in an individual's thinking and ability to socialize with others. Uranus seeks to differentiate, rather than resemble, and so siblings can be seen as extremely different from oneself, for good or bad.

AUDIENCE: William James said, "My brother is a queer boy."

LYNN: In modern language, that would mean something else and might still be accurate. But notice how there is refusal to identify with Henry. There is a need to see him as different, as other. Uranus in the 3rd gives a filter that automatically takes a counter-position.

AUDIENCE: But Uranus and Mars are in Pisces. What effect would the sign have?

LYNN: The combination of Piscean energy in the 3rd house and these rather hard-edged planets would be bizarrely sensitive. Uranus seems to have finely tuned antennae, picking up and responding to quite subtle variations of energy, and Pisces would open up the range of awareness even more. There could be almost too much mental stimulation here. Notice the mutual reception between Uranus and Neptune, a generational aspect also present in Henry's chart. How did William see his siblings? Another brother—I think his name was Robertson—was wounded in the war. Henry James was very complex, and slightly neurotic; Robertson was wounded; and Alice, as we said, became a total invalid. All of them are suffering in some way, carrying a Piscean archetype, and William turned his understanding towards healing, first as a doctor, later as a psychologist and philosopher, through opening up the awareness of the human psyche. In this family you have a division of light and dark, the strong and the weak, tough-minded and tender-minded. Of course, these polarities exist within all of us, but the James family seemed to split around this central axis.

Distributing roles in a family

In families, children are often attributed different roles: "She's the smart one, she's the beauty, he's the athlete, she's impossible, he does whatever he's told." Often these kinds of labels stick, and a child has very little room to break out into another identity. A planet in the 3rd may have more influence early in life, when you are exploring your identity through the people around you. Even if a 3rd house Mars is projected— say you have a bullying older sister to contend with—the mechanism is probably much more profound than it appears at first glance. We may very well induce a particular response in those close to us, a response that may have a great deal to do with what we carry in our minds about the world. How many of you have looked at twins' charts? Have you noticed how they split up the chart between them?

AUDIENCE: I have an experience of twins who have really divided things up. One went into the underground movement, the other into a position of authority. They have an equally strong need to be respected, but use different value systems. Each twin sees himself as "light" and the other as "dark."

LYNN: You make them sound as though they come from a similar core, but have taken radically different directions, as if one is identified with Saturn and the other with Uranus. It seems as though twins split up the resources available in the chart. The twins that I have worked with have had strong 7th houses, perhaps because they are so continually together. The mirroring function of the 7th house is far more powerful than the 3rd's more oblique connection, as we saw earlier, and except in cases where twins have been split up, they are rarely separate. I recently visited a friend whose fraternal twin boys are five weeks old, and it's fascinating to see how they are already differentiated in the mother's experience. She sent out a birth announcement, a photo montage of the twins, and one is in the light and one is in the shadow It was really quite striking. When I pointed this out, she said, "Oh, don't say that." But really, anyone else would notice it immediately. What's even more fascinating is that the twin in the shadow weighs a kilo less and is much more difficult than the one in the light. There is already a division of resources.

AUDIENCE: How far apart are they?

LYNN: They were born by Caesarian, so there is only one minute of difference. But the older one is actually in the light. They "feel" very different from each other, despite the common horoscope.

AUDIENCE: I know some twins, and when they were kids, one of them was always smiling in photos and the other was always serious. But when they grew up, they totally changed.

LYNN: Yes, because in the presence of the other we are different from what we could be on our own. This is true for all brothers and sisters, but even more so for twins. Have you ever imagined what life would have been like for you as a child without a particular sibling? To get rid of that mean brother, or feel bereft without the one you admired? I think most "only" children spend a lot of time thinking about how things would have been different for them. And yet there have been few psychological studies on the effects of brothers and sisters on identity. Most of the work has centered around sibling rivalry or focused on twins, who are really a special case. In fact, scientists are amazed that, given the close biological similarity between brothers and sisters, they actually have so little in common. Siblings are even more biologically similar than children are to their own parents, since they share more genes. They are genetically, culturally, and environmentally similar, unless they have been separated from birth, and yet it is astonishing how different brothers and sisters really are. I think that is something very interesting to turn around in your mind.

Birth order

A great deal has been written about the importance of birth order in families, although the theory is somewhat disputed. Are any of you familiar with this?

AUDIENCE: Isn't the eldest supposed to be the most responsible, while the youngest is always a bit indulged?

LYNN: Yes, but it's quite a bit more elaborate than that. The first child is the achiever, and carries the family need for productivity, success, and material accomplishment. There is generally, according to this theory, an identification between the first child and the father. In astrological terms we should expect to find a strong Saturn signature, and I have found this to hold true to some extent. Parents expect a great deal of themselves and put more pressure on a first child, there's more tension about getting it right.

The second child carries the emotional needs, conscious or unconscious, of the family system, and often is connected to the unexpressed emotional issues of a family. If a second child is in trouble, the mother may not be doing very well. In the James family, Henry, the second child, clearly embodies something lunar, and his writing expresses the inner landscape of his characters, giving a voice to women in particular. He was constantly pouring out all the impressions he was getting through an intense and very compressed Plutonian perspective. William, on the other hand, with all that Capricorn, has a very strong father reference, an archetype of order, of responsibility, an ability to deal with the world. Saturn in the 1st conjunct the Ascendant ruler gives a strong backbone, a vertical aspiration to the chart. William also spoke of the inner life. He invented the concept "stream of consciousness," but his effectiveness in the world is of another kind, and he wrote of "usefulness," "pragmatism," and "cash value."

AUDIENCE: Does the birth order carry on down?

LYNN: It does. The third child is considered to carry the relationship and communication needs of a family, linking siblings and parents, making sure they maintain contact, and this child often mirrors the health of the parental couple. The fourth child breaks the pattern in some way He or she needs to be more individual, and this push to be different can create the family black sheep or give great originality. The fifth is a fun child, and the sixth is a unifier, keeping everyone together. With the seventh you start over again, so the seventh is like a first, and you'll remember the expression, "the seventh son of a seventh son." When I do workshops on genealogy, we look at the birth order sometimes, and find it stimulating to play around with. Alice James didn't seem to have a lot of fun, but as a child she was teased and petted and responded with lively wit and humor. Can anybody here relate to this quick system sketch? No? Yes? And does it suit your family?

AUDIENCE: With modifications.

LYNN: When the model deviates, there are often underlying issues, and it's worth looking at the parents' relationship. Or crises may occur in a family around the birth of a child—miscarriages, stillborns, and children who have died in infancy or later will, of course disrupt birth order.

AUDIENCE: Is there more information about this somewhere?

LYNN: Walter Toman was the first to write about birth order, and his work has been enlarged upon by Sulloway and Leman.[11] But a lot of the people in the field object to this approach as an oversimplification. It's even been attacked as pseudo-science. I think the best approach is to interview people, and try it out on your own family and with those you know. A couple of years ago I set up a study group where we explored the charts of families. We met one Sunday a month, to work on the charts of a particular family and pull out the family myths. The group felt that birth order theory held true in their examples, to a certain degree. Everyone would get a pile of charts—brothers, sisters, parents, grandparents—a month ahead of time, and look for the patterns. We will explore genealogy work, the larger family patterns, in a later seminar.[12]

---

11 See the Bibliography for these and other references on family dynamics.
12 See Part One of this book.

AUDIENCE: Did William James marry?

LYNN: He married very late, a woman called Alice, the same name as the sister, and became a father late in life. I think he married in midlife, after the Uranus opposition.

AUDIENCE: It is all very Capricorn.

LYNN: Yes, the sons fulfilled their father's need for recognition. Alice, on the other hand, eventually transformed her hypochondria into a fatal illness, breast cancer. After her parent's death, Henry spent a year with her in Boston. He wrote of that time: "My sister and I form a harmonious enough couple, and I feel as though I were married." Later she came to England to be near him. They were close, and he was with her at her death. Early on, William was the most important person in Henry's life; later he transferred that intimacy to another sibling. During those years, he developed a close friendship with Robert Louis Stevenson, who was dying, probably of tuberculosis. Henry would spend his time with one invalid or the other.

It seems that his Scorpio Moon, Sun-Pluto, and Pisces Venus had a strong connection to other people's suffering. The entire family unconscious is coming out in his novels, where he writes about how one person controls another through subtle manipulation or influence. He portrays the battle between rationality and emotion, convention and freedom— freedom to be one's true self. The Moon in the 3rd allows him to give voice to the powerful emotional currents in his family. Many of his novels are about how people free themselves from family or from their culture, and his most powerful characters are women.

AUDIENCE: I get the feeling that Uranus in Pisces indicates an almost collective level of sacrifice. In the 3rd, a sibling is sacrificed to define the collective. There is Piscean sacrifice there.

LYNN: What you are saying is interesting. There does seem to be something they're both working on, something about sacrifice and individuation in the collective. Both of them are part of a generation that have Uranus and Neptune in mutual reception, which asks questions about the boundaries of the individual.

AUDIENCE: It feels bigger than just their family.

LYNN: In this case, the family becomes representative of something larger. It's quite unusual to have two brothers who are as immensely successful as William and Henry James, with their accomplishments in completely different fields. They have been called pioneers in the American rediscovery of Europe, but they also stood for "the cultivation of the self and the spiritualization of values."

"SILENT FOR SEVEN YEARS"

One of the richest sources of material about family relationships can be found in fairy tales, and a great deal of writing has been done on how they help children explore and talk about the darker undercurrents in their own psyche. Folk wisdom shows us many templates of sibling relationship, from the shared terror and complementary resourcefulness of Hansel and Gretel to the envious, denigrating stepsisters of Cinderella. It's an interesting exercise to think of our own family experience in these terms—a touch of exaggeration here, a simplification there, and we have the outlines of a tale. I've chosen a story from Italo Calvino's collection of *Italian Folktales*.[13]

> One day a weary father was returning home, to be greeted by his young sons: "Papa, Papa!" He was in no mood to play, and gruffly told them to go away, but they insisted, and kept pulling on his legs till he shouted, "The Devil take you both!" The ground opened up, and the Devil snatched the boys away.
>
> At first the contrite father said nothing to his wife and daughter, but as the night wore on, he was obliged to tell the story

---

13 Adapted from Italo Calvino, *Italian Folktales,* "Silent for Seven Years," Harcourt Brace, 1980.

The parents wept, but their daughter resolved to try to find her brothers and free them if she could. She crept out into the forest, and came to a chateau with an iron door, where an elderly gentleman lived. When she asked if he'd seen her brothers, he told her, "Go into that room with twenty-four beds, and look." She rejoiced to find them tucked into sheets and blankets. "Oh, you're safe!" she exclaimed. The brothers told her to take a closer look, and peering beneath the bedclothes, she saw countless flames. "If you do not speak for seven years, you will save us. But in that time you will go through fire and water."

True to her word, she went out into the world mute, and many strange adventures befell her. She married a prince, who fell in love with her mysterious and silent beauty, but was cast out by a scheming mother-in law who pretended she'd given birth to a dog instead of a baby. She did not speak, even at this great injustice, remembering her brothers' fate. Saved from death, her hair shorn, and dressed in a man's clothes, she was picked up by a ship and joined the crew as a man, firing her share of cannon, and fighting in a long war.

Back on land, she stumbled upon a tumbled-down house, and went in, taking small bits of food. But the house belonged to a gang of murderers, and she was caught and forced to stay with them. When they planned to rob the king, her former husband, she sent a warning note, but was herself caught and arrested as one of the gang and sentenced to death. Postponing the hour of her execution by writing notes, still disguised as a man, she was climbing the steps to the scaffold when two warriors rode up: her brothers, free at last. They told the story of her great courage, and she was able to accuse her mother-in-law and prove her innocence, though her own infant had been killed. She was reunited with her husband, and her brothers became prime ministers and close advisors to the king.

What does this story have to say. about sibling relationships? The story first describes the hell of thoughtlessness, words that wound and carry long-term consequences. The father's curse unleashed a terrible fate, and many of us know the psychological impact of violent language, when an exceptional moment of bad temper is burned into a child's memory of events. We can be held prisoner psychologically by the fear and distress of such a moment. The solution in this case is silence. In the magical logic of the folk tale, silence is the antidote to the destructive power of words. In this tale, the parents are never mentioned again after the beginning of the story; the problems are worked out between the brothers and sister, and this can often be the task left to children of abusive parents.

But the silence perpetuates loss and, carried on for too long, the sister would also lose everything. Her initial good fortune, falling in love with the young king, cannot be complete while her brothers are still held prisoner. In much the same way, siblings often hold themselves back, at least in part, while a brother or sister is in distress. Her own child is sacrificed as a result of her vow not to speak up, and perhaps this tells us that merely doing the opposite of what a parent did is inadequate to cure a great injustice in a family. Or in astrological terms, Venus is not enough. We could also say that her ability to be a mother was blocked by her brothers' suffering and the initial "bad" parenting. The sister changes her identity and develops masculine qualities, fights like a man, lives like a man. She must internalize the positive masculine values that have been imprisoned with her brothers and misused by the father. She must develop not only passive resistance through silence, but an active will to fight.

However, even that is not enough, for she is later held captive by the murderers, again connected to the hidden and destructive forces within a society and an individual psyche. Eating the murderers' food may symbolize a tendency to nourish herself through vengeance or violence. Once again, she chooses to protect those she loves over her own safety, and is judged as a murderer; she carries the destructive projection of others. It is only when the brothers arrive and are able to speak the truth that she can let go of the need to carry both masculine and feminine. She again becomes the companion of the king, and the destructive feminine, the wicked mother-in-law, is hanged in her stead.

I could have chosen any number of stories, but this one appealed to me because it reflects the diverse strategies that siblings may follow in order to correct an injury in a family. It illustrates the invisible bonds that link brothers and sisters in difficulty, and shows how their fates can often move in tandem over time and distance. It may also give us some clues for understanding the communication or lack of it within a family system.

SISTERS, SISTERS

The next example I've brought is that of two sisters, Marion and Anna, who have gone through periods of silence in their own relationship. But they started out almost twinned, and spent the first part of their adult lives wearing the same clothes, sharing the same friends, seeing life and other people in a very similar way.[14]

Missing air

The elder sister, Marion, has both Mercury rising and the 3rd house strong. I think we would all agree that this combination is going to make communication extremely important. And yet there is no air in the chart. This absence of air can be seen in the context of a family pattern, since all the woman in her family have a strong earth signature and very little air. Marion has no planets in air, her sister Anna has only Jupiter, and their mother has the Sun in Gemini as a singleton by element.

Now, air has to do with the space between things and the ability to stand back from the world—it helps to make things less personal. It also has to do with the movement and exchange of energy within systems. So we might imagine some difficulties for the members of this family in finding and maintaining space. Meanwhile, we usually speak of air in terms of intellect, communication, the ability to manipulate ideas. It could be that all that earth is much more "hands on"—something has to be worked with, experienced internally in order to be absorbed. In

14 Both birth times come from birth records.

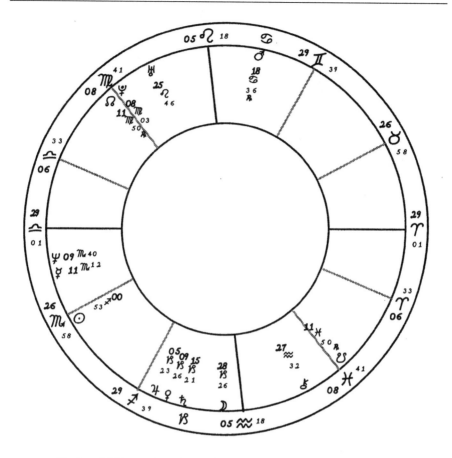

Marion, 23 November 1960, 5:30 am CET San Sebastian, Spain

this family, the women in particular are relying on something other than pure intellect. Things need to be put into practice. Both sisters married men with little air and very strong fire signatures; they were not looking for distance, but rather, a more powerful, passionate experience of the world.

There is no air, then, in Marion's chart, and at the same time, with Mercury-Neptune in Scorpio in the 1st house, she has a rather overwhelming permeability to the unspoken and unseen currents of life. Her curiosity will infallibly take her to places where others would instinctively hide, and she could easily be submerged by an unceasing flow of perceptions, impressions, feelings. All that Capricorn, particularly

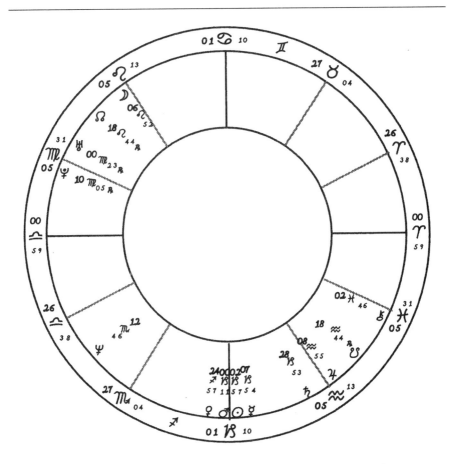

Anna, 25 December 1961, 1:00 am CET, San Sebastien, Spain

Saturn in the 3rd, will need to order this flow, and perhaps seek to stop it, to shut it off. Mercury-Neptune can feel crazy because it sees things that others pretend are not there, or it can disconnect from the raw emotional content of Scorpio into a pretend world. At its best, Saturn will help make these perceptions explicit, but it could be a barrier of rationality and control. Initially Marion may not have had the language to translate her perceptions, and if she did, would they be acknowledged by the people around her?

AUDIENCE: Perhaps the other family members are very practical, and stifled her imaginative tendencies.

AUDIENCE: Earlier you spoke of how similar she was to her sister. Would that be a function of Neptune in the 1st house? I could easily imagine Neptune creating a confusion of identity.

LYNN: Anyone with Neptune in the 1st house can give themselves over to a dream identity, and in this family the mother seems to have had a dream of closeness for her daughters. But Marion also has Saturn in the 3rd house, which is not a signature for fusion. Much of her work on herself has been about separating from her sister. There are other planets in the 3rd house, notably Moon and Venus, which tend to closeness, and she shares Venus in the 3rd with her sister. The story of these sisters seems to move between closeness and cut-off—they have had periods where they didn't see or speak to each other for nearly a year.

AUDIENCE: Does that mean there's an alternation between the different planets in the 3rd?

Planetary containment

LYNN: It's certainly one of the possibilities. Whenever planets are massed closely in a house or sign, it becomes important to look at their micro-relationships—what is called planetary containment. This gives a more finely tuned interpretation, and helps a story unfold. Here, Venus is between Jupiter and Saturn, which is not the same thing as coming from a conjunction with Saturn and moving towards Jupiter. Can you see that? It makes it much more likely that the sibling relationship is wide open to begin with, then closes down, and that this kind of movement from open to closed will be a pattern in all relationships. The Moon comes after Saturn, quite a bit further along in the house, and it's interesting to find two parental significators, suggesting a shift into caretaking roles. Of course, if there were several siblings, these roles would most likely be divided up among them. But Saturn limits and closes off, and then the Moon softens things.

We know that Neptune in the 1st house can make it quite difficult for Marion to establish a clear sense of self, and for other people to see her as she really is. The Ascendant ruler, Venus, is pulled between two contradictory energies conjunct Jupiter, generous, open and optimistic; conjunct Saturn, it describes someone more controlled, perhaps even inhibited. Initially this can give a choice in the way we see her; and perhaps she must choose internally as well. Her work will have to turn around finding a way to be both open and contained. She can be very talkative, or turn mute, unable to express herself at all if she feels judged. Again, she is both open and closed. We are moving between Jupiter and Saturn. Which is going to be stronger?

AUDIENCE: Saturn is dignified in Capricorn, and Jupiter doesn't do too well there.

AUDIENCE: Venus-Jupiter would be friendly and loving, and then Mars in the 9th house opposition Saturn would push away, or dominate. Half of her wants to be aggressive, but the other half gets pulled back into Saturn/Capricorn obligation.

AUDIENCE: There's a lot of contraction and anger in this chart. Maybe this is what William James called "tough-minded." But then it's covered up by that Neptune in the 1st.

AUDIENCE: Couldn't there be some kind of restriction in early life? Perhaps there was a trauma around a move. As a result, the need for travel and freedom could be extremely powerful.

3rd/9th house oppositions

LYNN: Oppositions from the 3rd to the 9th house often result in internal or external warring. This kind of aspect structure can give an endlessly questioning mind, a need to fit together things which often wish to stay apart. Sometimes there is early exposure to different cultures, different religions, even different political points of view. An individual who ignores these tensions can suffer psychologically, often feeling extremely restless, distracted, and even split internally. The attempt to hold a fixed point of view will often pull in conflict from outside, until an individual addresses their internal contradictions. The impulse to travel can be seen as a need to change horizons, to step out of a limiting world-view, as we have seen in the earlier examples. Planets in these houses demand mobility, either physical or mental, preferably both. There is a 3rd/9th house story here. Any ideas about what it might be?

AUDIENCE: Mars and Saturn could be linked to her father, perhaps through a struggle with religion, or maybe he travels for his work. Didn't you say the father was born in Spain?

LYNN: Yes, and he was born in 1934. 3rd/9th house oppositions mean there can be a conflict between different visions of the world, different belief systems, different languages and different cultures. These conflicts can be within the family, within the individual, or with the world outside. When you see active planets in an opposition to the 3rd house, you have to ask, "Is there a difference of opinion in this family? Is there something around change of culture, change of universe?" You probably have a good idea of what happened in Spain in the 1930's.

AUDIENCE: Does that mean the family were on different sides during the Spanish Civil War?

LYNN: No, but the Civil War played a huge role. The story has to do with forced emigration and flight. The father was barely three when the war reached their part of Spain. His father was interned in a camp, and his mother had to flee Franco's forces on foot with small children, under a hail of bombs, travelling roads littered with dead bodies. They lost all their possessions, and the house where the family had lived for generations was burned to the ground, while a small sister was left behind with an aunt for several years. As adults, all the children, and there were eight brothers and sisters, ended up living in widely different places.

Spain in the 1960's, when Marion was born, was still a society under constraint. Under Franco you couldn't even say things in front of your children; if they repeated them, someone at school might tell their parents, and they might turn you in to the Fascist police. The environment demanded secrecy and caution, and so when Marion was two and a half her parents moved to France, taking Anna with them. They gave up their home, and left Marion behind with relatives for four months.

Notice the powerful repetitions of exile and separation in the family story. This kind of resonant event often happens when a child reaches the age a parent had at the time of a traumatic experience. For Marion, we now see that the pattern of closeness and separation began very early on, anchored by what, for her, was a period of traumatic abandonment. Four months is a very long time for such a young child, even in a familiar environment with a loving aunt, and the sense that her sister was chosen over her must have been terribly wounding. Then, in Paris, when she rejoined her parents, there was a new language to learn. The opposition in her chart begins to make itself clear—the Cancer/Capricorn emphasis, and the Moon's conjunction to the 4th house cusp, are indications of a story stretching beyond her own experience, into the family past. Although the details of these stories were unknown to her until relatively recently, they left a strong emotional imprint. She remembers her anxiety, not knowing whether her parents would come back or not, since no one thought to explain things to such a small child. The Moon in the 3rd gives a powerful emotional memory, and she is using all those planets there to reconstruct the family history through writing. Her Mercury-Neptune sensed something, and through persuasive, gentle, and yet very persistent questioning she slowly unraveled the family secrets.

Marion has lived most of her life in France, but still considers herself Spanish. She doesn't even have a French passport. On the maternal side, there is a history of displacement and immigration as well. Her Spanish great-grandmother defied her wealthy family and eloped with the man she loved, leaving everything behind for a new life in France. Both sides of the family have these threads of disconnection, separation from the family of origin—again, that 3rd/9th house pattern. Where there is fusion, there is often an anxiety about separation and loss, and perhaps this gives us a clue to Marion's and Anna's need to stay so close together.

Shared planets: problems of identity

From the beginning, Marion's verbal precocity tagged her as "the intelligent one." While her sister, a fine, delicate child, was dressed in pretty clothes like a princess, Marion was given books and ran wild, a short-haired tomboy, for the first twelve years. Her temper and willfulness got her the nickname, La Tigressa. As adults, both sisters are lovely, soft-spoken and feminine, and Marion now has long thick hair down to her waist. The sister, Anna, speaks very little, but erupts in explosive bouts of bad temper, much like the father, while the mother, a schoolteacher, talks easily. We begin to see a 3rd/9th house pattern of ease and frustration in expressing ideas, no doubt accentuated by the father's Spanish origins and her mother's Geminian fluency in both languages.

At adolescence, the two sisters were thrown together more. Their parents would say, "We only have enough money to buy one coat this year," and they would take turns wearing the old and the new one, like sisters in a fairy tale. They shared one bicycle between them, and one stereo; they shared friends as well. Marion, who is in analysis, says that she sometimes has the impression that together, she and her sister made up one woman. Her mother saw her femininity and beauty mirrored in the younger daughter, while Marion reflected her intelligence. Interestingly enough, both sisters have Libra rising, and both have Venus in the third. The sisters went from having quite different identities to being so similar that people would confuse them.

AUDIENCE: That reminds me of the song: "Sisters, sisters, never were there such devoted sisters...When a certain gentleman arrived from Rome, she wore the dress and I stayed home." It's like a joke.

Venus in the 3rd house

AUDIENCE: Could we talk more about Venus? How would it fit in here? Presumably she would try to get other people to agree with her?

AUDIENCE: I have a 12th house Moon, and my sister and I share our

Venuses. She acted as though we were the same, and had the same feelings. She has Pisces on the 3rd house cusp.

LYNN: It seems that Venus in the 3rd may activate issues around identity, especially for sisters. I'm not sure that brothers with Venus in the 3rd would have the same issue.

AUDIENCE: I have Venus in the 3rd, and I feel very connected to my sister, but it's also conjunct Neptune, which probably makes it stronger.

LYNN: Wouldn't most of us expect a loving relationship with a brother or sister when Venus is in the 3rd house? Perhaps we find love in our early environment, and that keeps us close to home. Venus prefers to function through consensus, but she has Saturn for company in Marion's chart, and may be a bit more embattled, a bit less harmonious. Mars in the 9th in opposition rarely shies away from confrontation.

AUDIENCE: I have Venus conjunct Mars. My feeling is that my sister always thought that I was the popular one, and it took a long time, until our twenties, for that to recede. We were close, but there was always this underlying rivalry.

LYNN: There is another possibility, too—perhaps having the same planet in the 3rd house as a sibling, whether it's Venus or Mars, Jupiter or the Moon, might make it easier to identify with them, easier to see the world in the same way. But it will depend on the planet. You can see that Mars will increase any tendency to rivalry between siblings.

AUDIENCE: The idea of identification is interesting. My brother and I have Mars on the same degree, and other people have confused us, despite the fact that I think this is incredibly difficult to do.

LYNN: Castor and Pollux were connected along Martial lines. They fought and competed, ran races and wrestled, but in the end they were deeply twinned and stayed together. The question I have is whether

Marion and Anna have deeply similar values and a profound affection, or whether they were under unconscious pressure to be connected. This kind of enmeshment can be a response to separative currents in a family, disconnections that were unresolved in previous generations. For some years, Marion would find herself in conversations with someone she didn't know, feeling slightly offended by their over-familiarity, and slowly realize they'd mistaken her for her sister. They both worked in the cinema, one in costume, the other as a dresser; then they changed roles. Marion went to London to live for a while; Anna followed six months later; Marion went to Spain; again Anna followed. Later, in Paris, they lived in the same building, in different apartments. Anna would find a job on a film, then bring Marion in. They could never get very far apart from each other without reconnecting, almost as if they couldn't be separate.

Anna's Moon is square Neptune, an indicator of powerful emotional needs, and her Mercury is quincunx the Moon, which is not particularly easy for self-expression. Marion provided the words, stories, explanations. Marion shared friends with Anna, in part because her mother disapproved of those she chose for herself. But in the past few years she began to see that she was really stealing them, becoming closer than Anna was, so she took more distance. Anna often had affairs with Marion's men friends, and even insisted on going to see Marion's analyst; Marion felt powerless to say no. She had always been responsible for Anna, the littler one, helping her dress, cooking meals, taking her to school, despite their closeness in age. Fortunately, the analyst refused to work with both sisters. Things changed two years after Marion's son was born, when she and her partner bought a house. Anna stopped speaking to her for nearly a year, a silence that was never explained. They became close again when Anna became pregnant with her own son.

AUDIENCE: It sounds as if Marion might have overpowered her sister intellectually. Perhaps, with such a strong 3rd house, she tends to dominate communication with others, especially her sister, and then the Mars in the 9th could be anger coming from outside, breaking things open. I'm not surprised they don't always get along.

AUDIENCE: I almost see Saturn-Mars the other way round, as if the opposition gives an intellectual justification for suppressing anger. One must not be angry.

LYNN: Marion is clearly the more dominant sibling, but this is really a case of enmeshment, of over-involvement. Anna really only expresses herself when she doesn't agree, and then she gets very angry and unreasonable, which doesn't sound like Venus, does it? It certainly fits your interpretation of Saturn opposition Mars. Looking at Anna's chart, we find Scorpio on the 3rd house, with Venus in Sagittarius conjunct Mars in Capricorn, very close to and conjuncting a 4th house Sun-Mercury, which would suggest a strong connection to the father. Perhaps the father felt frustrated and inhibited by his wife's ease in communicating, and we see this pattern repeated between the sisters. The parents also have Mars connected to the 3rd house, an interesting juxtaposition of Mars and Venus in this family. Venus suggests that everyone get along, while Mars pushes to dominance. Still, the sisters have that 3rd house Venus in common, and when you share a 3rd house planet with a sibling, there may be an interface, a confusion, similar to the connection between twins. This blurring of identity is likely to be stronger with receptive planets like Venus, Moon, or Neptune, as well as signs like Pisces on the cusp of the house.

This relationship goes beyond rivalry, beyond mirroring and emulation. Anna feels that Marion always got more attention, more consideration than she did, and she is in a deep crisis, with transiting Uranus opposition her Moon. Perhaps she is truly beginning to separate from her dependency on her sister. Marion is trying to see what belongs to her and what belongs to Anna, and once again the sisters have stopped speaking to each other, but this time Marion has initiated the split.

You can begin to see that intense relationships between siblings can be traced to larger patterns within families, and that we must look beyond the 3rd house in order to understand, even in part, their place in the larger scheme of things.

8th house/Pluto patterns: closeness as a reaction to loss

I know another pair of sisters in their late thirties, both beautiful women, who live in the same building, share friends, fight and make up passionately; neither are married, as if the bond between them cannot allow enough room for another partner. Because of problems with the concierge, they still receive their mail at their parent's address, so symbolically, all their contacts with the outside world pass through the family. In 1961, when the sisters were tiny, the family left an established, comfortable life in Tunisia, propelled by the independence movement shaking the region. The cultural model for the *pieds noirs,* as they are called in French—blackened feet from their contact with North African culture—is very entwined and overlapping, with a strongly emotional connection to the family and almost daily contact through telephone or in person. The family's exodus also activates the archetype of exile inherent in their Jewish roots.

Their mother had been exceptionally close to her brother, but their relationship turned sour when he married an outsider—a Dutch woman. They stopped speaking to each other for many years. The father later sought to heal the split by loaning some money to this brother-in-law for a business deal, but he ended up getting swindled. You can see that the fusion-oriented relationship between the sisters is, at least in part, a response to painful, separative events in the family past.

On the father's side, one of his siblings had been given away to a childless aunt. The family story, with its themes of separation and fusion, is reflected by strong 8th house or Pluto patterns that run through the entire family, rather than a simple reading of the 3rd house. Why are some families or certain siblings closer than others? We may need to go more deeply into family synastry in order to understand this. These sisters and their father have Sun-Moon contacts, a traditional signature for closeness.

Marion began to write screenplays, and had some success with it, but then she fell into writer's block and depression, experiencing a creeping paralysis, an inability to take action of any kind—very expressive of that Saturn-Mars opposition. Until she could get the family history out into the open, she could not move forward in her life. She went into analysis, slowly uncovering things, slowly understanding what had been running her unconsciously. She could only unlock her will by bringing out what had been hidden. What made it more difficult was that her mother started to write when she did, which she took as a not-so-subtle form of competition. Virgina Satir said that every family has rules, and in this one, belongings and talents must be shared, a rule which inhibits the development of strong individuality. Marion's 1st house Neptune-Mercury gives an unusually powerful sensitivity to all the undercurrents in the family, making her profoundly receptive to the family unconscious. Now Marion is writing a novella set during the time of the Spanish Civil War, incorporating some of these family ghosts into the creative process. It is almost as if she could continue writing only by giving voice to these family secrets and grievances.

AUDIENCE: That sounds like Chiron in the 4th a wound coming from the family, and perhaps continuing in her own life.

AUDIENCE: It almost sounds as if she separates because she's overly connected to begin with.

LYNN: That's a good way of understanding Saturn in the 3rd—a need to have some kind of frontier between self and other, to counteract all this sensitivity If we look at the synastry between the two charts, we see that Anna has Mars, Sun, and Mercury conjunct Marion's Venus-Jupiter, aspects of strong love, connectedness, and passion. At the same time, her Saturn sits exactly on Marion's Moon, evoking feelings of responsibility, guilt, and protection, but leading, often enough, to a sense of emotional frustration. We can see why Marion might have difficulty feeling nourished in this relationship, yet there is a kind of connection that will probably never go away, despite the silences.

Strong planetary contacts and aspects between siblings may mean that more can be accomplished when they are together. A fascinating example is flight. Our capacity as a species to lift off from gravity was first successfully performed by two different sets of brothers. The Montgolfier brothers developed the hot air balloon, and the Wright brothers together developed the first airplane. Perhaps siblings working together in this way can go further than they might alone, like Castor and Pollux. On a more tragic note, we have Vincent Van Gogh and his brother Theo. We will look at their story a bit later.

Pluto in the 3rd house

Let's talk about some of the 3rd house planets we haven't yet looked at—like the Sun, Pluto, and Neptune. Would anybody like to talk about one of those? Pluto in the 3rd?

AUDIENCE: In the beginning of the seminar I said I had to explain my brother's language to my mother. But during the break another idea came to me. I would now say I found his voice within me. I have been thinking about what you said earlier. I never fully realized before that it was the child my mother lost that kept my mother from letting go of me. I have Moon conjunct Pluto in the 3rd She was speaking for me as if I had no thoughts, or was too weak to exist on my own. I struggled to find my own language as a child, and suffered from depression. When I left my mother I started writing, so when you say phrases like, "to give voice to feelings," it really hits home.

LYNN: It sounds as though Pluto cast a long shadow. Notice that, with Moon-Pluto, there is a danger of the mother taking over, almost inhabiting the child's psyche. A child with Moon in the 3rd may often be strongly connected to the mother's unconscious, so much so as to be disconnected to self, and a situation of this kind can lead to high levels of anxiety.

AUDIENCE: In therapy I felt badly at first about the things I said about my mother, but it helped me to have a better connection with her. She was angry, not violent, but sad underneath, and needed to live many things through me. I had this feeling of oppression, and felt inferior to my other brothers and sisters because they were a little bit more independent.

LYNN: Betrayal, imagined or real, is one of the key issues surrounding Pluto, so it's not surprising you would have felt uncomfortable breaking the privileged relationship you had with your mother by discussing it with a therapist. It's also interesting that, with Uranus also in the 3rd, you see your surviving siblings as freer than you are.

AUDIENCE: Initially I felt left out. Now each of us is strong in their own way.

LYNN: When Pluto is in the 3rd, a sibling may carry a very dark, shadowy energy. In your case, this is clearly linked to your mother's anxiety over the loss of a child. You didn't feel safe because your mother didn't feel safe. In your case, the Moon is the carrier for Pluto. But with or without other planets, the more shadowy aspects of the unconscious are going to be activated in a relationship with a sibling when Pluto is here. Does anybody else have Pluto in the 3rd? No one wants to admit to this!

AUDIENCE: I know a woman whose mother had quite a lot of problems, and it's clear that these have been passed along to her. She has no brothers and sisters, so how would you interpret her loaded 3rd house in that case? It contains Pluto, Saturn, and Mars.

LYNN: I would look closely at the model of communication in the family. Each planet in the 3rd demands expression, and the greater the number of planets, the more you are pushed to find words for them. We have also talked about Saturn in the 3rd as a feeling of isolation—having no one to talk to. Pluto-Saturn-Mars in the 3rd clearly indicates great tension around communication, in part because what needs to be said probably won't be pleasant. This could be a situation where a child has difficulty expressing her own misgivings or fears because of the mother's overcharged reaction to any negativity.

This combination could describe a barrier to expression, but could also give great persistence and concentration, and an ability to ferret information out of obscure places. It would be worthwhile to explore how things have functioned in preceding generations, and I would expect to find a number of secrets. The more you can step back and find perspective on this one, the easier it will be, because the greatest danger would be getting completely caught up in tormented patterns of thought. I would look at the aspects to Mercury in the mother's chart, and also the synastry between the charts, to find out if there is a scarring from lack of trust that has perhaps caused her to close off to the world. The child will need to give voice to something that feels heavy, depressive and a bit morbid. It is quite essential that she can do so, or she will, in turn, feel bound and closed off from others.

The family underworld

AUDIENCE: I have a feeling that Pluto in the 3rd and Scorpio on the 3rd are always symbolic of a contact with the family "underworld."

LYNN: That's a good way of looking at it. It doesn't take much imagination to conjure up the rage and jealousy this placement might indicate towards a sibling. Since this is a profoundly human experience, and not limited to those with Pluto in the 3rd, Pluto's presence is possibly an indicator of greater sensitivity toward these destructive impulses. Difficult events will be seared into a person's memory, while someone else might pass over them more lightly.

AUDIENCE: I'm beginning to feel very uncomfortable sitting here. I don't have Pluto in the 3rd. But Mars is in Scorpio in the 3rd, which means that Pluto is the ruler of the house, and it's in the 12th, in the center of a stellium in Leo. I can hardly describe how mean-spirited, how odious my brother was; how he would hurt me or humiliate me at every opportunity. It went way beyond sibling jealousy. I grew up with a torturer. He was seven years older and physically scary. Okay, my mother adored me, and I understand now that my brother must have felt left out, but he never grew out of it. Words became my weapon, and I cut and wounded him verbally as soon as I was able, so he began to keep a distance.

LYNN: Has your relationship with this brother changed over time?

AUDIENCE: I don't have to see him anymore, and I avoid him whenever possible. I haven't spoken to him in years.

LYNN: Would you say there's a similar pattern, when conflicts come up for you in other relationships?

AUDIENCE: If anything, I overprotect myself. I've become all too aware of how my words can be wounding, so I prefer to stay silent, even when I'm boiling inside. But sometimes I lash out, and feel badly afterwards. I can't always control it. I have this general sense of holding myself back, on many levels, and suspect that my depressions are in part linked to this.

LYNN: We may underestimate the power of jealousy and rage that inhabits a young child. The destructive potential of the species can flare up in nascent form, and it is rarely subtle among children. Since you are strongly 12th house, you may be identified with the position of victim; as you say, you tend to overprotect yourself, like a tender plant curling back into the bud for protection. Squares between planets in the 3rd and the 12th can often have this effect.

This brings us to a key component of the 3rd house: its connection to thinking and perception. To some extent, it describes the mental patterning that we carry within us and, along with the 9th house, Mercury, and Jupiter, how we elaborate our systems of belief. The 3rd house is more automatic, less conscious, and probably much more difficult to grasp because it describes, in part, the very tools through which we try to understand the world. Could it be that our first encounters shape and color our perception of the world? Or does the 3rd house describe an internal template which predisposes to a particular vision of things? In either case, the earliest interactions between outer experience and inner predisposition clearly shape our way of seeing and understanding.

Pluto in the 3rd, or ruling it, always looks to see more deeply into things. The presupposition is that something is hidden and needs to be uncovered. Pluto has a definite taste for stripping things down to essentials, for destroying pretense, for looking into obscure places. If the initial connections, as in your case, are extremely difficult, an individual's perceptions may be tuned to danger, to the psychological underside. This in turn can become a habit of perception that filters through almost all relationships, which means that we live in a hostile, threatening environment and must act accordingly. In the most extreme cases, this can result in a paranoid model of the world.

AUDIENCE: Didn't someone say that paranoids are usually right?

LYNN: If you went to school expecting other boys to be hostile towards you, you almost certainly set that situation up through unconscious cues in your behavior. And if you did get teased or attacked, it reinforced your perception. A paranoid expectation often activates the corresponding behavior in someone else. An even deeper issue with Pluto has to do with anxiety—anxiety that things are not what they seem to be. Precisely because Pluto contains such volcanic emotions, it tends to be prone to splitting the world into absolutes of Good and Bad. A friend of mine in Paris, Christian Fenninger, believes that this splitting is the main way Pluto defends itself. In your case, it certainly sounds as though your brother carries a powerful negative projection. Whether he deserves that projection or not is another matter.

AUDIENCE: I can guarantee that he was an unmitigated monster!

LYNN: Remember, we're talking about Mars in Scorpio in the 3rd, which corresponds to the lacerating and cutting images that you used earlier. Pluto can often be more obscure, harder to get one's thinking around. Its placement in the 3rd very often means a sibling is carrying something heavy, whether it belongs to them or not. I have this placement in the birth chart, and my sister suffers from depression. Many years ago, when I began analysis, I dreamt that she was in the subway carrying a very heavy suitcase. I said, "Do you want me to help? Look, we can take the elevator." She said, "No, I want to take the stairs." I said, "Well, I'm taking the elevator." I didn't see any point in struggling with this heavy baggage when it was possible to take the elevator. I've always seen this dream vignette as especially evocative of Pluto in the 3rd. The image of the subway, the underground, is the underworld, and there is very heavy baggage to be dealt with on one level or another. My sister is the carrier of that baggage, and in my work as a consultant it is fundamental for me to speak about what might be in the suitcase. Pluto in the 3rd house enables me to give voice to something which may be frightening for those who come to see me. My sister is weighed down by that suitcase, and perhaps there are things in there to be brought to consciousness. But the dream also reveals a choice that I made in relation to her suffering—not to stay down there unnecessarily.

AUDIENCE: I hadn't given much thought to the weight of my dead sibling until today. I'm beginning to see that he or she may have been a guide to the underworld for me.

LYNN: It seems very clear to me that the lost brother or sister has never been properly mourned, and so you were drawn down to this heavy, grey, lifeless place, your mother's depression. That dead child needs to be psychically evacuated, and because you have Pluto in the 3rd, this task falls squarely on your shoulders. When that work is done, Moon-Pluto will help you to go more deeply with others, to accompany them in their own underworld journeys.

Mercury-Pluto: power and knowledge

Pluto placed in the 3rd or 9th often describes an urge to power through some kind of special knowledge. It goes without saying that this is frequent enough among serious students of astrology! Pluto here often develops a penetrating mind, but although observational acuity may keep our own anxiety at bay, it may bring a degree of sharpness that's uncomfortable for others. Pluto here can terrorize others through withholding communication, or through pointed and penetrating comments. In my family, the women were all extremely verbal, and not particularly good listeners—rather off-putting for other people. My father spoke very little, perhaps because there wasn't much room. Words were a tool for fascination, even domination, somewhat similar to Mars placed here. No opportunity to mark a point was passed over, whether through shouting someone down or seizing on another's discomfort until they began to squirm. Sometimes Pluto in the 3rd can cast a chill, because it has an uncanny instinct for another's weak spot. Clients with this placement, or with Mercury-Pluto combinations, often describe how they learned to use words to protect themselves from aggression. Stripping another verbally down to the bone is quite an effective defense!

AUDIENCE: Could there be a tendency to obsession and depressive, repetitive thoughts? How could someone with Pluto here relieve the pressure that they may feel at times?

LYNN: If a perception cannot find its way out, it drags you down to uncomfortable places over and over again. At its most extreme, a disconnection occurs, and obsessive habits of thinking or acting are set up. To relieve this, true communication becomes absolutely necessary, and that means not just pushing empty words around, but touching deeply and being heard by the other person. Pluto also needs to deliver the communication to the right place.

AUDIENCE: With Pluto there, the world looks darker than for other people. It's a way of thinking in itself.

LYNN: Exactly The need to penetrate beneath the surface of things can make it hard to relax. Certain kinds of mental patterns seem to run endlessly, pulling one's thoughts into difficult places. But an individual with Pluto in the 3rd needs to get all the way down to the core, by whatever means possible. If we go back to the idea that the 3rd house is our first doorway to connection with others, Pluto here means we will quickly encounter the more destructive impulses in human nature. Given its unsavory side, it's easier to see the danger in others—easier than to see it in yourself, of course. If your sibling cooperates by trying to strangle you or hit you over the head with a shovel as mine did, the pattern of projection finds a convenient object. This activates your Plutometer, and soon you are sniffing out, and perhaps selecting, destructive behavior in a sibling, and in others. One can easily see how this could be a handicap later in life, although useful under certain circumstances.

GERTRUDE STEIN
AND HER BROTHER LEO

We also need to keep things in perspective, because I have seen charts where Pluto in the 3rd is neither morbid nor monstrous nor destructive—where siblings are healthy and have warm, friendly relationships. At times this signature gives sibling relationships full of passionate intensity, and no other can rival the depth of connection they share.

Let's look at another example. I came across an excellent book called *Sister Brother*, by Brenda Wineapple,[15] which tells the story of a tightly fused sibling pair, Gertrude Stein and her brother Leo. They were emotionally devoted and intellectually linked, great collectors and enthusiasts of modern art. They lived together as a couple of sorts until the age of the Uranus opposition, when they broke completely and irrevocably.

Gertrude's chart[16] gives Pluto in Taurus in the 2nd, but still conjunct the 3rd house cusp, and for me, the story of the Steins is a powerful illustration of a Plutonian involvement with a sibling and its continued resonance, emotional and intellectual, later in life. Gertrude has four planets in Aquarius in the 12th house, and she struggled for many years to find her path, following her brother to Harvard, dropping out of medical school, then following him again, this time to Europe and their apartment in Paris. It was often said that Leo was the more intelligent of the two, while Gertrude had the stronger character, and yet she felt overshadowed by him for many years. Her Sun-Mercury conjunction

---

15 Brenda Wineapple, *Sister Brother*. Bloomsbury Press, London, 1997.
16 Birth data for Gertrude Stein from Lois Rodden, *Profiles of Women*, AFA, 1978. Birth date for Leo from *Sister Brother* (op. cit.).

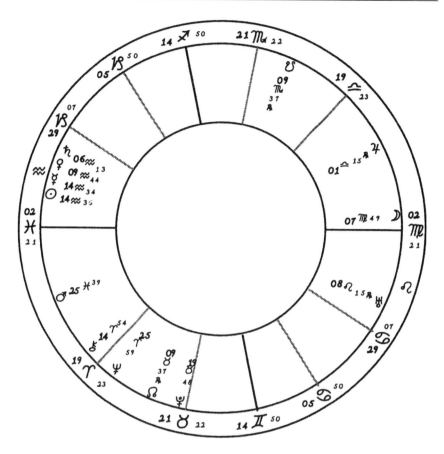

Gertrude Stein, 3 February 1874, 8:00 am LMT, Pittsburgh, PA

is square Pluto, while her brother had a conjunction of Pluto, Sun, and Mars in Taurus. Both of them were given to absolute judgments and opinion by proclamation.

It was Leo who began to collect modern art, starting with Cezanne, and rapidly acquiring a stunning collection of early Matisse and Picasso. They held court on Saturday evenings, when visitors could come to see the work. It was Leo who spoke passionately about the paintings, who became the high priest of modernism, although he and Gertrude purchased all the works together. We don't usually associate Pluto with fusion-oriented relationships, although it is quite often involved in cases of influence or fascination, where a dominant personality holds another

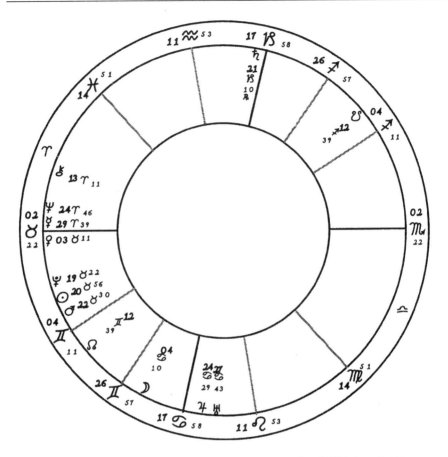

Leo Stein, 11 May 1872, "about four in the morning," Pittsburgh, PA

in thrall. With Pisces rising and an angular 7th house Moon, as well as Jupiter in Libra in the 7th house, Gertrude Stein did not like to be alone. Her 3rd house Pluto looked like fusion to start with, but there were dinosaur-sized power issues rumbling under the surface.

Cutting off from a sibling

Trouble between siblings was also part of the family history. Their father had emigrated from Germany with his family as an adolescent, and had eventually gone into business with his five brothers, but that venture shattered at the beginning of the Civil War, when three of the brothers chose the Confederate cause. The remaining two, Daniel—their father—and his brother, Solomon, sided with the Union, and made a small fortune manufacturing uniforms during the war. For ten years the families either lived together in the same house or side by side. Shortly before Gertrude's birth, the two brothers had a major falling out, with Daniel selling his share to Solomon for one dollar "to correct a mistake."

The strong 12th house in Gertrude's chart reflects her father's withdrawal from the business, a kind of early retirement. He soon took the family to Europe, where they spent four years, first in Vienna, then Paris. Gertrude learned German, French, and English at the same time, before the family moved to California to start a completely new life. This experience of "exile," prefiguring her later life as an expatriate, fits with the ruler of the Gemini 4th house in the 12th In Leo's chart. This same mobility is reflected by a conjunction of Jupiter and Uranus in the 4th, and, like Henry James, he has a watery 3rd house Moon. The illness and death of their mother when they were still young, as well as complementary temperaments, bound them tightly together. In this respect it's interesting to note that both brother and sister have the ruler of the 3rd house in the 12th, perhaps a reflection of the fusion between them.

Leo Stein was a fascinating and gifted talker, spinning passionate and obsessive theories about art, the nature of perception, and metaphysics. But he was never able to give concrete form to any of his talents, dropping out of law school, abandoning painting, expounding with brilliance but never putting ideas into published form—never, that is, until he was seventy-five and Gertrude was dead. Mercury is rising in his chart, conjunct Venus in Taurus, a classic configuration for aesthetic sensibility, heightened by the conjunction with Neptune. They form a T-square to a powerful Capricorn Saturn on the MC, opposing Jupiter-Uranus in Cancer. There was always another, bigger, more ineffable, more inclusive explanation of things, and he grew disenchanted with each one in turn. Over time his passions became increasingly obsessive and bizarre, and around the time he and Gertrude grew apart he was fasting for days on end in an attempt to purify body and consciousness. His rigidity and intensely inward focus can be seen as a reflection of the powerful Saturn and Pluto themes in his chart.

Meanwhile, Gertrude became increasingly massive physically, and more and more fixed in her theories of personality and literary experiment. Although Leo discovered both Matisse and Picasso, and introduced many people to their work, he rejected cubism. Gertrude became increasingly identified with Picasso. And then there was Alice B. Toklas, who replaced Leo as her life partner. Until this time, Leo had always been the determining influence in Gertrude's thinking. She separated from him first intellectually, then emotionally Wineapple writes:

> For three decades she (Alice) and Gertrude Stein lived at 27 rue de Fleurus without Leo and without, they said, any mention of him. He *was persona non grata,* the "one we don't see!" Gertrude Stein was given to dismissing things and people. Eventually she severed relations with more than one sibling and most of her family, banishing old and some new friends with a peremptoriness both startling and bold. (Composer Virgil Thompson, later reinstated, once received one of Stein's calling cards on which she'd written under her engraved name that she "declines further acquaintance with Mr. Thompson.") But nothing was as complete, unremitting, or profound as her separation from a once beloved Leo.[17]

When asked why he was spending less and less time with her, he spoke of her relationship with Alice, saying he had "seen trees strangled by vines in the same way." Although we can easily read feelings of jealousy and abandonment into this comment, it accurately reflects a very uncomfortable dimension of Pluto, which has a tendency to set up a subtle dimension of host and parasite in relationships. This seems to spring from a belief that there isn't enough life force to go around, that another's substance must feed and support one's success; Gertrude later said that there was room for only one genius in the family.

Plutonians sometimes bind others to them in order to feel powerful. When this happens, they may grow increasingly dominant, while those close to them seem to shrink in substance and vitality. And yet the apparently submissive partner has incredible underground power. When a Plutonian pulls others out of their own orbit, subtly usurping

---

17 *Op. cit.* (Note 16).

their energy, they may become tyranny-prone, or increasingly manipulative, in order to maintain an illegitimate position. The outward reason for the break was that Leo dismissed her writing, labeling it "damned nonsense," and Gertrude brooked no criticism of herself or her creative process. His response to her writing "destroyed him for me, and it destroyed me for him." You can hear Pluto, in that word "destroy" and the absolute quality of her judgment.

But imagine how much power Leo's opinion must have held for her, that she needed to cut him out of her life so irrevocably. This splitting off of warring feelings or opinions then marked her relationships with others for the rest of her life. She was warm, generous, and funny, as long as she was held in an idealized position. When she wrote *The Autobiography of Alice B. Toklas,* she completely eliminated Leo from the story. As Alice later said: "She really had put him and the deep unhappiness he had caused her so completely out of her mind that finally he and it no longer existed." You can understand from this why Pluto is so often found, along with Scorpio energy, in families where people break off all contact completely, where they haven't seen each other or spoken for many years. Although Leo made an attempt to reconnect with his sister after the First World War, she never answered his letters. The silence between them lasted till their deaths—thirty-five years.

So she killed him off in her mind. Perhaps Pluto in the 3rd house is pushed to eliminate a brother or sister from the idea of self, to uproot their influence. Mysteriously enough, this placement sometimes describes fated events that change a sibling's life. I have witnessed how these disruptive events affect others. A man with Pluto in the 3rd, opposition Venus and square Mars, had his life rocked by the death of his brother-in-law in a plane crash. Within two years, his only brother became ill. It was early on, when AIDS was almost unknown, and the horror of the epidemic was just beginning to surface. How can we understand this kind of fate? His marriage ended not long after his brother died, as if the couple's purpose together had been about this shared experience of loss.

Pluto in the 3rd means that someone close to you, or in your environment, is likely to touch bottom, or even center themselves in areas in life that may seem frightening. In doing so, they open the door to the underworld, and you become aware of the presence of these issues much more acutely than other people. Gertrude Stein may have been disturbed by her brother's depressions, his constant self questioning, and needed to distance herself from that dangerous territory. And she accomplished more, published more than her brilliant brother. She went back to America on a literary tour and was "lionized." Pluto and Neptune seem easier to project onto a sibling, perhaps because they take much longer to assimilate, or perhaps they're simply too big *not* to project. Sometimes I will ask people with Neptune in the 3rd if they have a brother or sister who got lost for a while, metaphorically speaking, to drugs or alcohol.

Not of this world: Neptune and Chiron in the 3rd

AUDIENCE: I have Neptune there, and my sister ran away; she was literally lost for a time.

AUDIENCE: Could there be boundary issues with Neptune in the 3rd?

LYNN: Most likely, since Neptune here usually gives a porous structure to the psyche. But siblings might not even notice these blurred frontiers with Neptune. A brother or sister can be "too good for this world," too sensitive to survive or be understood by others. I always think of the sister in Tennessee Williams' play, *The Glass Menagerie*—she limps and is terribly fragile, and she delights in her collection of glass animals.

AUDIENCE: My youngest sister has had a long history of drug use. We keep trying to pull her out of it but she sinks back down every time. I have Neptune in the 3rd house.

AUDIENCE: What about Chiron in the 3rd?

LYNN: You probably work with Chiron more than I do. Let's see if anyone has this placement and might be able to give us clues. You do? Is there anything you can relate to, in terms of siblings?

AUDIENCE: I have a very difficult relationship with my brother. We barely speak to one another.

LYNN: There seems to be a wound around communication. Does that carry over into other relationships?

AUDIENCE: No. I have a lot of friends. I have the Moon in Sagittarius in the 2nd, so I am quite friendly.

LYNN: I know one woman whose 3rd house Chiron is in Pisces, so we have a Neptunian overlay, and her brother has had a history of problems with drugs, both as a small-time dealer and a user. He flipped out on LSD and had to be hospitalized for awhile; he couldn't get "back" on his own. He is what family therapists call the "identified patient," a technical term for the family scapegoat. This certainly fits with what we would expect to find symbolically. Although I'm still observing Chiron, when I look at my files and remember clients who have come with stories of the suffering and illness of a brother or sister, I have quite a number of cases with Chiron in the 3rd house. There seems to be a strong tendency for a sibling to carry the family wounding.

AUDIENCE: If you have more than one planet in the 3rd, which planet is which sibling?

LYNN: My first instinct would be to take the planets in order, or perhaps in pairs, if they are close together. But these kinds of attributions need to remain fluid, because they fundamentally describe an inner landscape. In the example we were looking at earlier, Marion had four 3rd house planets and only one sibling. We saw that her attitude towards her sister changed over time, and even went through certain phases described by those planets. As we go along in life, certain planets are activated by progression, and that might be one way to look at these internal and external shifts. Because sibling relationships are defined so early, at a time when we are psychically somewhat primitive, it can be more difficult to keep them flexible and alive. We could talk about this for a long time.

Jupiter in the 3rd house

AUDIENCE: And Jupiter in the 3rd?

LYNN: There is an idealization with Jupiter, as with Neptune, but without the fragility. This can be quite difficult if it's projected, because the best of you already belongs to someone else. I remember doing a workshop in the east of France and a participant shared the story of his brother, "the angel." A first child had died in infancy, and the parents kept pictures of him all over the house. The parents would say, "Your brother was so wonderful, and he is watching over us, looking down on you from heaven. Remember your brother He would do it like this." The perfect brother was always present, but no real contact or exchange could take place. So he had this sense that he could never be good enough, and this idealized brother became the source of a lot of suffering.

Does anybody here have a brilliant sibling who is good at everything? Yes? What do you have in the third? Nothing? What do you have on the cusp?

AUDIENCE: Aquarius. But my sister had Jupiter in the 3rd, and she thought I was brilliant. So we were actually both generous to each other.

LYNN: I like that notion of generosity for Jupiter in the 3rd. Sometimes you'll find a teaching relationship between siblings, an opening of doors and possibilities. We saw this between the two sisters, Marion and Anna. However, Jupiter likes the top of the heap, and can lord it over a sibling, even when benevolent. One man, an Aquarian with four planets in the 3rd, among them Venus, Jupiter, and Sun conjunct, had a brother older by seven years, and this brother was annoyingly talented at many things. Praised and gifted, he was the "creative" one, and the younger boy felt that he could never compete on the same level. A brilliant student, good in science, math, and music, he became a journalist and psychologist. Most of his friends were artists, and it was only in his late forties that he realized his talent for photography could match, and even surpass, his brother's more spontaneous gifts as an art director. The older brother was probably unaware of his role as an obstacle, since this scenario was mostly played out in the younger's imagination. Despite his doubt, those around him had long been convinced of his talent.

Sun in the 3rd house

AUDIENCE: Would the notion of creativity be linked to the Sun in the 3rd?

LYNN: Quite possibly. Remember the song, "You Are the Sunshine of My Life"? With Sun in the 3rd, a sibling may be radiant or brilliant, or simply intensely alive. But it is your Sun, and the Sun will always speak to a drive deep within oneself. In the 3rd, you are asked to bring the solar radiance into ideas, connections and words. If you can't do that, and you are dazzled by a sibling's virtuosity, that can be very, very difficult. Again, the best of you belongs to someone else, because you've given it away.

AUDIENCE: I know someone who's got Sun in the 3rd, and there is a loving relationship between the siblings. They go around together.

LYNN: Admiration and appreciation can be mutual when the Sun is in the 3rd house. A brother or sister may lead the way to who you really are, so the Sun's potential gift in this house is a revelation of your true nature in your earliest relationships. From the very beginning, you can be yourself. We all know brothers and sisters who prefer each other's company because no one else, even a husband or wife, knows them as well. If all goes well, the 3rd house Sun individual goes on to light up those around him or her, through openness and clarity of perception. But it can also stay contained within relationships of proximity, because it becomes impossible to find that ease outside your intimate circle.

If your brother or sister was your hero, they can cast a rather long shadow, so paradoxically, the Sun in the 3rd may never feel strong enough to fully emerge into the world. To understand the dynamic, you'll need to look at more than one chart. If one sibling has the Sun and the other Pluto, you'll know they're not experiencing these things in the same way. Or if you have Sun in the 3rd and your brother's Saturn falls right on it, you can feel squashed, stifled, compressed, and bound. But that doesn't mean the relationship is inauthentic. One can identify positively with a brother or sister, and find a reflection, an aspiration in the relationship. We must remember that the Sun needs challenge to emerge fully, and there may be more competition with this placement than we might initially expect.

Some families seem more linked than others. Their bonds are close and constant. Others hardly acknowledge their siblings, speak with them rarely, see them even less. Erin associated Uranus with emotional distance in families, and Neptune with exaggerated closeness, and most of us will fall somewhere in between this two extremes—moving closer, then apart, and then back together again.

BEYOND THE 3RD HOUSE: SYNASTRY BETWEEN SIBLINGS

It is important to point out that sibling relationships are much bigger than the 3rd house alone. I'd like to look briefly at two brothers who were intensely linked, and yet neither have planets in the 3rd house. In order to do this, I usually set up a bi-wheel, with one of the charts at the center and the planets of the other distributed around the outside of the first wheel. But it is also possible to set up a table listing the inter-chart aspects, and this may help you if you're not used to seeing things only visually.

Vincent and Theo

Let's put up the bi-wheel with the chart of Theo Van Gogh as the center. The second chart is Vincent's.

First, we immediately notice many conjunctions linking the two charts. Vincent's Sun and Venus fall very close to Theo's Ascendant. How would we interpret this?

AUDIENCE: I always learned that these were very warm contacts, bringing a sense of ease and well-being from the very beginning.

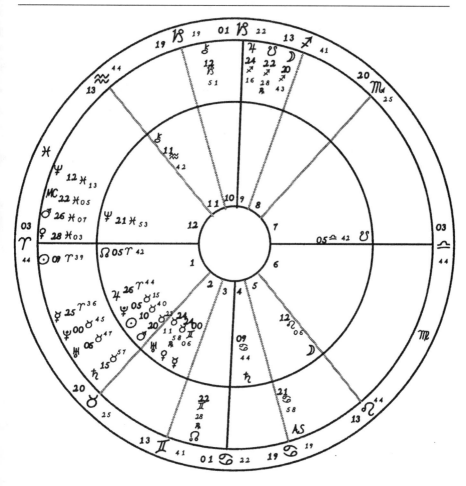

Center: Theo Van Gogh, 1 May 1857, 3:30 am LMT, Groot Zimdert, Holland
Perimeter: Vincent Van Gogh, 30 March 1853, 11:00 am, Groot Zundert, Holland

LYNN: That is very often the case, and it may have more weight here because Vincent's Sun is unaspected except for a square to Chiron. An unaspected planet has great difficulty finding its measure. It can be much too strong or much too weak. Theo's Ascendant then becomes a friendly place for Vincent's Sun. It connects directly with his brother's creative force, a force that is immense and yet unintegrated. Theo, like his brother, has a tight square between Sun and Chiron, which points to a wounding of the solar principle, some pain or difficulty in the unfolding of that inner life force. In Vincent's words:

Our inward thoughts, do they ever show outwardly? There may be a great fire in our soul, but no one ever comes to warm himself at it, and the passers-by see only a little bit of smoke coming through the chimney, and pass on their way. Now, look here, what must be done, must one tend that inward fire, have salt in oneself, wait patiently yet with how much impatience for the hour when somebody will come and sit down near it—to stay there, maybe?[18]

It was Theo who stayed closest to Vincent's inward fire. Interestingly enough, the Sun also rules Vincent's 3rd house, the house of siblings. Theo also has a Sun-Pluto conjunction, and we have seen that Pluto tends to high intensity, and strongly charged relationships in families.

The Sun-Chiron square in both brothers' charts no doubt points to their father's difficulty existing in the shadow of his own successful and intellectually brilliant father, a churchman, also named Vincent. Talking about the Van Gogh family gets very complicated because the names Vincent and Theo repeat. We'll have to make a genogram.

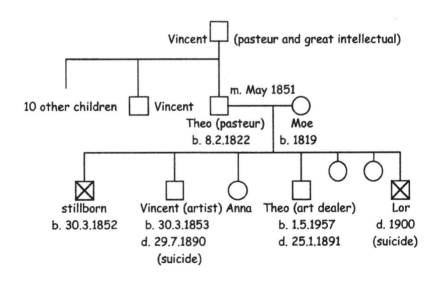

18 Mark Roskill, ed., *The Letters of Van Gogh*, Fontana/Collins, London, 1963.

One of the grandfather's younger sons, Theo, followed him into the church, but seems to have been something of a disappointment, relegated to a poor parish and forgotten. It was natural that he name his first son Vincent, and this child, a stillborn, was born exactly one year to the day before our Vincent, the painter. So Vincent began his troubled life with the same name and birth date of that dead child, cloaked in someone else's identity, trailing the death behind him. It's no wonder his solar energy lacks support in the chart.

Their father's brother, Uncle Vincent, was a successful art dealer, and both his nephews came to work for him at various times. There is already a pattern of success and relative failure between brothers in the father's generation. Uncle Vincent and their father Theo had married two sisters, so the Van Goghs qualify as a highly enmeshed family.

Let's put up the table of aspects made between the charts of the two brothers (see page 264). There are mutual Saturn-Sun contacts between Vincent's and Theo's charts. Vincent's Saturn falls on Theo's Sun-Mars conjunction, and Theo's Saturn exactly squares Vincent's Sun. This suggests some reworking of the father principle in their relationship. Although Vincent was always a source of worry and concern for his younger brother, and a heavy charge financially, it is not so much the difficulty of the relationship that is striking as the support and devotion of Theo, who provided the means for his brother's survival and creative expression. Saturn in Cancer is quite strong in Theo's chart, not far from the IC, in the 4th house and sextile his Sun -much more integrated than in Vincent's chart. Although it would seem that Theo sacrificed himself for his brother (his Neptune is on Vincent's MC), it may be that their destinies were inextricably linked, that they mysteriously kept each other alive, harnessed to a common purpose. Or did Vincent's fire consume Theo's substance? Vincent's breakdowns began soon after the news of Theo's engagement, accelerated when Theo's son Vincent was born, and Theo himself died almost six months to the day after his brother.

During a difficult period, Vincent wrote to Theo:

And men are often prevented by circumstances from doing things, imprisoned in I do not know what horrible, horrible, most hor-

	☉	☽	☿	♀	♂	♃	♄	♅	♆	♇	MC	AS	☊
☉	001 S ⚺ 01				000 A ∠ 27	001 S ⊓ 24	005 A ☌ 17	003 S ☌ 52	001 A ☌ 33	009 S ✶ 54			001 A ⋈ 47
☽	002 S △ 27	008 A △ 37		000 A ⚏ 56	000 S ⚏ 59		003 A □ 50	005 S □ 19	000 A ⊼ 06				001 A ✶ 46
☿	000 A ✶ 58			002 S ✶ 02	003 S ✶ 58				000 A ⚺ 39			000 A ✶ 55	
♀	000 A ∠ 19		000 S ⚺ 37	003 S ✶ 04	001 S ✶ 09	000 A ⊼ 42	009 A ☌ 01		000 A Q 45		002 ✶ 53	004 ✶ 22	
♂	000 S ⋈ 44	000 A ⊼ 21			005 A ✶ 43		004 S ☌ 26				001 ✶ 41	000 ✶ 12	
♃		005 S △ 59	001 S ☌ 08	001 S ⚺ 18	000 A ⚺ 37	002 A △ 28			000 A ∠ 28	004 A ☌ 01		006 □ 08	004 ✶ 16
♄	000 S □ 05							002 S ✶ 56	002 A △ 29				
♅	000 A ∠ 27		001 A ⚺ 24	003 A ✶ 51	001 A ✶ 56	000 A ⊼ 04	008 S ☌ 14		000 A Q 01	002 ✶ 06		003 ✶ 35	001 S ⚺ 43
♆		001 S □ 08		006 A ☌ 10	004 A ☌ 14	002 A □ 23	005 S ✶ 55	000 A ∠ 05	009 S ☌ 39	000 S ☌ 12	001 A △ 16	000 □ 35	
♇		000 A ⚏ 29	009 S ☌ 38	000 A ⋈ 52				001 A ☌ 32		004 S ☌ 29	001 ∠ 50		
MC	008 □ 16		005 △ 46	003 □ 19	005 □ 14	007 ☌ 06	000 ⚏ 25	005 △ 24		000 △ 36	009 □ 17		008 ⚼ 54
AS	006 ☌ 03			005 ☌ 32	007 ☌ 27	009 □ 19							
☊	003 S ☌ 57			007 A ☌ 38	009 A ☌ 34			000 S ⋈ 15	001 S ⚺ 05				

Table of synastry aspects
[Vincent's planets run across the top, Theo's down the side.]

rible cage...Do you know what frees one from this captivity? It is very deep, serious affection. Being friends, being brothers, love, that is what opens the prison by supreme power, by some magic force. But without this one remains in prison.[19]

How could Theo, with an exact Venus-Uranus conjunction in Taurus, resist such an appeal? Vincent goes on:

---

19 *Ibid.*, p. 126.

We are rather far apart, and we have perhaps different views on some things, but nevertheless there may come an hour, there may come a day, when we may be of service to one another.

If we look at the relationship with Vincent's chart at the center, we see that five of Theo's planets fall in Vincent's 11th house, a house which is linked to our potential. We will be speaking of these issues very shortly. A source of tremendous suffering for Vincent was the lack of friendship in his life. With Pluto, Uranus, and Saturn in the 11th house, he was too intense, too demanding for anyone to deal with him for very long. So Theo became that friend, that brother. Theo's

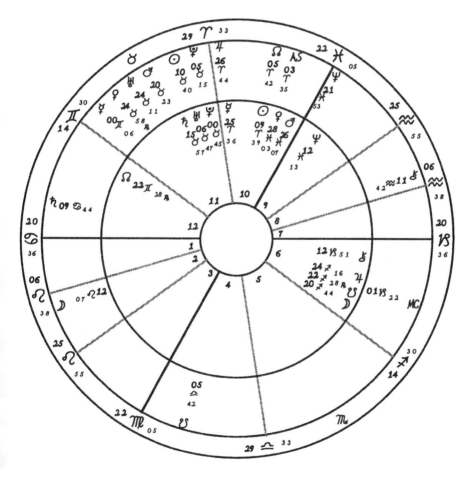

Center: Vincent Van Gogh Perimeter: Theo Van Gogh

Moon falls in Vincent's 2nd house of finances, and this worked out very literally. He was his brother's sole financial support for the last six years of his life. His Moon is also square Vincent's Saturn-Uranus conjunction. And Theo has Jupiter on Vincent's Mercury, often a sign of a teaching or helping relationship, and an aspect that points to their voluminous correspondence. It is worth noting that both brothers, whose lives were dedicated to painting, have a very powerful Venus. Vincent's is exalted in Pisces with Mars on the MC, and Theo's is in rulership in Taurus.

There is much more to say—the misfit complementarity between Theo's earth emphasis and Vincent's fire, the similarity in chart structures, with many planets massed in a few signs, the differences in house emphasis, nodal connections. Once again, there is very little air in the two charts, as we have seen in other fusion-oriented relationships between siblings. But I would like to move on to the 11th house before we use up all our time.

As you can see, sibling relationships, like any relationship, can't be limited to a single house, even if the 3rd house provides clues to their nature. What I would like you to retain is this notion of how our very first interactions with others affect our way of seeing the world and emerging into adult relationships. A difficult early connection with a sibling may propel us into the 11th house, and that could end up being more appropriate for our life's work. Take a moment to think about whether you enter into contact with others through your 3rd house, your 7th, or your 11th, and reflect on which is more comfortable for you and which is more difficult.

THE 11TH HOUSE

Can any of you imagine living without friendship? It seems such a fundamental part of our lives, and yet you will find almost no reference to it in the psychological literature. It's fascinating to think of friendship as somehow outside the psychological landscape. But then, where does it belong? Any ideas?

Freedom and choice

AUDIENCE: Freedom and choice play an important role in choosing friends. Friendship isn't conditioned by the past, is it?

LYNN: Not usually. In many ways, psychology concerns itself with our conditioning, addressing both the innate nature of the mind and the emergence of individual personality—how and why we become who we are. However, the meaning of the word psyche is soul, and friendship is surely the soul's concern. The library places works on friendship in children's literature, philosophy, and ethics. Friendship concerns the choices we make about our lives, what kind of human being we wish to be, and what we value most. Most of you know that philosophy means "the love of wisdom," from *sophia*—wisdom and *philia*—love. The Greeks spoke of three kinds of love: *eros*, *philia*, and *agape*. *Eros* is a piercing, irresistible desire for the beloved that both uplifts and shatters an individual, while *agape* is "the love of god for man"—what we might call unconditional love. *Philia* lies somewhere in between these two, both less hot and less cool.

Certain key ideas belong to the 11th house: friendships and groups; hopes and wishes. We don't really speak of hopes and wishes much any more, probably because our society favors decisions of the will over wishing, and many books have eliminated this, or changed it to something more tonic, like "projects and goals." It seems to me we may have lost something there, and I'd like to take this up later.

As we said, friendships are freely chosen. Unless our life is extremely circumscribed, they emerge out of an open terrain. We step into unknown territory, even if, in the beginning, that may be the school selected by our parents, in a town where people are more or less culturally similar. In making our first connections, we step away from our families towards a zone of what Goethe called "elective affinities." Perhaps some of these early relationships can last a lifetime, though many of them have more to do with proximity than real choice. At what age do most of us make our first friends? And at what age do friends enter our lives "for keeps"? A friendship with the boy or girl next door may have more to do with the 3rd house than the 11th.

When I ask people about this, many remember very early childhood friends, age four or five. Later, a different kind of friendship forms, around nine, ten, twelve.

AUDIENCE: My first important friendship was around eleven or twelve. That's the Jupiter return isn't it? Until then my family moved around a lot, and friendships were broken.

LYNN: Yes, that makes a certain sense. At the first Jupiter return we step out of the first circle of family into a second transitional twelve-year period on the way to adulthood. It probably signals a readiness for another dimension in friendship, especially because the approach of adolescence will bring so much confusion. Our identity changes so fast that we need people who can give us information about who we might be growing into. Cervantes said, "Tell me what company thou keepest and I'll tell thee what thou art." Early on, our friends may help us grope towards this sense of who we are, or represent choices about which direction to take. And as we said earlier, Jupiter has its joy in the 11th, perhaps because of the openness they share in common.

How many people here are closer to their friends than their siblings? I see it's the vast majority. That in itself is interesting, don't you think?

The 11th/4th house quincunx

Astrology attracts people who need to step away from a conventional path, so we may be a group with a built-in bias towards the 11th house. Very few of us had parents who were astrologers. Our passion generally moves us away from our families, occasionally creating waves of shock and protest. I like to think about this in terms of the quincunx relationship of other houses to the 4th house. There are two of them: the first with the 9th house, which has to do with moving beyond the explanations and pictures of the world that were transmitted by your tribe. You may physically leave or acquire beliefs and knowledge that mark you as somehow different. You then become a teacher, if things go well, or a contaminant and a threat if your home circle feels endangered. I sometimes imagine life in a small town several centuries ago, and the way people would respond when a young man came back from university or a voyage to foreign parts. Would he be greeted with suspicion, or curiosity?

In the 11th house we step out of a small, protected circle into a relationship with the world at large. As the second, transformational quincunx to the 4th house, it can bring a profound change in our relationship to the tribe. We align ourselves with outsiders, and this becomes a kind of caricature in adolescence when we dump our families in favor of our friends. Many cultures still favor blood ties, and remain suspicious of strangers—one reason why relations with in-laws are treated with elaborate ritual and caution. Choosing a friend, especially one not bound to us by self-interest, requires a certain courage, and a belief in humanity. We could say that the 11th house helps us let go of the past, to step out from our need for security. Relationships formed here require trust, and in trusting others we trust to our own future, our becoming.

The *OED* defines "friend" as "one joined to another in mutual benevolence and intimacy." Do you think that's overly optimistic?

AUDIENCE: It sounds like Neptune in the 11th!

LYNN: There are other definitions: "One who wishes another well. A sympathizer, a favorer, a patron, a helper or a supporter." You can see why the 11th has a political side, since it has to do with how we link to other human beings, both individually and collectively. As students of the CPA, you are part of an 11th house group, even if that group exists around the 9th/3rd house axis of teaching and learning.

Strangers: the 8th house

If the friend is found in the 11th, where would you put the stranger in the chart?

AUDIENCE: The 8th.

AUDIENCE: The 12th house, because of its link with the unknown.

AUDIENCE: The 9th house rules things that are unfamiliar.

AUDIENCE: Wait a minute! To me, being a foreigner is very familiar!

LYNN: In French, the word for "stranger" and "foreigner" is the same — *l'etranger*. That could argue for the 9th, although linguistically the French call this a *faux ami*![20] The 12th has more to do with our own unconscious, or our response to the collective. I would choose the 8th house, since it concerns areas of intimate exchange with others, and touches on the mysteries of life. The 8th is a relationship house, after all, very much concerned with issues of trust and betrayal. I asked about the stranger because I'm really curious to know how we recognize that someone is a friend. Most friends begin as strangers, after all. How do we choose the other? Why do we seek out a particular person, and what is the basis for our choosing?

AUDIENCE: I suppose you look for reflections of what you happen to perceive in yourself—mirrors, and sometimes masks.

LYNN: Friends will reflect something of you back to yourself, but is it only that? Aren't we also attracted to those who are different from us?

AUDIENCE: It is easier to see yourself in relationship to other people.

The 11th house: Uranus or Saturn?

LYNN: Ah, so you are looking for something you haven't seen in yourself yet. The whole question of the 11th house turns around what you believe to be possible in your relationships with other people. Clearly, this will be affected by the way they see you. I'm sure all of us have had the experience of being with someone who sees us as stupid, incompetent, or clumsy, and find ourselves becoming mysteriously dumber, helpless, or a threat to fragile objects in response. That is not to say that

---

20 *A faux ami* is literally a "false friend"—a word that looks familiar but has an entirely different meaning from the word you know in your own language.

---

friends will see only wonderful things in you, but, at least initially, they tend to warm to your better qualities.

I interviewed some people to prepare this seminar, and I wanted to look at the role culture plays. So many of you here come from other countries, and while I don't know all of the different cultural models, I do know that the whole idea of the friend in France requires time, and time is Saturn. They say with disdain that, in America, you can become an instant friend, fast food, fast friends.

AUDIENCE: But that is really possible as well.

LYNN: For some of us, it is. You might think of it as the Uranus versus Saturn approach to friendship, after the two rulers of Aquarius. Americans lower their boundaries with each other much faster than Europeans, and that is also true of those who have lived in the States and become more Americanized. In France you have to go through a series of rituals, like a boat going through the locks. You go through the first step and then you wait, and see if everything is safe. You get through the next step, and then you wait again. Once you get admitted into the inner sanctum of friendship with a French person, you are expected to stick around. It is very rare that friendship just happens.

AUDIENCE: It is much easier in England. You just have to wait for three hundred years.

LYNN: Where are you from?

AUDIENCE: Switzerland.

LYNN: I am sure they are very speedy aren't they? All this is to say that friendship has a cultural context, an external reference system, and so it includes ideas about human nature: can we trust another not to betray us? Is everyone "out for himself/herself?" Cultures that take their time about friendship may be harboring long memories, collective reasons for caution. Thomas Hobbes, the 17th century philosopher, saw human life as "nasty, short, and brutish"; for him, everyone acted out of self-interest, and friendship, like politics, sprang from self-preservation. I found an interesting quote in French: "*Est-ce que l'homme est un loup ou un dieu pour l'homme?*" Is man a wolf or a god for other men? Humanity as a wolf is the 8th house, the devouring, ravaging stranger, capable of raping, pillaging, burning. The fear that another might despoil you, destroy you, or do you harm lies close enough to the surface for most of us. And this danger is a reality in human relationships. We have only to watch the news or read the press for a few weeks to find the ravager in Rwanda, or Kosovo, or a small American Midwestern town where a teenager has just shot his schoolmates.

If you have an 8th house planet that makes a square to one in the 11th, the question, "Can I trust other people to really be my friend?" will have a lot of power. It will cross your mind more frequently than for other people. This fear, which may be grounded in reality, can interfere with your ability to believe in other people.

Pluto in the 11th house

AUDIENCE: Could that be true of Pluto in the 11th? I know someone who has Pluto in the 11th and has fallen in with a bad crowd.

LYNN: Pluto will often activate issues around the shadow. In French, there is an expression, "*Entre chien et loup*," literally, "between the dog and the wolf," a poetic way of talking about dusk, or twilight. Each day, after sunset, when things shift from light to dark, it becomes difficult to distinguish dog from wolf, and this shadowy time has a psychological correspondence with the underworld, Pluto's realm. How do we know if someone near to us is a loyal dog or an untrustworthy wolf? We can never absolutely penetrate the heart of another person, and this zone of doubt most probably lies in the 8th house. 12th house doubt tends to target the self, although it can include almost anything, being global and formless.

Because of Pluto's tendency to reach beyond the individual, there can be anxiety around groups, mass gatherings, or a particular class in society. This could manifest as the "them" of paranoid discourse. The

11th has a collective dimension, and I've seen Pluto in the 11th in the charts of both anti-racist campaigners and Nazis alike. Jackie Robinson, who broke through the color barrier in sport, had Jupiter conjunct Pluto in the 11th. He was often turned away from hotels, slandered, refused service, yet he held true and initiated a change in society, in group consciousness. The 11th house has to do with the world we are bringing into being, both collectively and individually, and planets there tell us how we may affect this process. This sense of future or potential is extremely fundamental to the 11th house.

The 11th house and the future

Would anyone here like to talk about the difference between the future described by the MC and the 10th house, and the future described by the 11th house? Have you thought about this?

AUDIENCE: I would say the 10th house has more to do with status, with your place in society, while the 11th house is much wider.

AUDIENCE: In the 10th house you become president of the company, and in the 11th you start doing charity work.

LYNN: That describes the traditional social function of the 11th pretty well, but the 11th house is even more inclusive than that. We may set a goal and reach it in the 10th house, but the 11th represents "not yet fulfilled potential."

AUDIENCE: Capricorn is more structured than Aquarius's vision.

AUDIENCE: The 10th feels much more personal, more immediate. The 11th is about the collective.

LYNN: That's true. We could say that it's not just your unfulfilled potential, but that of society as well. How might that be connected to friendship?

AUDIENCE: I get the idea of a seed for the future. The charity would help things grow. The 10th is where you achieve something personal, and then, in the 11th, you try something new. You plant a tree.

LYNN: Like planting a tree when you are seventy years old?

AUDIENCE: After you die, people you have never met will come and appreciate it; others will water it.

AUDIENCE: Maybe it is about growing things. With friends, you grow. Capricorn is more structured, but when you include another person, you have to be aware of more. It's a two-way exchange.

LYNN: The vertical arrow that we put on the MC is always pointing somewhere. We can see it as the path our life follows; as long as we are alive, it carries direction and intention. We move along the path of the MC, but it is largely an individual path, connected to purpose and accomplishment. For some of us, that will automatically include other people, or big world events, but the focus in the 10th is on the role we play. Once you have accomplished something, whatever it may be, the 11th house is the next step.

Sun in the 11th house

AUDIENCE: Would it be the next step that you can't take as an individual or through a pre-established structure, a next step you have to take with a group of people?

LYNN: That sounds very Aquarian!

AUDIENCE: I am a Cancer with Sun in the 11th.

LYNN: It's great to hear you put it into words, to hear your Sun in the 11th house speaking. There's an innate sense of connectedness to other people. With the Sun placed here, one's identity comes through being part of something larger, through the ability to link with others, to feel the spark passing from one person to another, to participate in something that brings a whole group along with it. I have known 11th house Suns who do this mostly socially—they're out at the clubs, gossiping and partying, and yet they're still creating links, seeking a certain solidarity. But many 11th house Suns do what the books tell us. They find themselves joined to others in some humanitarian aim.

AUDIENCE: If a goal cannot be accomplished by an individual alone, or within a structured organization, it will have to be done in a mutually supportive group of friendship.

LYNN: Friendship can happen through a group, but not necessarily Remember, we speak of "a friendship."

AUDIENCE: But we say, "a group of friends."

LYNN: This is an interesting dialogue. We're tapping into the individual/collective nature of the 11th house, and both are clearly present. We may join groups and form friendships for similar reasons, but the dynamic is slightly different. Most of us have more than one friend, and these friends are not necessarily friendly with each other. We'll talk more about the larger dimension of the 11th house a little later.

The ruler of the 11th house in the 8th house

Since Uranus and Saturn share rulership of Aquarius, one way of looking at friendship is to explore these two planetary models. Some friendships happen almost instantaneously, and others develop slowly over time. But even the fast-forming ones need time to take root in your life. Saturn's co-rulership of the sign tells us that friendships are not absolutely free. There are certain principles, certain requirements involved, but these are rarely consciously elaborated. How do we know when someone will be a friend? How do we choose?

AUDIENCE: I have Taurus on the 11th, and Venus, the ruler, is in the 8th in Aquarius. For me, a friend is somebody with whom I feel there is both love and power. The issue of domination or fearfulness doesn't enter into it—simply two people sharing power.

LYNN: So the 8th house issue of power defines friendship for you, perhaps because it is part of your consciousness, something you're working on. You're not looking for complementarity, tenderness, or compassion, but for equal strength. Confucius said, "Have no friends not equal to yourself." How do we know when someone has this kind of parity, an equivalence in whatever quality we hold precious?

Any other examples?

AUDIENCE: I have Sun-Venus-Saturn in the 8th, squaring Neptune in the 11th, and Venus rules the 11th house. Boundaries are very difficult.

LYNN: Yes, I can imagine. You save your friends and pay their rent and help them out. Then, when you feel it is too much, you say, "That's it."

AUDIENCE: Yes, variations on that.

Neptune in the 11th house

LYNN: Neptune in the 11th seeks to find something limitless and infinite in another, so even without 8th house squares, boundary issues can rise up. The 11th house moves us into a new field of experience, and it may feel too big for us in the beginning. If we stay in the familiar territory of the 3rd, things remain more predictable, even when they're difficult. When you step out into the 11th, anything can happen. Planets there get activated, whatever their nature, as you move out into the world, into the unknown. The 11th house represents an alternative way of connecting to other people. When the 3rd house contains pleasant planets, you will most likely be drawn to what you already know, to those who have come from a similar place and experience. Planets like Saturn, Pluto, or Mars in the 3rd may automatically make the 11th look more attractive, but difficult planets in the 11th could keep us closer to home, too.

AUDIENCE: How do you know how to choose your friends?

LYNN: Do we really choose our friends, or do we find them? There seems to be something solar about friendship, which has to do with recognition of one's true nature. Usually, we worry less than in the 5th house about whether love is returned; the relationship is more spacious. Since the 3rd and 11th houses are trine in principle, there should be a flow or continuity between them, but friendships are really quite dissimilar from sibling relationships because of the element of choice. And in certain house systems, planets in the 3rd can even square the 11th.

AUDIENCE: With brothers, you can easily fall into a certain pattern. It's hard to be yourself. But with friends, your individuality has to come out, even if it's a struggle. I often feel friction at first, with someone who later becomes a friend. Confronting reality and facing the truth are fundamental in friendship, even if you have to fight to be accepted.

LYNN: Notice the words "struggle," "truth," "reality"—they express your 11th house Uranus quite well. You have to struggle to be yourself with others, and this colors your sense of what is possible with other people. If it were Pluto here, you might feel overpowered by others. At its harshest, no one can be trusted. The planet you have in the 11th is the attitude you have to what it is to be a human being—not just who you are, but who they are, who we are.

AUDIENCE: I find that relationships are always changing. There's a whole variety. There are the people I go towards, and the people who come towards me. Some are very good friends who are fabulously loyal and supportive, even if they are boring; they have got a quality of gentleness which is wonderful.

LYNN: You have Libra on the cusp, and Venus in the 3rd, which may explain your need for variety and movement. The 3rd house doesn't like boredom. I'm struck by your description of your kind, supportive friends as boring. Perhaps we can assimilate them to the Saturn-style friend—they function as a kind of scaffolding or support system. Uranus would then favor friendships that help you break loose and contact an inner freedom, and hopefully to be who you really are. It sounds as though you are still exploring yourself through all your different kinds of friendship.

Aristotle speaks of three different kinds of friendship: the good, the pleasurable, and the useful. He asks whether "like attracts like" or whether opposites attract, quoting a saying, "The parched earth longs for rain." He says that we need to study friendship, since it seems to be an auxiliary for happiness.

It's fascinating that people can spend hours and weeks and years in therapy, talking about their parents or lovers, but they don't talk about their friends unless something is wrong. You don't generally go around declaring your undying love for your friends. Isn't it interesting that there is something in all of our lives that we don't want to get too close to? I'm still looking for the link between friendship and the future. Do you have any thoughts?

AUDIENCE: You spoke of the wolf, the destroyer, as the square to the 11th house from the 8th. But where would the God part of the quotation fit in? Didn't you say the 9th was the house of God?

THE *BONUS DAIMON*

LYNN: One of the things that stimulated my thinking for this seminar was the connection, in the older texts, between the 11th house and the *bonus daimon*, and the 12th house and the *malus daimon*. This is really the heart of what I want to look at today. Have any of you run across this? In some texts they are referred to as the good angel and the dark angel, which conjures up cartoon devils and angels fighting it out on your shoulders—temptation and conscience. But the *daimon* carries a great deal more that this.

Daimon and destiny

I had already been working on this idea when I arrived in London this weekend, and somebody thrust James Hillman's new book, *The Soul's Code*, into my hand. As it turns out, this book is all about the *daimon* and one's calling—one of those thrilling coincidences that happens, sometimes, when ideas are working their way into consciousness. Then, in front of the library at Swiss Cottage, I found a new, bargain-priced paperback copy of the book, even though it hadn't yet been released in paperback in the stores. In it, Hillman says:

> The soul of each of us is given a unique *daimon* before we are born, and it has selected an image or pattern that we live on earth. This soul companion, the *daimon,* guides us here in the process of arrival. However, we forget all that took place, and believe we come empty into this world. The *daimon* remembers what is in your image and belongs to your pattern, and therefore the *daimon* is the carrier of your destiny.[21]

This is very heady stuff. In the astrological model, we associate destiny with the 10th house, so my question has to do with why the ancients would place the *daimon* in the 11th.

AUDIENCE: Is this the Saturn side of Aquarius?

LYNN: In the sense that it carries a pattern, yes. But remember that, even though we have been speaking about the rulers of Aquarius and their connection to friendship, the Greeks wouldn't have been thinking in this way. The ancient astrologers didn't necessarily connect the houses to the signs in the way we do. That's a modern approach, helpful in the beginning, but it may blur your thinking in the long run. The 11th house and Aquarius have a great deal in common, but its also useful to see where they are dissimilar.

Interestingly enough, the ancients believed that everyone was assigned a *daimon,* but you could have one that was good, bad, or

21 James Hillman, *The Soul's Code*, Bantam Books, London, 1997.

indifferent. You didn't necessarily get one that was helpful, and to some extent the quality of your life depended on the kind of *daimon* you got. Remember *It's A Wonderful Life,* the Frank Capra film where Jimmy Stewart plays a man in deep inner turmoil, on the verge of suicide, who is assigned a guardian angel who hasn't yet got his wings? He got an immature *daimon,* who makes a number of mistakes before he figures out how to turn him around. A difficult *daimon* can plunge you into suffering and difficulty, and connect you to your purpose through struggle and error. This is how I would understand the *malus daimon,* or the 12th house. Even something that seems to be terrible can lead you to a connection with your fate. You can't necessarily judge an event off the top.

The word for happiness, in Greek, is *eudaimonia daimon* with *eu* (meaning "well" or "good") in front of it. Think of "euphoria." Your capacity for happiness was determined by the kind of *daimon* you ended up with. If you got a good one, you were in luck. *Webster's Dictionary* translates *daimon* as "attendant spirit." The guardian angel of Christianity carries an echo of the *daimon* in a more sugary form. It's hard to imagine your angel getting you into trouble, but the *daimon* isn't necessarily nice. It would be interesting to do a whole seminar on these attendant spirits, good and bad, and their implications for the understanding of fate in our lives. Hillman cites Plato and the myth of Er. Where once you have chosen your lot or fate in life, Lachesis the Measurer, one of the three Moirae, presents you to your *daimon.* The *daimon* then accompanies you to the other Fates, who weave the pattern and fix your destiny. The *daimon* remembers what you are supposed to do and who you are supposed to become.

All this was running through my mind as I watched *Wilde,* the film about Oscar Wilde. The film shows his obsession with a lover, a relationship that eventually shatters his reputation and his health, and leads him to jail, exile, and destruction. Wilde had the Moon in Leo in the 11th, exactly square Uranus, perhaps the carrier of his brilliant success, and he had many influential, well-disposed friends. The Moon in Leo would certainly describe a flashy attendant spirit, a generous muse. We would see his neglect of his wife, and his headlong fall into an unsuitable and disastrous love affair, as a reflection of Neptune conjunct the 7th house cusp in Pisces, square a 10th house Saturn. The 12th house is empty, but ruled by the Sun, connected to that Moon in Leo through rulership. Wilde had a dramatic *daimon* for both good and bad.

AUDIENCE: So the *daimon* is connected to the soul purpose—you carry it with you from birth onwards, into the future, the 11th house.

LYNN: Yes. In this model, someone or something helps you along the path. The good *daimon* functions like a spiritual friend, and its attention is on your purpose.

AUDIENCE: Why don't we know about this idea?

LYNN: A great deal of the astrological tradition was lost between the fall of the Roman empire and the re-transmission of these ideas from Islamic culture. The *daimon* is also a pagan concept, not entirely welcome in the overwhelmingly Christian world-view of medieval Europe, where Christ is our direct link to God. Fooling around with spirits and genies conjures up the doubtful environment of magic and witchcraft. People still believed in them, but they probably faded into the fringes of collective consciousness.

On another level, the Greeks believed we forgot ourselves and all that came before, at the moment of birth. The *daimon's* purpose is to remind us of what we are meant for. The Romans spoke of the *genius,* the tutelary spirit who accompanies us at the moment of birth. The emperor would have a special altar, and give prayers and offerings to his *genius.* It was only in the 17th century that the word "genius" would begin to be applied to a person and his abilities, reflecting our increasing separation from this world of gods and spirits, as well as the growing sense that we alone are responsible for what we accomplish. I suppose we could think of the *daimon* as a guide, but it isn't quite that. The 9th house normally signifies our teachers and guides, but it's more concerned with understanding; the *daimon* really belongs to a separate category.

AUDIENCE: Does this mean it picks your friends for you, and you don't know why it has?

LYNN: I suspect that friends and the *daimon* may be playing the same role.

AUDIENCE: Maybe it's because I have Aquarius on the 11th, but it seems to me that friends are part of inventing yourself. You learn to be better, you learn with new friends, you choose your new life. I am talking with my Venus-Saturn. I learn something of value through these outside connections

LYNN: Each person looks for certain specific things in friendship. Some have many, many friends, all quite different from each other; others have only one or two close friends. I asked a friend of mine, a Gemini with an 11th house Sun, "What would it feel like for you if you only had one friend?" "Oh, I would feel as though I were on very shaky ground," she answered, adding, "What I really like in my relationships with my friends is the contrast I feel with them." With Sun in the 11th, she defines herself, learns about herself, through comparing how she feels with each one. She will get a different piece of herself from each person she meets and becomes close to, and this is perhaps accentuated by the Gemini tendency to fragment into many selves.

AUDIENCE: I found that my friends helped me to become myself. Friends are more supportive than family or lovers. They helped me to see my essence and find my creativity.

Friends as daimons

LYNN: We have been slowly working our way to an idea about friendship, beyond the Hallmark greeting card sentimentality that it is somehow connected to the seed of potential inside each of us. Human beings can act towards each other as wolf or *daimon*, destroyer of our wellbeing or midwife to our essence. In friendship, we approach the side of the angels or the demi-gods, and this was literally enacted by the Romans, who would raise a benefactor to the status of divinity after his death. I have been liberally drawing from a text in French by Jacqueline Lagrée, where she explores classical thinking about this division in man between bestial and divine. There is a saying in Ancient Greek, *anthropos anthropou daimonion*, meaning, man is a demi-god for man. Literally, one man is another's *daimon*. Here we have the 11th house link between friendship and the *daimon*: in small, subtle ways or through direct material assistance, a friend brings something out in you, helps you to move closer to your essence and purpose. Friends are those who connect you to the *daimon*, who do the *daimon's* work. Do we really choose our friends? Or do we somehow recognize something in them, an indefinable quality that we would be hard put to describe even after many years? A vibrant friendship connects you to your aliveness, it reconnects you to your hope, even when that hope is unformulated or unknown. Hopes and wishes: remember those initial attributes of the 11th house. In the Mexican film, *Like Water for Chocolate*, the narrator speaks of the small flame that burns inside each of us, and how these flames can be lit by those we encounter. Don't you hear echoes of the Promethean fire?

For the animistic mind, one that sees the world as full of spirit, as ensouled, the friend may be harboring the divinity. Or to paraphrase Elvis, be a *"daimon* in disguise." Somehow, our friends connect us to this 11th house future—what we are supposed to be doing, not where we have been and what we have done, but what is next, and still to be accomplished. Orson Welles once told of a dream where he came upon a cemetery. As he wandered through the graves, he noticed something strange. All the dates showed an extremely short lapse of time between birth and death—1822–1826, 1930–1934. In the middle of the graveyard he came across a very old man, and asked him how it was that he could live so long in a village where all the others had died so young. The old man answered, "It's not that we die young. Here, in this cemetery, we don't count the years of a man's life, but those during which he kept a friend."

Endings and beginnings

Many of us have had the painful experience of friendships dying. Some just fade away, and others degenerate into unsatisfying or conflicting relations. Often enough, clients have come and recounted a massive shift in their relationships, from having many friends to a time when they see almost no one. How can we understand this kind of major life change?

AUDIENCE: There are times in life when you need to stand on your own, rather than look to someone else to do things for you.

AUDIENCE: Doesn't it depend on whether both people are growing, and growing in a similar way at the same time? If you grow and they don't, then it falls apart. But if both people are committed to growth, the friendship can stay alive.

AUDIENCE: It also sounds as if you're saying that, in a time of major life change, when a person's goals and direction change, his or her friends may fall away because they were linked with the old direction.

LYNN: Like any relationship, a friendship contains its share of projection and self interest. It would be rather naive and self-serving to assume that a friendship ends simply because someone is no longer on the same path. But this can be part of the reason for separation between friends, and they may even reconnect later when their lives draw close again. Once a friendship belongs strictly to the past, it ceases to carry its 11th house function of future unfolding, and it becomes more difficult to keep it alive.

Not all friendships have equal weight in our lives. From hanging out and having fun, to those with whom there is a deep and lasting soul connection, we find a hierarchy of sorts, circles that increase in intimacy and decrease in number as they move to the center. The *daimon* sends those that are closest, or who do its work.

AUDIENCE: I don't believe this literally.

LYNN: We're using a story, an explanation from classical thinking, to help understand what links us to other human beings. Run with the metaphor; ask yourself if you have something like Saturn in the 11th, and what that will mean in terms of the idea of the *daimon*. You said earlier, "Friends have similar values and they are moving towards a similar future," but that is not necessarily true for everyone.

I know a woman who has created a welcoming place in the heart of Paris, a tea room where people love to come. With Saturn in Cancer in the 11th, she feels she doesn't really know how to receive love, even though she knows how to give. She has Moon in the 5th, opposing Saturn. Her life has often been out of control, especially financially, and her business was turned around by an employee and friend, who came in and played Saturn, helping her create order out of the chaos. She feels totally disconnected to rules and deadlines, payment schedules and laws, and yet she has created something enduring which serves a whole community, and she has many friends.

In fact, the business was begun initially by three friends, but she is now sole owner. As a child, she says, her primary goal was to control other people, to get them to do what she wanted. There is a great deal of rather paradoxical information about Saturn here. On the one hand, she enjoys control and is probably good at it, but on the other, she's created a situation in which controlling is impossible for her. Her Saturn is activated when she's involved with other people, but she doesn't feel it belongs to her.

AUDIENCE: So the *daimon* brings her people who help her get structured, but getting structured is really what she needs to learn?

LYNN: That's part of it. Since the 11th carries both your potential and something you encounter outside yourself through others, it may take time before you recognize it as your own. It may be projected. But if all your friends play the same role for you, you may need to look at whether they aren't pointing to something you need to develop in yourself.

Friends often surprise us. One woman I spoke to has friends who have been in her life for over thirty years. She said, "Well, somehow, and I have no idea how this happened, almost all of them now prac-tice Zen—totally independently, and different kinds. In the beginning, none of them did." In this one particular, her friends have all ended up on a similar path, as if an invisible pattern existed all along. Imagine my surprise when a friend of long date, someone with his feet firmly planted in a very down-to-earth world of dollars and cents, a high level businessman, suddenly turned his interest towards astrology and ended up becoming a professional. It may be that we are drawn to people who are living out something that we carry within us in embryonic form. A friend contains an aspiration.

AUDIENCE: Is that mutual?

LYNN: Yes, it seems to me that mutuality is a fundamental part of friendship, even if one individual may play a particular role more fre-quently.

Perhaps there is a kind of pattern recognition when we meet a friend. Without even being aware of it, we "see" something in the other that corresponds to our own pattern. Have you noticed how the 11th house or Uranus is strong in the charts of engineers? They have an ability to see something and create a plan which will bring a bridge, an engine, a microchip into being. They "see" the thing before it comes into physi-cal manifestation, and they find a way to build it, drawing up plans and specifications. Visionaries and futurists imagine the seed of the present growing into the future, and though the 9th house holds meaning and connects us to an ideal, the 11th holds the pattern. I remember reading Rudolf Steiner many years ago. He writes about looking at an acorn and trying to see the oak tree inside it; we know it contains the potential to become an oak, but this is not at all obvious from its physical appear-ance. Hillman takes up this acorn metaphor for the *daimon*.

Think of Aquarius as fixed air. The idea is fixed, held into place, something like the unveiling of DNA, the coding underlying our physi-cal form. It's fascinating that, since the conjunction of Neptune and Uranus in Capricorn, this form behind the form is being revealed. Now that both planets are in Aquarius, we are engineering new life, creating new seeds, and there is an immense collective responsibility involved. Here is another idea: "When mortals do good, they imitate the gods." At the market I go to in Paris, Friday is the day for the Moslem beggars, the turbaned blind men who call out in Arabic. If you give them a coin, they will call down a blessing on you, for in the Islamic tradition, alms-giving moves you closer to God. Here is an echo of Jupiter, which has its joy in the 11th house. For the Egyptians, even the harvest or animals were gods, because they assisted the life of mankind. A cat was a god because it got rid of the mice and protected the harvest; the wheat was a god because it was a divine source of nourishment. They were per-haps minor gods, but gods nonetheless. It can be hard to get you mind around these ideas, because we're not used to conceiving of the world in this way Whatever was good or beneficial had its source in the divine. Seneca said, "Any man, slave or free, poor or rich, wise or unwise, has through good will the possibility to help another to be virtuous, to find happiness, to imitate the gods." In other words, anyone can play the role of the *bonus daimon* in the life of another. Admittedly, benefactors and friends are not exactly the same, and there is a great deal of discus-sion in Aristotle and other classical writers on whether friendship is based on self-interest or is a good in itself.

One way of thinking about this is that an 11th house planet only expresses itself fully when it is connected to the group in some way, or used for something bigger. If you have difficult planets in the 11th house, you may not believe that other people can help you. In some cases this can mean that people protect themselves from the outside world, from those that are not part of the inner circle. Frequently enough, I've seen 11th and 4th house tensions when someone comes from an ethnic group that has drawn a cordon around itself, living apart from the larger soci-ety. These wider issues of identity also belong to the 11th house—how we fit in society, how we fit into a particular group, even an idea of how the world should be. And yet all of these are an extension of friendship, which moves from the personal level to affect the world at large. "What might be possible in my relationships with someone with whom I have no reason to be connected?" Here in this room, we all share an interest in astrology, and that can be a basis for friendship, because generally there is a shared terrain between friends. But it isn't friendship. Is that clear? If we are able to connect with others in an 11th house way, we can affect the world differently.

AUDIENCE: Surely this is 7th house? I'm feeling a bit confused about the boundaries between the two.

LYNN: Didn't you say you had a relationship between planets in the 3rd and 7th? There may be more mix between those, perhaps, than for other people. Are there other people who have this confusion, who see this as 7th house?

AUDIENCE: Not necessarily confusion. There has got to be an overlap, because they are the three airy houses. Friends can become lovers. The 7th house reflects something back to us too.

Once in three hundred years

LYNN: I've brought some citations from Montaigne, a famous French essayist and humanist philosopher of the Renaissance, and these might help us get more clarity about these different kinds of relationships. He wrote one of the most celebrated essays on friendship, and describes the different kinds of love, between father and child, between brothers, lovers, and friends. In very beautiful French, he describes love between a man and a woman as "...*plus actif, plus cuisant et plus aspre; mais c'est un feu temeraire et volage, ondoyant et divers, feu de fiebvre, subject à accez et remises, et qui ne nous tient qu'à un coing.*"[22]

AUDIENCE: How do you spell that?

LYNN: Translation, "...hotter, harsher and more energetic. It is nonetheless a brazen and unsteady fire, given to flaring up and dying down like an outbreak of fever, it engages only a 'corner' of us." Friendship, however, has a "steady, satisfying warmth, is universal and complete,

---

22 Montaigne, Edition Thibaudet-Rat, Paris, Gallimard, coll. Bibliotheque de la Pleiade, 1967.

all gentleness and polish, with nothing rough or piercing." Notice how he contrasts friendship with the "piercing" of *eros* {*poignant* in French, literally, "stabbing")—tempestuous, hot, 5th house falling in love. The 7th house usually has this quality of piercing—remember its association with war. But friendship, for the Greeks, was not *eros*, it was *philia*. Why are you laughing?

AUDIENCE: If you have *homophilia*, then suddenly *eros* is back in. I don't think you can draw the line that clearly.

LYNN: Many forms and variations of *philia* existed, and yes, one was *philia erotica*. So there is such a thing as erotic friendship.

AUDIENCE: In a way, I can relate to what you say. What I know about the Greeks is that they were into respect and simplicity. So friends were not allowed to be so passionate that they lost their sense of boundaries. It was taught this way. I am talking about the relationship between an older and a younger man.

LYNN: Yes, *philia* seems to maintain some distance, even when sex is involved, but this is not true of *eros*. Even in the quote from Montaigne, you feel that the erotic sentiment is out of control, unbounded, slightly dangerous, whereas the sentiment of friendship is equated with warmth and well-being. It uses the same energy, but without any danger of it burning out of control, and it's interesting to think again of Saturn and Uranus in this respect.

AUDIENCE: You were speaking in very fiery terms.

LYNN: Not me that was Montaigne's metaphor. Interesting, though, because he had only one planet in fire, Jupiter in Sagittarius, so there is a need to pull fiery energy in from others. Even if we call the "air" houses the houses of relationship, that doesn't mean that fire is an inappropriate image. We carry a torch for someone, we burn with desire, we spark an idea and we acknowledge the warmth of our feelings.

AUDIENCE: Didn't Montaigne write about one friend in particular, and that friendship ended tragically?

LYNN: Yes, it's true. When he was twenty-four, the age of the second Jupiter return, he met La Boetie, and from the very first moment they were extremely close. Montaigne's Essais are required reading in school, and in talking to French people about friendship, I realize they have all read it, because they tend to unconsciously quote it back to me. Asked why such a strong bond existed between these two individuals, Montaigne replied, "*Parce que c'était lui, parce que c'était moi*"—"Because it was him, because it was me." There was an immediate mutual recognition between the two men, and although they shared a great deal intellectually, this is a relationship of essence. All the rest, shared values and beliefs, love of learning and philosophy, spin out from this central core. Both men were drawn to the humanist values of the Renaissance, with its underpinnings in classical thought. They believed that a human being had the potential for a perfect friendship.

Montaigne speaks of transparency in friendship, the ability to see through the surface of manners and masks directly into the heart of the other. You are not hiding yourself from the other person, which, of course, occurs frequently in the 8th. To the extent that you are able, you are transparent in friendship—you let yourself shine through. Perhaps you'd be interested in having a look at Montaigne's chart?[23] Let's put up his chart, with the positions for La Boetie around it in a bi-wheel.

An extraordinary friendship should already be potentially described by the natal chart. Montaigne has an exalted Moon in Taurus in the 11th house, and four planets—Pluto, Mars, Venus, and Mercury in Aquarius, so it's not surprising he would place great value on friendship. Remember, he used the words "steady" and "satisfying." These correspond well to the Moon in Taurus, ruling the Cancer Ascendant. This is a chart with high ideals. The Sun conjuncts Neptune in Pisces and squares Jupiter in Sagittarius. For almost all of La Boetie's day of birth, the Moon is in Pisces conjunct Montaigne's Sun, a profoundly soulful contact, which often corresponds to the instant recognition Montaigne

---

23 Time given by Montaigne as "between eleven and noon" in *Essais*.

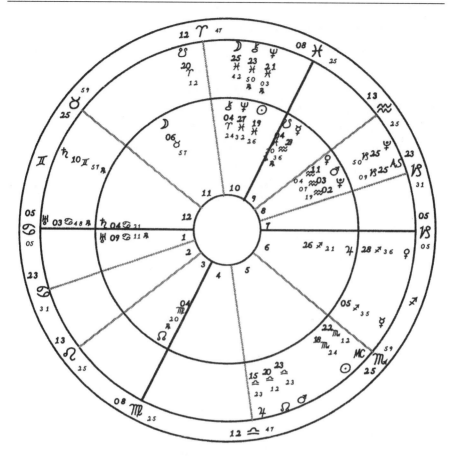

Center: Michel de Montaigne, 28 February 1533, 11:30 am LMT, Bordeaux
Perimeter: La Boetie, 1 November 1530, (no birth time, noon is used), Sarlat

describes. We feel immediately at home with someone whose Moon conjuncts our Sun.

The other principle contact between their charts is La Boetie's Venus conjunct Montaigne's Jupiter in Sagittarius. Their friendship centered around a love of learning and philosophy, a belief in humanity during a period of civil war. The Uranus-Ascendant contact is typical of fast-forming relationships, and we hear Moon-Neptune and Sun-Neptune in Pisces when Montaigne speaks of losing themselves in one another's depths. It was a friendship which happens "only once in three hundred years."

La Boetie died four years later, a great shock for his friend, who went through a dark, disconsolate time. This did not prevent him from exercising his appetite for the fair sex, for Montaigne was a sensualist and a wry, forthright commentator on sexuality in his Essays. But no other relationship, no lover, no child, certainly not his wife, ever equaled the perfect understanding he shared with La Boetie. This is a fascinating expression of the Moon's square to three 8th house planets—Pluto, Mars, and Venus—in his birth chart. With Moon square Venus, and Venus in Aquarius, physical love and ideal love were disconnected.

The 11th house and projection

AUDIENCE: Surely the 11th house is projection?

LYNN: It depends on how you look at it. It is certainly more likely to contain our positive projections, our "hopes and wishes," and among them, our desire for the Friend. Above all, it concerns our ability to be the best of ourselves with someone else. As we open up to another, something unfurls inside, or, as one Buddhist teacher puts it, we water the seeds of well-being, of trust, of joy. The 11th represents a growing space, defined by freedom, and yet, with certain rules and requirements, so that both people can flourish. Of all the airy houses, the 11th gives the maximum amount of space, without losing closeness. At least, that is the ideal. And this house is about ideals—about the ideal of self and other—and that can mean we are busy showing our best and nicest face, tucking more shadowy impulses away.

AUDIENCE: I'm beginning to wonder whether there isn't a psychological necessity in friendship, almost in the same way that nurturing from the mother is a psychological necessity. There is a need for an atmosphere free of uncomfortable control, and without ambivalence. The erotic 7th house is more ambivalent, somehow.

LYNN: Imagine a world where you could never let your guard down outside the family. The image that comes to mind is one of wild cubs playing. The claws and teeth are there, but in an environment without harm, and this suspension of vigilance probably has all kinds of beneficial effects, physical, psychological, emotional. It strikes me that we don't really spend much time thinking about this safe space of friendship, which may say something about just how important it is. In much the same way, I don't imagine people spoke much about the relationship with their mother two hundred years ago. And how much more restful to carry a positive projection than a negative one!

The rules of friendship

AUDIENCE: Could you go back to this idea of rules and regulations in friendship? That seems odd to me somehow.

LYNN: Just think of all the things a "real friend" would never do -sleep with your lover, betray your secrets, not return your phone calls, humiliate you in front of other people. The list is long and implicit. Watch what happens when one of these "invisible" rules gets broken! Most of us would immediately agree about some of them, but others, more personal, can be crossed unawares. Then, oops! Suddenly you're back into 8th house territory, uncomfortably aware of sharp teeth and hidden knives.

All of us have dangerous zones, mined territory left over from our past and only partially healed. They may not be clearly sign-posted, even if we are acutely aware of them. A friend may unintentionally step into one of these places and generate, unawares, a whole flood of negative projections, fears, and painful ghosts. Like any relationship, friendship includes an exploration of unconscious content. In addition, there is this small matter of the ideal you are supposed to live up to!

AUDIENCE: This helps explain why so many odd misunderstandings happen in friendship. Would rivalry be an 8th house issue too?

LYNN: It might have its origin elsewhere; in many house systems, planets from the 3rd can easily square the 11th house. Unresolved sibling issues will often pop up in friendships, especially with planets or signs linked to the energy of the past. This can be terribly useful and easier to resolve than with the real family member, if a bit confusing. Remember, projection helps us to learn about our own unintegrated psychic content, good or bad. And all of us have both wolf and angel in varying proportions.

When we do project a planet in the 11th house, we are offering the other person a particular role, much as we do in the 7th house. Jupiter here might bring friends who teach you about generosity, while with Mars, they could fight your battles or show you how to contact your courage. In a similar vein, we might be inviting friends to play the role of *daimon*. At the very least, they shine a light on something that we hope to grow in ourselves.

Does anybody have the chart of a friend they'd like to present? Let's try to see how this will work out in practice.

TERMS OF ENGAGEMENT

Equality and admiration

HERMIONE: Here is my chart and that of my friend Sarah. We've known each other for nine years.

LYNN: We'll start by looking at some chart fragments. Sarah has Neptune on the cusp of the 11th, at 3° Scorpio. Both of you have strong 3rd house placements. Sarah has Mars, Mercury, and Venus in Pisces there, and Hermione has a 3rd house Sun in Libra. Just from these elements, we can get an idea of what kind of friend Sarah might be. Any ideas?

AUDIENCE: Limitless.

AUDIENCE: Inspiring, with a strong aura of understanding and compassion.

LYNN: Sarah has Sagittarius rising and Mars in Pisces, and all of this is very large and limitless, somehow Hermoine has Leo rising and a 24°

Cancer Moon. Nothing is in the 11th house, but Taurus is on the cusp, and Gemini intercepted. So friendship will be carrying a Venusian need, and Venus is in Virgo in the 2nd house. How might that get expressed in friendship?

AUDIENCE: A friendship couldn't be with someone who is on the other side of the Atlantic Ocean.

LYNN: That's right. One would expect a strong, present relationship. With Taurus on the cusp and Venus in Virgo, the earthy emphasis would go for direct contact, which might not be the case with airy signs here.

HERMIONE: She is just two or three minutes' walk away.

AUDIENCE: Leo is very strong-willed, and Taurus is stubborn. Would Hermione tend to dominate in the friendship?

LYNN: Remember, she is a Libra. I'm not sure you should give so much weight in character analysis to that Taurean 11th house. However, with Gemini intercepted in the 11th, she will seek out someone she can really talk to. It probably won't be that easy for her. Are you more of a listener than a talker?

HERMIONE: No, both.

LYNN: So there's a sense of receptivity in this relationship. From what we see of Sarah's chart, the 3rd and the 11th are very watery. Would you say that your friend has a lot of compassion? Is that one of the things you admire about her? Has that compassion come into her life through difficulties?

HERMIONE: I would say so.

LYNN: Neptune rules the 3rd here. Are those difficulties linked to a sibling?

HERMIONE: We are both eldest children. She stood in for her father, who left, and became a surrogate "man" about the house. She was caring, someone for her mother to lean on. Her little sister is, I would say, fairly difficult.

LYNN: We spoke of Pisces or Neptune connected to the 3rd house. Here, as the ruler, it again indicates a sibling whose sensitivity makes it hard for them to deal with the world. In Sarah's case, the ruler of the 3rd is connected to the 11th, which gives tolerance for suffering and a willingness to include that in relationship. A person who has Neptune in the 11th has Neptune to offer to their friends, and friendship carries the dream of perfect understanding. Along with it might come the Neptunian underside of unreliability and disappointment, but there is a direct relation to the dream.

Notice that Sarah's Ascendant ruler, Jupiter, is conjunct Saturn in Capricorn—very responsible and parental. What is it that you offer this friend?

HERMIONE: There is a sort of balance. She has no air, I have Libra and am pretty airy, while with Sun in Aries and Moon in Leo, she is very fiery and a great inspiration to me. She has a lot of ideas that she can't coordinate.

AUDIENCE: With all her fire and lack of air, she probably has trouble getting distance, and you help her clarify things.

LYNN: Sarah has an abundance of creative energy, but somewhat jumbled. Notice that your Venus in Virgo, ruling the 11th, also helps her sort things out. It sounds as though her 11th house Neptune has great receptivity to what you bring. You don't save her, which could be the case with Neptune here, but you do understand her. I get the sense that you steady things. Are you both equally steady in this relationship, or are you steadier than Sarah?

HERMIONE: Funny you should say that, because one of the things I most appreciate about our friendship is that I know I can count on her, no matter what. I hadn't really thought about it, but I suppose that has to be mutual.

LYNN: With Taurus on the 11th, consistency has to be incredibly important in friendship. It reminds me of something Rumi said: "Friend, our closeness is this: Anywhere you put your foot, feel me in the firmness under you."[24] Now, Neptune could be lived out quite differently, since it hopes for so much from other people, senses their fragility and responds to it. Not holding back, investing so much care, feeling the connection and then being disappointed when friends don't live up to our hopes—someone here spoke about this earlier, with squares from planets in the 8th, but it's as if we are asked to have faith, feel let down, and then still have faith again in the redemption of human nature. I don't know if your friend Sarah has had this experience with other friends. Neptune is quite well aspected here, so I wouldn't necessarily expect that, but it could be an issue.

HERMIONE: Some of her other friends are not very practical.

LYNN: That lack of practicality may reflect her own aspiration to be without boundaries, to follow the dream—not so easy for someone with the Ascendant ruler conjunct Saturn. But notice how Hermione speaks of Sarah with admiration, particularly her fiery qualities. It seems to me that most of our friends have something we admire but haven't developed to the same extent that they have. They respond to something in us in a similar fashion, although all this stays quite under the surface, for the most part.

During the tea break, someone passed on a quotation: "A friend is someone who leaves you with all your freedom intact, but obliges you to be who you fully are." Freedom and obligation: Saturn and Uranus. These are the building blocks that we use to create a space for friendship. Although we use the word "friend" for all kinds of more

---

24 Coleman Barks, *The Essential Rumi,* HarperCollins, San Francisco, 1995.

casual connections, this true space of friendship nurtures authenticity, and invites our true self to emerge. In sibling relationships, you may not even have your own room, let alone any psychological space, and in the not-so-distant past, many brothers and sisters even slept in the same bed. We move from bodily and genetic connectedness to an invisible, loosely defined connection in which friends meet and move apart. You and Sarah have strong 3rd houses, and live nearby, so this closeness may have a very "sisterly" quality. It's interesting that you are both eldest children; generally they have a more hierarchical relationship with siblings. Perhaps together you have created the space and mutuality of equals.

According to Desmond Morris, the anthropologist who did all that work on body language, people who are extremely different socially rarely manage to maintain a friendship. Some kind of equality seems to be a prerequisite, though just how much probably depends on the proportion of Saturn to Uranus. Marguerite Yourcenar, the French novelist who was both strongly 11th house and Uranian, said that she saw no difference as a child between her friendship with the gardener's son and her friendship with her wealthy cousins. Later, she counted among her friends carpenters, sailors, nurses, and former cleaning ladies, "between eighteen and eighty-eight," saying there was no difference between them and her intellectual or artistic friends. "We are all alike, and we move towards the same fate."

Closeness versus freedom

Now, has anybody here experienced a period in their lives when friends fall away?

CHRIS: Constantly! I have started to think a lot about that over the last couple of months. I make friends on the spot, and I always make a new friend when I meet them. They can be completely different. Someone will come around the corner and I'll say, "Take care. Everything's fine." Great—I've got a new friend. Forty-eight hours later, I haven't got the faintest idea where they are. The way I would look at this is that my friends are only there when I need them. I know that at the end of the day, I have to sort myself out anyway when I am in trouble, but they are never there when I just want to have some support.

LYNN: You have Aquarius on the 11th house cusp, with Chiron there. Where is Uranus in your chart?

CHRIS: In the 5th, in opposition to Chiron.

LYNN: Real stability in friendship?

CHRIS: That's what I was complaining about!

LYNN: His friends are galloping off over the horizon!

AUDIENCE: Or if his friends don't, then he does.

LYNN: Does that mean that you do not know how to be stable?

CHRIS: I'm actually quite stable, but you may have to ask somebody else.

LYNN: Have you moved around a lot?

CHRIS: All of my life. I once worked out that Chiron might describe the loss of Louis, my bosom buddy and "true brother" when I was four years old. We punched each other's noses, maybe once a week, but immediately made up. Then my family moved countries, and I lost contact with him. I mourned him, thinking, "One day I'll meet Louis again."

LYNN: Did it feel like a soul connection?

CHRIS: I know it was the only friendship that I've had that I regard as being really close. No matter what, we were inseparable, physically and otherwise. We were at school together, and though I have friends in Tokyo, in New York, here in London, it never happened ever again. So twenty-five years later, I looked him up. I may see most of my friends every two years or so, since I move around.

AUDIENCE: There's a lot of space—perhaps too much.

LYNN: How long do you tend to stay in one place?

CHRIS: Nine or ten years.

LYNN: Constancy, dependability, loyalty—these are the things that come up over and over again when people speak of friendship. Would people here agree? Why do you think it's different for you, Chris?

CHRIS: I have it when I really need it—we are there for each other in times of crisis. But I don't have friends to go to the movies with and have a laugh. The casual, light part of things is missing.

LYNN: Doesn't it sound as though there's an overload of Uranus, and not enough Saturn? Uranus loves breakthrough, excitement, and change—it will always favor freedom in relationship whereas Saturn builds the scaffolding, the support that helps you become who you are day after day.

AUDIENCE: Uranus can disconnect to escape suffering. I have it in the 8th, and going into relationships is so difficult. I don't want to meet what I did with my mother. Aquarius can have this strategy of moving away out of fear of being wounded.

LYNN: Uranus in Chris' chart, as ruler of the 11th, understands this intimately. Notice that Chris needs to go quickly, as if he hasn't integrated time into a relationship. It sounds like you are in a hurry.

CHRIS: Of course, I have got Aries rising.

AUDIENCE: My question is, how can you maintain sufficient space to breathe well in friendship? That intimacy feels slightly constraining. I had a very close, intense friendship that lasted a year. We were like sisters, we had so much in common, and I'd always dreamed of having a sister, since I'm an only child. Then the friendship ended very suddenly, without a real explanation. Afterwards I would run into her, and so I ended up moving out of the area. It was left unresolved. I find it very curious how two people can be so close, and then very abruptly find themselves disconnected. And this has happened more than once.

LYNN: Friendship needs boundaries. Do you know the saying, "A hedge between keeps friendship green"? When everything happens all at once, the substance of friendship can be burned up, just as it can in a passionate love affair. Once again, Saturn plays a role.

AUDIENCE: I have all my personal planets in the 11th, in Aries.

LYNN: With siblings, you can fight, get mad, ignore each other, and yet the link remains. This moving away and staying connected at the same time may be harder to learn without brothers and sisters. Your chart asks you to discover yourself through relationships outside the family You may very well be the pioneer—Aries, the first one to have enough confidence to emerge into the outside world. Sometimes difficult planets in the 11th will indicate that you come from a family that does not know how to make friends.

Does anyone here have that experience? Those of you who have raised your hands have come from different countries with your families. There is always a struggle for integration into the community at large when you're an outsider. Sometimes there can be a powerful identification with a sub-group as a kind of protection.

AUDIENCE: My parents were immigrants. We had family jokes about our lack of guests or people coming to our house.

LYNN: The 11th house can speak about your relationship to society as a whole; it shows where you open the door to the outside world. Now, if somebody comes from a family where that didn't happen, you will either need to knock down the barrier in a big way, or confront a fear of others on a more personal level. Otherwise you will be constrained to stay close to the family model.

AUDIENCE: My family didn't go out very much. They had so-called friends, but I wouldn't honor them with that name. It's so much more important for me. I find that friends with a shared interest cluster around you. Most of my friends are vegetarians, not just astrologers. I change friends a lot, though I have got two old school friends that I have known since I was six. We have kept in touch all this time.

AUDIENCE: Friendship, like anything, changes. It's not static. It gets to a threshold situation and sometimes moves through it. At other times, it doesn't. I have a lot of very Scorpionic friends, and Capricorn friends for whom change is quite an issue.

LYNN: That seems strong when we find an 8th house square, either natally or by transit. A relationship transforms or dies. Lets go back to something we said before—that somehow, friendship contains something to which we aspire. Imagine that you enter into a friendship and have a wonderful experience; you absorb something you hadn't been able to contact before. Let's say that, through a particularly intense relationship, you learn something from the other person. But then the reason for the initial attraction no longer applies. What is left?

AUDIENCE: That sounds very opportunistic.

LYNN: When we are younger, it can be like that. Think of all those adolescent friends that get left behind. Until you know who you are, a friendship may be like a signpost, a means to find your true direction, but usually an exchange of some depth happens along the way, and the relationship blossoms in new directions. You discover the other at the same time that you discover yourself.

HERMIONE: The sign on the cusp of the 11th house seems powerful. Sarah has Scorpio there, and I have Taurus. We are both quite fixed in the sense that we look for loyalty. Not that we are incapable of changing—but it is different from people with, say, Gemini or Sagittarius there.

AUDIENCE: I have a rather improbable friendship with a woman, a "Marilyn Monroe" type, Gemini-Scorpio, and though I was quite distant at first, we eventually became close. Presumably this has something to do with my loaded 11th house, where I have the Sun on the cusp in Pisces as well as Mercury, Moon, and Mars in Aries. I'm curious as to how you would see this.

LYNN: It sounds as though she helps you to contact something in your feminine identity. Moon-Mars conjunct in Aries may describe a woman who knows how to get what she wants, who owns her desire. Marilyn Monroe had Venus in Aries. It's probably worth doing some reflecting on this. With a best friend, things become 7th house. If you spend all your time with that person, and you talk to each other five times a day, you are moving into a 7th house, not an 11th house, structure.

But it does happen that a solid, valuable friendship disappears from your life. When I spoke to people about this, it seemed most frequent when major changes had taken place—career, marriage, divorce, a move. We suddenly disconnect, and a key friendship no longer holds any charm for us, because the friend expects to find us the way we used to be. If friends can't reflect the new self back to you, the relationship may not survive.

AUDIENCE: You are almost describing before and after the Saturn return—a time when I lost quite a few friends. But one has remained, my oldest friend, a woman I met when I was twenty I'm now thirty-four. Her Moon is exactly on my Venus, and my Moon is in her 3rd house. It is the most fabulous friendship I ever had.

AUDIENCE: It strikes me that, with Uranus going into Aquarius, there is something now about family ties becoming looser. Does that mean that the energies are going to go to friendship?

LYNN: At the moment, a certain amount of research in psychology seems to show that parents have less impact on personality than people have tended to believe. Whatever its truth, this probably reflects a change in the collective archetypes, something that seems to follow Neptune's sign shifts. With both Uranus and Neptune now in Aquarius, you can observe this crossover to a new "idea" it's a fascinating process! As Neptune enters a sign, it lights up that area of experience, and heightens in some way the intrinsic values of the sign. Since Aquarius concerns the relationship between the group and the individual, our social models are likely to change. Notice the new dominance of socialist governments in Europe. The family has to do with our past, after all. Aquarius looks to the future, creates Utopias, invents new models.

AUDIENCE: So we spend all this time talking about our mothers, then we think, wait, what about the father? And now we have to start looking at our friends!

LYNN: Plato says the family is part of the soul's necessity, even when we are convinced there had to be a better way. They provide the biological and chemical soup, the emotional and material conditions for what needs to emerge inside us in the very beginning. We leave our families eventually, but the *daimon* comes along with us, putting people and situations on our path. The Sufis have a symbol—a winged heart—and they speak of the Friend, the one who leads you to your true nature. Friends may enter our life through serendipity, which means finding something you're not necessarily looking for When Jack in "Jack and the Beanstalk" sells his cow for those beans, the vendor plays the role of the *daimon*.

It was Gertrude Stein who told Hemingway to go to Spain and see the bullfights—she pointed the way. Since we've already looked at her

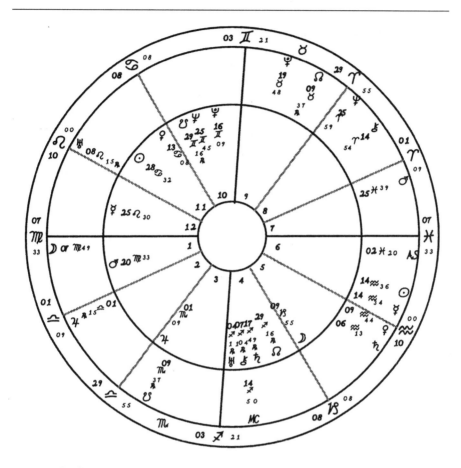

Center: Ernest Hemingway, 21 July 1899, 8:00 am CST, Oak Park, IL
Perimeter: Gertrude Stein

chart earlier, it may be interesting to look at her synastry with Hemingway.[25] Gertrude Stein's Aquarian planets fall in Hemingway's 5th and 6th houses. We could say she served his creativity. Her Moon exactly conjuncts his Ascendant, so he would bring out a nurturing energy in her. But unresolved maternal issues might also pop up, sooner or later And Hemingway has Cancer on the cusp of the 11th house. What was his mother like? She was a fascinating and dominant figure, not at all conventionally maternal she was beautiful and creative, and never

---

25 Hemingway's data from Lois Rodden, *Astrodata II*, *op. cit.* (Note 9).

stooped to performing ordinary chores. This corresponds well to a 5th house Capricorn Moon. Ernest both loved and hated this mother He has Pluto on the MC. Pluto opposes Saturn and squares Mars, a highly charged T-square, pointing to issues of compressed rage around authority. With this T-square he sought to prove his courage over and over again, as the wounded war journalist, the hunter, the "macho."

He and Stein spoke often and at length about writing. She encouraged him to simplify his language, to leave journalism, to become a novelist. Friends describe him as being surprisingly docile with her. But Hemingway, even more fiercely than Gertrude Stein, had a tendency to turn on those who helped him. With Venus and Sun in the 11th house, his benefactors were many, but it was said of him that as soon as he began to love someone, he felt the need to kill them. It is worth noting that Stein and Hemingway have Mars in opposition to each other's Mars. When the honeymoon was over, they both went to war, insulting each other verbally and in print. Hemingway speculated on the weight of Stein's breasts and talked about her "fat ass," an interesting way to reject the "nurturer."

AUDIENCE: This doesn't sound like Venus in the 11th to me. I wonder why it worked out that way for him? Did the T-square create a disconnection of some kind?

LYNN: It would seem so. Perhaps it has to do with Hemingway's inability to accept his own vulnerability. That Moon opposition Venus may describe a mother who alternately held him close and pushed him away, but she always decided. If you have difficulty with the qualities represented by the sign on the cusp of the 11th, friendship may get a bit tricky for you. Trust is a necessity for friendship, so a strong Pluto can also be problematic. During the tea break, Carol, who has Pluto in the 11th, was saying that until recently she could only see Pluto in other people's charts; it didn't seem to be functioning in hers. But what does this say about where she is going, and what needs to be integrated? Her friends, or her community, will teach her about Pluto. And in the long run, she may have a transformative impact on the group.

AUDIENCE: Saturn in the 11th has a bad reputation, doesn't it? No friends, dour friends, but I haven't found that to be true.

AUDIENCE: It's supposed to be strong in the charts of policemen.

LYNN: Your favorites. Any policemen here?

Saturn-Neptune in the 11th house

AUDIENCE: I have Saturn-Neptune in the 11th.

LYNN: My first thought would be about whether your father was able to find his place in society. Saturn might indicate a discomfort with the world at large, while Neptune can give that feeling of being "at sea."

AUDIENCE: That's true. He was an island.

LYNN: Here, Saturn has to do with an attitude received from the father, and since Saturn will always demand attention and hard work, it heightens the need to break through our fear of being rejected by others. With Saturn here, you may have had a parent who was unable to form a relationship with the outside world, and remained an outsider. This often happens in immigrant families. Paradoxically, it could also mean that your family identifies with a rather exclusive group, a class or caste apart. Saturn and Neptune together turn up the heat on this issue of inclusion or exclusion. The lack of model generates a certain amount of insecurity and a need to work at finding a place in the group. A Saturn in the 11th person can become highly skilled at this, but may never feel absolutely comfortable.

Jupiter in the 11th house

Jupiter in the 11th is much more likely to be optimistic about other people. As the "greater benefic," it will tend to bring grace and good fortune through friends. We could see them as acting in lieu of the *bonus daimon.* It can help an individual leave difficult 4th and 3rd house planets behind. According to Firmicus Maternus, "The greatest good fortune and great fame—consular or proconsular power -result from Jupiter in the 11th house."[26]

AUDIENCE: It sounds like Jupiter in the 11th would bring the best kind of *daimon.*

Moon-Venus in the 11th house

AUDIENCE: I'd like to ask about a rather complicated structure in the 11th Moon and Venus are conjunct in Taurus, but intercepted, and they form a yod with Neptune in Libra and Chiron in Sagittarius.

LYNN: That's a lot to take in all at once, Julie. Let's start by looking at the Moon-Venus conjunction—warmth and affection in abundance, with perhaps a wee bit of possessiveness. Someone with this structure is going to have a tremendous amount emotionally invested in their friends. They may mother them, or they may ask their friends for mothering, understanding, and comfort. A relationship will build familiarity and loyalty over time. Is this you?

JULIE: Yes. That's quite accurate. I lost a long-term friend when I gave birth to a child. She knitted the first pair of socks, and then I never heard from her again. I guess she must have seen me as a mother.

LYNN: Perhaps you brought out the need for mothering in your friends, without being totally aware of just how strong it was. Moon-Venus is quite powerful emotionally, and it sounds as though you were working out some unresolved mother issues in that relationship. The suddenness of the change could be the yod working to break through an illusion about the relationship. The implicit agreement might have been that you would always take care of her, but with a real baby demanding

---

26 Julius Firmicus Maternus, *Matheseos Libri VIII*, trans. Jean Rhys Bram, Ascella Publications, Mansfield, UK, 1995.

your attention, this illusion bit the dust. This abruptness seems to be common with the yod, which pushes for a change in levels. With a simple quincunx, the tension remains subdued, and less likely to burst out in this way.

JULIE: I never saw her again.

LYNN: She never called or wrote? With Moon in Taurus, that must be quite difficult. Is Pluto square the Moon?

JULIE: Yes. I think the child took over.

LYNN: So you didn't seek her out either. Perhaps she pulled away to see if you would come after her, but there must have been something lop-sided in the friendship all along. Normally, Moon and Venus in Taurus would be incredibly loyal, but Pluto prefers things to be absolute and final: "I never saw her or spoke to her again."

Your Neptune in the 4th probably describes a lack of solidity some-where, a disconnection with the family that created a need to go out and nurture yourself in friendship and group relationships. Does that make sense? With the luminaries in the 11th, a sense of self must come from outside, and the family alone can't give that.

JULIE: I have had years of communal living.

AUDIENCE: Like Julie, I have Neptune in the 4th. My family didn't sup-port my creativity and artistry, but my closest friend was an artist. She's fiery, though I'd say there's something wobbly about her at the same time. I have Mars in the 11th, by the way.

Mars in the 11th house

LYNN: It's so interesting that your friend nourishes you exactly where something was missing. I would expect Mars to be more stimulating, though, perhaps even competitive. Was there a lot of friendly rivalry?

AUDIENCE: You could say that, mostly, I feel energized by her. We often painted together.

LYNN: Aries on the cusp of the 11th, like Mars placed there, can draw slightly challenging relationships into your life. They will dare you to take risks, or force you to stand up for yourself. Often friends will spur each other on, not necessarily in direct competition, but there is a strong sense of stimulation, even emulation. A relay race comes to mind, with one person passing the baton to the other. The combined group effort goes beyond what an individual might have accomplished. But when the competitive spirit comes up, it needs to be conscious, or it can pull the relationship apart. Do you think that's what happened?

AUDIENCE: It's very common for me that friendships end. I have a lot of friends with very strong 8th houses and Plutos.

AUDIENCE: In the synastry of friendships, would you often find the Sun or Moon in the 11th of the other person?

LYNN: That seems likely, along with the same kind of classic synastry connections you might find for romantic relationships. I have the charts of two men in their forties, who have been friends from childhood. Michel's Leo Moon is exactly conjunct Jean's Sun, and both have Pluto there as well. This kind of Sun Moon connection creates an instant fit, like that perfect pair of shoes you never want to throw away. Jean, a brilliant student, was fatherless, and became quite close to Michel's father, a sensitive and literary man. Michel's father once told him that his friendship with Jean was his greatest success—a slightly ambiguous compliment, since Michel struggled in school, unlike his gifted sisters, and was somewhat dazzled by Jean's intellectual finesse.

As they grew older, Jean changed countries and pulled away, feeling he no longer had much to say to Michel, who seemed stuck in his work and emotional life. But their children have brought them together again, since they both place a great deal of importance on fathering. Astrological theory would have it that the Sun has a more central position in the relationship, which is certainly borne out here, but Pluto's presence may, in part, explain why one friend has a more dominant role. They both have fire signs on the 11th house cusp, fire Moons, and fixed Suns, and they honor friendship greatly, attaching great importance to the ideal. Venus and Sun, rulers of Michel's Ascendant and 11th house, are conjunct in the 1st in Scorpio, suggesting that his sense of self came through this ability to construct friendship.

If we look at this in terms of the *daimon,* you could say that Michel helped Jean to contact Michel's father. Coincidentally, the friendship began to unravel around the time of Michel's father's death. Both men loved travel early on, and married women from other countries. But Jean has acquired a new nationality, while Michel still lives in the same neighborhood in a building owned by his mother. Jean has Sagittarius on the cusp of the 11th, and needs a sense of discovery in friendship. He now brings his experience of other cultures to his relationships. Michel occasionally speaks of leaving France, and perhaps this will happen one day—it wouldn't be entirely surprising. Often, the lives of friends loosen over time, then interweave again later, forming odd and unexpected parallels.

The sign on the cusp of the 11th will describe an energy that you are looking for in friendship, along with the planets found there. Julie's Moon-Venus in the 11th may mean she needs the freedom afforded by choice in order to get really close. For a time, her ability to express love came out with non-family members more strongly, and drew her to community living. The 11th house has a quality of invention, and Rani found a new model of intimacy in the group. Her work in friendship may have to do with defining just this boundary between freedom and intimacy.

We are trying to elaborate the 11th house, but it's important to remember that exploring the synastry between two charts will always give a more satisfying "take" on any relationship, including friendship. Just as someone with Saturn in the 7th will always experience a Saturnine element in partnership, someone with Saturn in the 11th will explore Saturn in friendship. Certain people will feed that Saturn more than others, but the whole chart is always involved.

SEEDING THE COLLECTIVE

LYNN: The 11th house was also a house of wealth in the older texts, but Firmicus speaks particularly of the ability to affect a great number of people. One's life touches the collective. I've always wondered about Anne Frank's chart in this respect. She has north Node conjunct Jupiter in the 11th in Taurus, as well as Sun-Mercury further along in Gemini. How can we understand this?

AUDIENCE: You could say that she became the "voice" for a whole group of people. Through her diaries, the world was able to understand what was lost.

LYNN: That's a very good point.

AUDIENCE: She hardly had a positive experience of humanity in general!

LYNN: And yet, optimism about human nature pervades her diaries, despite her tragic fate and suffering. You cannot read her without a feeling of hope. A part of the 11th house stretches beyond us, beyond individual intention, even beyond the span of our own life. Planets here have the possibility of reaching the collective and seeding it. Neil Armstrong has Uranus in the 11th, and he took a "giant leap for mankind" Mozart had Neptune in the 11th, opposing his 5th house Sun-Saturn-Mercury, and as a talented child he was society's darling.

Tremendous creativity poured through him, and yet his adult music went unappreciated by his contemporaries. Neptune symbolizes the lack of response, the disappointment in a fickle public, even his rejection by the Freemasons after writing *The Magic Flute*. Yet the inspiration that continues to move through his music, long after his death, is also Neptune.

The 11th house carries a dimension that reaches into the future, and awakens something in the group soul. Van Gogh, who was virtually without friends while he was alive, had Pluto, Uranus, and Saturn in the 11th. At one point he was forced to leave the village he'd been in because people became deeply afraid of him. His work and life continue to disturb and move people greatly. On a totally different note, Woody Allen stirred up a collective convulsion around sexuality and betrayal with the events in his personal life, and he has Pluto in the 11th.

In his book *The Twelve Houses*, Howard Sasportas wrote of the 11th house, "Our individual minds are connected not just to the minds of those close to us, but to all other minds."[27] Friendship, where we first step away from tribal and biological identity and reach outside ourselves with a generous heart, constitutes a first experience of this collective sensitivity. In the 11th house we give back, not out of a desire for personal aggrandizement, but because giving back is as natural as breathing in and out. We become aware of being bigger, having more dimension, taking in more of the world. Strong 11th house planets can stretch our connectedness, bridge time and space, through a grid of consciousness that links many individuals. So the 11th also has to do with our relationship to society and humanity as a whole. We leap off the purely personal into something quite bigger than ourselves.

AUDIENCE: Could you talk about the Moon's Nodes here, particularly the south Node? Would it point to self-denial?

LYNN: With the Moon's Nodes, you often have to open up your thinking and embrace paradox. The north Node in the 5th asks that you focus on personal expression, rather than looking toward companionship. You are asked to breathe life into your own creativity, no matter what others are doing. The south Node in the 11th may indicate a particular sensitivity to the group mind and lots of easy connections to others. You may not have to work hard at belonging. The south Node brings many gifts, and these are only problematic when they stifle the development of the complementary polarity.

AUDIENCE: So, in the 5th house, we have to give because we need to

---

27 Howard Sasportas, *The Twelve Houses*, The Press, Wellingborough, UK 1985.

315

express something; and in the 11th, we contribute in a way that isn't self-interested.

A cell in the larger body of humanity

LYNN: The 11th house ultimately links us to others in such a way that we begin to- lose our sense of separateness. Howard talked about being "a cell in the larger body of humanity." The Buddhists call this inter-being, the awareness that all other life forms underlie our own existence. I had a wonderful experience of this when I moved into a house on a small courtyard, with a number of dwellings in close proximity. When I arrived it was rather barren, but I imagined it, in my mind's eye, filled with plants and flowers. I haunted plant stores, becoming slightly obsessive about buying flowers and greening the courtyard.

In the beginning, people were a bit taken aback by this, because the French are rather territorial. A curmudgeonly plumber, who spent much of his time drinking with the local low life, began to feel threatened. "In the 1940's we had the German invasion, and now we are getting the Americans taking over the courtyard with their flowers!" He probably preferred the Germans, but fortunately, he was ready to retire, and sold his space to my plant-loving neighbor. She and I did a lot the first year, and then, when the others realized it actually improved things, they began to participate too. People who had lived there for years and never put a plant out started gardening, and by the third summer this spontaneous collective process had utterly transformed things. In the beginning, people would say, "It would be great if you had this all to yourself," but I preferred sharing it. I wanted to plant those flowers, but the fact that other people benefited from it was an added bonus. They came round, and we ended up creating that flowered space together, along with a sense of community and warmth.

AUDIENCE: Where would you put relationships with people in care? They don't actually choose to live with each other, but they are stuck with each other.

LYNN: Institutionalized care would generally be the 12th house. If you are simply sharing a space, like roommates or foster-children, it probably becomes 3rd house, unless there is a sense of group bonding. My neighbors were 3rd house, relationships of proximity, but the courtyard became an 11th house experience when we brought the group energy into it.

The 11th house brings us to an experience of connectedness. It echoes the fundamental meaning of Aquarius—being an individual among others without fear of losing oneself, giving without feeling as if something is being taken away. I took the Eurostar to come to the seminar, imagining I'd be able to work on the train. This man sat next to me, made a series of calls on his mobile phone, and then pulled out a tape recorder and began dictating into it. "Paragraph two. The quote for that was 1.5 million. Thirty acres on the ground floor." He took my rueful smile for friendliness, and we started a conversation in which 11th house themes kept bubbling up. One of the things he mentioned was how he deals with salesmen. "No matter what you are doing in your life," he said, "you have to take time out for other people. So if a salesman calls me selling photocopiers, a horrible job, I'll stop and say, 'Well, I don't need one, but I really appreciate you calling me. Thank you very much, and please feel free to call me again.'"

AUDIENCE: Pisces on the 11th?

LYNN: I don't think so. This was a successful businessman in his mid-thirties. He said, "If you're doing something with your life and you're not giving anything back to other people, then what's the point? I work for myself in business, and I refuse to work with anybody I don't like." At the end of the train ride, I asked for his birth data, and as it turns out, he had five planets in the 11th house. Everything in the conversation had to do with how you give back, or how you are connected to other people, and here was this helpful encounter to jog my thinking for the seminar

The 11th house isn't just about friendships. It shows how our friends link us to ourselves and our purpose, to the unfolding of our inner nature and potential. The Greeks believed that, when you help someone fulfill their destiny, you have then stepped into the *daimon's* role. It doesn't matter whether it was intentional or incidental, big or small; you have helped fate to move that person forward. We are all constantly rubbing off each other, sparking things through word or gesture, moving each other along. And sometimes it happens on a larger scale, seeding the potential for all of us, for human beings to become what they may. That's what the 11th house is about.

There's a lot more to say, but we will stop now.

BIBLIOGRAPHY

Ancelin Schuetzenberger, Anne, *Aie, mes aieux!*, Desclee de Brouwer/La Meridienne, Paris, 1993-1999.

Aristotle, *Les Grands Livres d'Ethiques*, trad. Catherine Dalimier Arlea, Paris, 1995.

Bank, Stephen P. and Kahn, Michael D., *The Sibling Bond*, Basic Books, New York, 1997.

Barbault, Martine and Gestas,Catherine: *La Memoire Ancestrale en Astrologie*, 2006 Editions du Rocher, Paris

Barbault, Martine et Gestas, Catherine: *Des Frères et des Soeurs*, 2009 Editions Buissiere, Paris

Berry, Jean-Francois: *Le Chant De Resonance*, 2007 Editions du Brenagel, Saint-Andre-de-Sango

Boszormenyi-Nagi, Ivan, and Spark, G. M., *Invisible Loyalties*, Harper & Row, New York, 1973.

Bowen, Murray, *Family Therapy in Clinical Practice*, Jason Aronson, New York, 1978.

Calvino, Italo, *Italian Folktales*, Harcourt Brace Jovanovich, 1980.

Clark, Brian, *The Sibling Constellation. The Astrology and Psychology of Sisters and Brothers*, Arkana, London, 1999.

Costello, Darby, *The Astrological Moon*, CPA Press, London, 1996.

Ebertin, Reinhold, *The Combination of Stellar Influences*, Ebertin-Verlag, 1960.

Edel, Leon, *Henry James. A Life*, Lippincott, Philadelphia. Vol 1 *The Untried Years, 1843-1870* (pub. 1953) Vol 2. *The Conquest of London, 1870-1882* (pub. 1962) Vol 3- *The Middle Years, 1882-1895* (pub. 1962) Vol 4: *The Treacherous Years, 1895-1901* (pub. 1965) Vol 5- *The Master, 1901-1916* (pub. 1972).

Elniski, James, "Finding One's Twin," *Twins, Parabola*, Vol. XIX, May 1994, Number 2.

Firmicus Maternus, Julius *Matheseos Libri VIII*, trans. Jean Rhys Bram, Ascella Publications, Mansfield, UK, 1995.

Graves, Robert, *The Greek Myths*, Penguin, London, 1992.

Greene, Liz, *The Astrology of Fate*, HarperCollins, London, 1985.

Greene, Liz and Sasportas, Howard, *The Development of the Personality*, Samuel Weiser Inc, York Beach, ME, 1987.

Haley, Jay and Hoffman, Lynn, *Techniques of Family Therapy*, Basic Books, New York, 1967.

Hand, Robert, *Horoscope Symbols*, Schiffer Publishing Ltd, 1987.

Hellman, Lillian, *An Unfinished Woman, A Memoir*, Little, Brown, Boston, 1969.

Hillman, James, *The Soul's Code*, Bantam Books, London, 1997.

James, Henry, *Autobiography*, ed. Frederick W. Dupree, Criterion, New York, 1956.

Kenzaburo, *A Healing Family*, trans. Stephen Snyder, Kodansha International, 1996.

Kerenyi, C, *The Gods of the Greeks*, Thames & Hudson, London, 1982.

L'Amitié, Les Editions Autrement, Nr 17, Paris, février 1995, especially Jacqueline Lagrée, "L'homme, un loup ou un dieu pour l'homme?" pp 16-134.

Lazard, Madeleine, *Michel de Montaigne*, Fayard, Paris, 1992.

Lerner, Harriet Goldhor, *The Dance of Intimacy*, Harper & Row, New York, 1989.

Lindbergh, Anne Morrow, *Gift From the Sea*, Vintage Books, New York, 1991.

Lindbergh, Reeve, *Under A Wing: A Memoir*, Simon & Schuster, New York, 1998.

McGoldrick, Monica and Gerson, Randy, *Genograms in Family Assessment*, W. W. Norton, New York, 1985.

Mellow, James R. *Hemingway, A Life Without Consequences*, Perseus Press, 1994.

Montaigne, Michel de, *Essais*, Edition Thibaudet-Rat, Paris, Gallimard, coll. Bibliothèque de la Pleiade, 1967.

Rodden, Lois, *AstroData II*, AFA, 1988.

———, *Profiles of Women*, AFA, 1978.

———, *Profiles of Women*, AFA, 1979.

Roskill, Mark, ed., *The Letters of Van Gogh*, Fontana/Collins, London, 1963.

Sasportas, Howard, *The Twelve Houses*, The Aquarian Press, Wellingborough, 1985.

Satir, Virginia, *People Making*, Science and Behaviour Books, USA, 1972.

Selvini, Mara, *Family Games*, Karnac Books, London, 1989.

Sharman-Burke, Juliet, *The Family Inheritance*, CPA Press, London, 1996.

Smiley, Jane, *A Thousand Acres*, Ballantine Books, New York, 1991

Sullivan, Erin, *Dynasty: The Astrology of Family Dynamics*, Penguin Arkana, London 1996.

Toman, Walter, *Family Constellation*, Springer, New York, 1976.

Whitaker, Carl A., *Dancing With the Family*, Brunner/Mazel, New York, 1988.

Wineapple, Brenda, *Sister Brother*, Bloomsbury Press, London, 1997.

Wolfe, Thomas, *You Can't Go Home Again*, HarperCollins, 1988.

Yeats, W. B., *Selected Poetry*, ed. Norman Jeffers, Pan Books Ltd., London, 1974.

Zazzo, René, *Le Paradoxe des Jumeaux*, Editions Stock, Paris, 1984.

ABOUT THE AUTHOR

LYNN BELL began to be interested in astrology as an adolescent in Chicago, and the passion never went away. She learned to calculate charts and dropped out of graduate school to pursue personal esoteric studies, after studying Sociology and Literature. Books were her teachers, and though she began practicing early on, she only succumbed to astrology as a profession in her late twenties, after much resistance. Her work in astrology has always been centered around the consultation—teaching came after ten years of practice.

She has lived in Paris since 1978, and has lectured and taught workshops in many cities throughout France. She began teaching for the CPA in London in 1995, and is now a regular tutor there. A friend of the Reseau d'Astrologie Humaniste, she also taught classes for Agape, and helped create the AFAP, an association which promotes psychological astrology in Paris and brings speakers from abroad.

Since *Planetary Threads* was first published, her work has taken her to five continents, most recently Hong Kong and Taiwan, and she has spoken at most of the major astrological conferences in the world. She is co-author of *The Mars Quartet*, with Darby Costello, Liz Greene, and Melanie Reinhart; and author of *Cycles of Light: Exploring the Mysteries of Solar Returns*, both CPA Press. Among the many places she has been fortunate to teach are the Faculty of Astrological Studies summer school at Oxford, the LSA in London, and Heaven and Earth workshops in Bali. Outside the world of astrology she teaches for Caroline Myss at the CMED Institue, and Wisdom University's New Chartres School.

Her articles have appeared in *The Mountain Astrologer* and other publications, and she is a regular speaker at conferences in France, as well as in Holland, the UK, Norway, and the U.S.A. Personal work in analysis, training in Eriksonian Hypnosis, and other therapeutic techniques have all enriched her work as a consulting astrologer with an international clientele. This is a revised edition of her first book.